# DESIGNING SECURE SOFTWARE

# DESIGNING
# SECURE
# SOFTWARE

## A Guide for Developers

### Loren Kohnfelder

**no starch
press**

San Francisco

Printed in the United States of America

First Printing

25 24 23 22 21    1 2 3 4 5 6 7 8 9

ISBN-13: 978-17185-0192-8 (print)
ISBN-13: 978-17185-0193-5 (ebook)

Publisher: William Pollock
Production Manager: Rachel Monaghan
Production Editor: Katrina Taylor
Developmental Editor: Frances Saux
Technical Reviewer: Cliff Janzen
Cover Illustrator: Rick Reese
Cover and Interior Design: Octopod Studios
Copyeditor: Rachel Head
Compositor: Jeff Lytle, Happenstance-Type-O-Rama
Proofreader: May Huang

For information on book distributors or translations, please contact No Starch Press, Inc. directly:

No Starch Press Inc.
245 8th Street, San Francisco, CA 94103
phone: 1-415-863-9900; info@nostarch.com
www.nostarch.com

*Library of Congress Cataloguing-in-Publication Data*

```
Names: Kohnfelder, Loren, author.
Title: Designing secure software : a guide for developers / Loren Kohnfelder.
Description: San Francisco : No Starch Press, 2022. | Includes index. |
    Summary: "An introduction to computer security that focuses on basic
    security concepts, like threats and how developers mitigate them. It
    covers the process of reviewing design documents with security in mind
    and explores techniques attackers use to exploit systems and how to
    protect against them with secure coding and development practices"--
    Provided by publisher.
Identifiers: LCCN 2021032322 (print) | LCCN 2021032323 (ebook) | ISBN
    9781718501928 (print) | ISBN 9781718501935 (ebook)
Subjects: LCSH: Software engineering. | Software architecture. | Computer
    security. | Application software--Development.
Classification: LCC QA76.758 .K675 2022  (print) | LCC QA76.758  (ebook) |
    DDC 005.1--dc23
LC record available at https://lccn.loc.gov/2021032322
LC ebook record available at https://lccn.loc.gov/2021032323
```

[S]

In memory of robin.

Dedicated to all the software professionals
who keep the digital world afloat, working
to improve security one day at a time. Their
greatest successes are those rare boring
days when nothing bad happens.

# About the Author

Loren Kohnfelder began programming over fifty years ago. As an undergraduate at MIT, his thesis "Towards a Practical Public-Key Cryptosystem" (1978) first described digital certificates and the foundations of public key infrastructure (PKI).

His software career spans a wide variety of programming jobs, from punched cards, writing disk controller drivers, a linking loader, video games, two stints in Japan, to equipment control software in a semiconductor research lab. At Microsoft, he returned to security work on the Internet Explorer team, and later the .NET platform security team, contributing to the industry's first proactive security process methodology.

Most recently, at Google, he worked as a software engineer on the security team and later as a founding member of the privacy team, performing well over one hundred security design reviews of large-scale commercial systems.

# About the Technical Reviewer

Since the early days of Commodore PET and VIC-20, technology has been a constant companion (and sometimes an obsession!) to Cliff Janzen. Cliff spends a majority of the work day managing and mentoring a great team of security professionals, but strives to stay technically relevant by tackling everything from security policy reviews to penetration testing to incident response. He feels lucky to have a career that is also his favorite hobby and a wife who supports him.

# BRIEF CONTENTS

# CONTENTS IN DETAIL

# 3
# MITIGATION

# 4
# PATTERNS

# 5
# CRYPTOGRAPHY

# PART II: DESIGN

**93**

## 6
## SECURE DESIGN

**95**

## 7
## SECURITY DESIGN REVIEWS

**109**

# PART III: IMPLEMENTATION  127

## 8
## SECURE PROGRAMMING  129

## 9
## LOW-LEVEL CODING FLAWS  145

## 10
## UNTRUSTED INPUT  167

# FOREWORD

The book you have just started to read is unusual in many ways. Small and carefully written, it is a very technical book with very little code. It's a security book designed for those other than security experts. And as Loren discusses, it is a deeply personal perspective on technology, written by someone who has shipped large commercial products, invented important security technology, and worked extensively in product security.

In 2006, I joined Microsoft, and was handed responsibility for how we threat modeled across all our products and services. The main approach we used was based on Loren's STRIDE work. STRIDE is a mnemonic to help us consider the threats of Spoofing, Tampering, Repudiation, Information disclosure, Denial of service, and Elevation of privilege. It has become a key building block for me. (It's so central that I regularly need to correct people who think I invented STRIDE.) In fact, when I read this book, I was delighted to find that Loren calls on my Four Questions Framework much the way I call on STRIDE. The Framework is a way of approaching problems by asking what we are working on, what can go wrong, what we are going to do about those things, and whether we did a good job. Many of the lessons in this book suggest that Loren and I have collaborated even though we never worked directly together.

Today, the world is changing. Security flaws have become front page news. Your customers expect better security than ever before, and push those demands by including security in their evaluation criteria, drafting contract clauses, putting pressure on salespeople and executives, and pressing for new laws. Now is a great time to bring better security design into your software, from conception to coding. This book is about that difficult subject: how to design software that is secure.

The subject is difficult because of two main challenges. The first challenge, that security and trust are both natural and nuanced, is the subject of Chapter 1, so I won't say more about it. The second is that software professionals often hope that software won't require design. Software seems infinitely malleable, unlike the products of other engineering disciplines. In those other disciplines, we build models and prototypes before we bend steel, pour concrete, or photo-etch silicon. And in contrast, we build code, refine it, and then release it to the world, rather than following the famous advice of Fred Brooks: you're going to throw away the first system you build, so you might as well plan to treat it as a prototype. The stories we tell of the evolution of software rarely linger on our fruitless meanderings. We like to dismiss the many lightbulbs that didn't work and talk instead about how the right design just happened to come to us. Sometimes, we even believe it. Even in writing this, I am aware of a risk that you will think me—or worse, Loren—to be an advocate of design for its own sake. And that I bother to disclaim it brings me to another challenge that this book ably takes on: offering practical advice about the design of software.

This is a book for a group of people who are too rarely respectfully and compassionately addressed: technical professionals new to security. Welcome to this part of the profession. As you'll discover in these pages, the choices you make about the systems you work on can impact security. But you don't need to become a security expert to make better choices. This book will take you far. Some of you will want to go further, and there's plenty of material out there for you to read. Others will do well simply by applying what you learn here.

ADAM SHOSTACK
President, Shostack + Associates
Author of *Threat Modeling: Designing for Security* (Wiley, 2014)
Affiliate Professor, University of Washington Paul G. Allen School of
Computer Science and Engineering

# PREFACE

*If you cannot—in the long run—tell everyone*
*what you have been doing, your doing has been worthless.*
—Erwin Schrödinger

Join me on a hike through the software security landscape.

My favorite hike begins in a rainforest, near the top of the island of Kaua'i, which is often shrouded in misty rain. The trail climbs moderately at first, then descends along the contour of the sloping terrain, in places steep and treacherously slippery after frequent rains. Further down, passing through valleys choked with invasive ginger or overgrown by thorny lantana bushes, it gets seriously muddy, and the less dedicated turn and head back. A couple of miles out, the trees thin out as the environment gradually warms, becoming arid with the lower elevation. Further on, the first long views of the surrounding Pacific begin to open up, providing a glimpse of the promise the trail offers.

In my experience, many software professionals find security daunting at first: shrouded in mist, even vaguely treacherous. This is not without good reason. If the act of programming corresponded to a physical environment, this would be it.

The last mile of the trail runs through terrain made perilous by the loose volcanic rock that, due to the island's geologically tender age of five million years, hasn't had time to turn into soil. Code is as hard and unforgiving as rock, yet so fragile that one small flaw can lead to a disaster, just as one misstep on the trail could here. Fortunately, the hiking trail's path along the ridge has been well chosen, with natural handholds on the steepest section: sturdy basalt outcroppings or the exposed, solid roots of ohia trees.

Approaching the end of the trail, you'll find yourself walking along the rim of a deep gorge, the loose ground underfoot almost like ball bearings. To your right, a precipice drops over 2,000 feet. In places, the trail is shoulder width. I've seen acrophobic hikers turn around at this point, unable to summon the confidence to proceed. Yet most people are comfortable here, because the trail is *slightly inclined away from the dangerous side*. To the left, the risk is minimal; you face the same challenging footing but on a gentle slope, so at worst you might slide a few feet. I thought about this trail often as I wrote this book and have endeavored to provide just such a path, using stories and analogies like this one to tackle the toughest subjects in a way that I hope will help you get to the good stuff.

Security is challenging for a number of reasons: it's abstract, the subject is vast, and software today is both fragile and extremely complex. How can one explain the intricacies of security in enough depth to connect with readers, without overwhelming them with too much information? This book confronts those challenges in the spirit of hikers on that trail at the rim of the gorge: by leaning away from the danger of trying to cover everything. In the interest of not losing readers, I err on the side of simplification, leaving out some of the smaller details. By doing so, I hope to prevent readers from metaphorically falling into the gorge—that is, getting so confused or frustrated that they give up. The book should instead serve as a springboard, sparking your interest in continued exploration of software security practices.

As you approach the end of the trail, the ridge widens out and becomes flat, easy walking. Rounding the last curve, you're treated to a stunning panoramic view of the fabled Na Pali coast. To the right is a verdant hanging valley, steeply carved from the mountain. A waterfall feeds the meandering river visible almost directly below. The intricate coastline extends into the distance, flanked by neighboring islands on the horizon to the west. The rewards of visiting this place never get old. After drinking in the experience, a good workout awaits as you start the climb back up.

- - - - - - - - - - - - - - - - - -

Just as I'll never get to see every inch of this island, I won't learn everything there is to know about software security, and of course, no book will ever cover this broad topic completely, either. What I do have, as my guide, is my own experience. Each of us charts our own unique path through this topic, and I've been fortunate to have been doing this work for a long time. I've witnessed firsthand some key developments and followed the evolution of both the technologies and the culture of software development since its early days.

The purpose of this book is to show you the lay of the security land, with some words of warning about some of the hazards of the trail so you can begin confidently exploring further on your own. When it comes to security, cut-and-dried guidance that works in all circumstances is rare.

Instead, my aim is to show you some simple examples from the landscape to kick-start your interest and deepen your understanding of the core concepts. For every topic this book covers, there is always much more to say. Solving real-world security challenges always requires more context in order to better assess possible solutions; the best decisions are grounded in a solid understanding of the specifics of the design, implementation details, and more. As you grasp the underlying ideas and begin applying them, the work becomes intuitive with practice. Fortunately, even small improvements over time make the effort worthwhile.

When I look back on my work with the security teams at major software companies, a lost opportunity always strikes me. Working at a large and profitable corporation has many benefits: along with on-site massages and sumptuous cafes come on-tap security specialists (like myself) and a design review process. Yet few other software development efforts enjoy the benefits of this level of security expertise and a process that integrates security from the design phase. This book seeks to empower the software community to make this standard practice.

With myriad concerns to balance, designers have their hands full. The good ones are certainly aware of security considerations, but they rarely get a security design review. (And none of my industry acquaintances have even heard of the service being offered by consultants.) Developers also have varying degrees of security knowledge, and unless they pursue it as a specialty, their knowledge is often at best piecemeal. Some companies do care enough about security to hire expert consultants, but this invariably happens late in the process, so they're working after the fact to shore up security ahead of release. Bolting on security at the end has become the industry's standard strategy—the opposite of baking in security.

Over the years, I have tried to gently spread the word about security among my colleagues. Invariably, one quickly sees that certain people get it; others, not so much. Why people respond so differently is a mystery, possibly more psychological than technological, but it does raise an interesting question. What does it mean to "get" security, and how do you teach it? I don't mean world-class knowledge, or even mastery, but a sufficient grasp of the basics to be aware of the challenges and how to make incremental improvements. From that point, software professionals can continue their research to fill in any gaps. That's the objective that this book endeavors to deliver.

Throughout the process of writing this book, my understanding of the challenge this work entails has grown considerably. At first, I was surprised that a book like this didn't already exist; now I think I know why. Security concepts are frequently counterintuitive; attacks are often devious and nonobvious, and software design itself is already highly abstract. Software today is so rich and diverse that securing it represents a daunting challenge. Software security remains an unsolved problem, but we do understand large parts of it, and we're getting better at it—if only it weren't such a fast-moving target! I certainly don't have perfect answers for everything. All of the easy answers to security challenges are already built into our software platforms, so it's the hard problems that remain. This book strategically emphasizes concepts and the development of a security mindset. It invites more people to contribute to security, bringing a greater diversity of fresh perspectives and more consistent security focus.

I hope you will join me on this personal tour of my favorite paths through the security landscape, in which I share with you the most interesting insights and effective methodologies that I have to offer. If this book convinces you of the value of baking security into software from the design phase, of considering security throughout the process, and of going beyond what I can offer here, then it will have succeeded.

# ACKNOWLEDGMENTS

*Knowledge is in the end based on acknowledgement.*
—Ludwig Wittgenstein

I wrote this book with appreciation of the many colleagues in academia and industry from whom I have learned so much. Security work can be remarkably thankless—successes are often invisible, while failures get intense scrutiny—and it's extremely heartening that so many great people devote their considerable talents and effort to the cause.

Publishing with No Starch Press was my best choice to make this book the best it can be. Without exception, everyone was great to work with and infinitely patient handling my endless questions and suggestions.

I would like to thank the early readers of the manuscript for their valuable feedback: Adam Shostack, Elisa Heymann, Joel Scambray, John Camilleri, John Goben, Jonathan Lundell, and Tony Cargile. Adam's support has been above and beyond, leading to a wide range of other discussions, putting in the good word for me with No Starch Press, and capped off by his generous contribution of the foreword.

It would have been interesting to record all the errors corrected in the process of writing this book, and it certainly has been a great lesson in humility. I thank everyone for their sharp eyes, and take responsibility for what errors may have made it through. Please refer to the online errata at *https://www.nostarch.com/designing-secure-software/* for the latest corrections.

I have benefited from great support from others outside the tech sphere as well, and a few deserve special mention with my appreciation: Rosemary Brisco, for marketing advice; Lisa Steres, PhD, for unwavering enthusiasm and enduring interest in this project.

Finally, *arigatou* to my wife, Keiko, for her boundless support throughout this project.

# INTRODUCTION

This book is a guide for software professionals who want to better understand concepts
essential to the discipline of software security
and learn how to practice the art of secure software design and implementation. Several of the topics
covered here I was fortunate to have innovated myself.
Others, I witnessed develop and take root. Based on
my own industry experience, this book is packed with
actionable ideas you can start using right away to make
the software you work on more secure.

Two central themes run through this book: encouraging software professionals to focus on security early in the software construction process,
and involving the entire team in the process of—as well as the responsibility
for—security. There is certainly plenty of room for improvement in both of
these areas, and this book shows how to realize these goals.

I have had the unique opportunity of working on the front lines of software security over the course of my career, and now I would like to share my learnings as broadly as possible. Over 20 years ago, I was part of the team at Microsoft that first applied threat modeling at scale across a large software company. Years later, at Google, I participated in an evolution of the same fundamental practice, and experienced a whole new way of approaching the challenge. Part II of this book is informed by my having performed well over a hundred design reviews. Looking back on how far we have come provides me with a great perspective with which to explain it all anew.

Designing, building, and operating software systems is an inherently risky undertaking. Every choice, every step of the way, nudges the risk of introducing a security vulnerability either up or down. This book covers what I know best, learned from personal experience. I convey the security mindset from first principles and show how to bake in security throughout the development process. Along the way I provide examples of design and code, largely independent of specific technologies so as to be as broadly applicable as possible. The text is peppered with numerous stories, analogies, and examples to add spice and communicate abstract ideas as effectively as possible.

The security mindset comes more easily to some people than others, so I have focused on building that intuition, to help you think in new ways that will facilitate a software security perspective in your work. And I should add that in my own experience, even for those of us to whom it comes easily, there are always more insights to gain.

This is a concise book that covers a lot of ground, and in writing it, I have come to see its brevity as essential to what success it may achieve. Software security is a field of intimidating breadth and depth, so keeping the book shorter will, I hope, make it more broadly approachable. My aim is to get you thinking about security in new ways, and to make it easy for you to apply this new perspective in your own work.

## Who Should Read This Book?

This book is for anyone already proficient in some facet of software design and development, including architects, UX/UI designers, program managers, software engineers, programmers, testers, and management. Tech professionals should have no trouble following the conceptual material so long as they understand the basics of how software works and how it's constructed. Software is used so pervasively and is of such great diversity that I won't say *all* of it needs security; however, most of it likely does, and certainly any that connects to the internet or interfaces significantly with people.

In writing the book, I found it useful to consider three classes of prospective readers, and would like to offer a few words here to each of these camps.

*Security newbies*, especially those intimidated by security, are the primary audience I am writing for, because it's important that everyone working in software understands security so they can contribute to improving it. To make more secure software in the future we need everyone involved, and I hope this book will help those just starting to learn about security to quickly get up to speed.

*Security-aware* readers are those with interest in but limited knowledge of security, seeking to deepen their understanding and learn more practical ways of applying these skills to their work. I wrote this book to fill in the gaps and provide plenty of ways you can immediately put what you learn here into practice.

*Security experts* (you know who you are) round out the field. They may be familiar with much of the material, but I believe this book provides some new perspectives and still has much to offer them. Namely, the book includes discussions of important relevant topics such as secure design, security reviews, and "soft skills" that are rarely written about.

Part III of this book, which covers implementation vulnerabilities and mitigations, includes short excerpts of code written in either C or Python. Some examples assume familiarity with the concept of memory allocation, as well as an understanding of integer and floating-point types, including binary arithmetic. In a few places I use mathematical formulae, but nothing more than modulo and exponential arithmetic. Readers who find the code or math too technical or irrelevant should feel free to skip over these sections without fear of losing the thread of the overall narrative. References such as man(1) are *nix (Unix family of operating systems) commands (1) and functions (3).

# What Topics Does the Book Cover?

The book consists of 13 chapters organized into three parts, covering concepts, design, and implementation, plus a conclusion.

## Part I: Concepts

Chapters 1 through 5 provide a conceptual basis for the rest of book. **Chapter 1: Foundations**, is an overview of information security and privacy fundamentals. **Chapter 2: Threats**, introduces threat modeling, fleshing out the core concepts of attack surfaces and trust boundaries in the context of protecting assets. The next three chapters introduce valuable tools available to readers for building secure software. **Chapter 3: Mitigations**, discusses commonly used strategies for defensively mitigating identified threats. **Chapter 4: Patterns**, presents a number of effective security design patterns and flags some anti-patterns to avoid. **Chapter 5: Cryptography**, takes a toolbox approach to explaining how to use standard cryptographic libraries to mitigate common risks, without going into the underlying math (which is rarely needed in practice).

## Part II: Design

This part of the book represents perhaps its most unique and important contribution to prospective readers. **Chapter 6: Secure Design**, and

**Chapter 7: Security Design Reviews**, offer guidance on secure software design and practical techniques for how to accomplish it, approaching the subject from the designer's and reviewer's perspectives, respectively. In the process, they explain why it's important to bake security into software design from the beginning.

These chapters draw on the ideas introduced in the first part of the book, offering specific methodologies for how to incorporate them to build a secure design. The review methodology is directly based on my industry experience, including a step-by-step process you can adapt to how you work. Consider browsing the sample design document in Appendix A while reading these chapters as an example of how to put these ideas into practice.

## Part III: Implementation

Chapters 8 through 13 cover security at the implementation stage and touch on deployment, operations, and end-of-life. Once you have a secure design, this part of the book explains how to develop software without introducing additional vulnerabilities. These chapters include snippets of code, illustrating both how vulnerabilities creep into code and how to avoid them. **Chapter 8: Secure Programming**, introduces the security challenge that programmers face and what real vulnerabilities actually look like in code. **Chapter 9: Low-Level Coding Flaws**, covers the foibles of computer arithmetic and how C-style explicit management of dynamic memory allocation can undermine security. **Chapter 10: Untrusted Input**, and **Chapter 11: Web Security**, cover many of the commonplace bugs that have been well known for many years but just don't seem to go away (such as injection, path traversal, XSS, and CSRF vulnerabilities). **Chapter 12: Security Testing**, covers the greatly underutilized practice of testing to ensure that your code is secure. **Chapter 13: Secure Development Best Practices**, rounds out the secure implementation guidance, covering some general best practices and providing cautionary warnings about common pitfalls.

The excerpts of code in this part of the book generally demonstrate vulnerabilities to be avoided, followed by patched versions that show how to make the code secure (labeled "vulnerable code" and "fixed code," respectively). As such, the code herein is not intended to be copied for use in production software. Even the fixed code could have vulnerabilities in another context due to other issues, so you should not consider any code presented in this book to be guaranteed secure for any application.

## Conclusion

The Afterword concludes the book and describes some ways that I hope it will make a positive impact. Here I summarize the key points made in the book, attempt to peer into the future, and offer speculative ideas that could help ratchet software security upward, beginning with a vision for how this book can contribute to more secure software going forward.

### Appendices

**Appendix A** is a sample design document that illustrates what security-aware design looks like in practice.

**Appendix B** is a glossary of software security terms that appear throughout the book.

**Appendix C** includes some open-ended exercises and questions that ambitious readers might enjoy researching.

**Appendix D** consists of a collection of cheat sheets that summarize key concepts and processes.

In addition, a compilation of references to sources mentioned in the book can be found at *https://designingsecuresoftware.com/* (and linked from *https://nostarch.com/designing-secure-software/*).

## Good, Safe Fun

Before we get started, I'd like to add some important words of warning about being responsible with the security knowledge this book presents. In order to explain how to make software safe, I have had to describe how various vulnerabilities work, and how attackers potentially exploit them. Experimentation is a great way to hone skills from both the attack and defense perspectives, but it's important to use this knowledge carefully.

Never play around by investigating security on production systems. When you read about cross-site scripting (XSS), for instance, you may be tempted to try browsing your favorite website with tricky URLs to see what happens. Please don't. Even when done with the best of intentions, these explorations may look like real attacks to site administrators. It's important to respect the possibility that others will interpret your actions as a threat—and, of course, you may be skirting the law in some countries. Use your common sense, including considering how your actions might be interpreted and the possibility of mistakes and unintended consequences, and err on the side of refraining. Instead, if you'd like to experiment with XSS, put up your own web server using fake data; you can then play around with this to your heart's content.

Furthermore, while this book presents the best general advice I can offer based on many years of experience working on software security, no guidance is perfect or applicable in every conceivable context. Solutions mentioned herein are never "silver bullets": they are suggestions, or examples of common approaches worth knowing about. Rely on your best judgment when assessing security decisions. No book can make these choices for you, but this book can help you get them right.

# PART I

## CONCEPTS

# 1

## FOUNDATIONS

*Honesty is a foundation, and it's usually a solid foundation. Even if I do get in trouble for what I said, it's something that I can stand on.*
—Charlamagne tha God

Software security is at once a logical practice and an art, one based on intuitive decision making. It requires an understanding of modern digital systems, but also a sensitivity to the humans interacting with, and affected by, those systems. If that sounds daunting, then you have a good sense of the fundamental challenge this book endeavors to explain. This perspective also sheds light on why software security has continued to challenge the field for so long, and why the solid progress made so far has taken so much effort, even if it has only chipped away at some of the problems. Yet there is very good news in this state of affairs, because it means that all of us can make a real difference by increasing our awareness of, and participation in, better security at every stage of the process.

We begin by considering what security exactly is. Given security's subjective nature, it's critical to think clearly about its foundations. This book represents my understanding of the best thinking out there, based on my own experience. Trust undergirds all of security, because nobody works in a vacuum, and modern digital systems are far too complicated to be built single-handedly from the silicon up; you have to trust others to provide everything (starting with the hardware, firmware, operating system, and compilers) that you don't create yourself. Building on this base, next I present the six classic principles of security: the three components of classic information security and the three-part "Gold Standard" used to enforce it. Finally, the section on information privacy adds important human and societal factors necessary to consider as digital products and services become increasingly integrated into the most sensitive realms of modern life.

Though readers doubtlessly have good intuitions about what words such as *security*, *trust*, or *confidentiality* mean, in this book these words take on specific technical meanings worth teasing out carefully, so I suggest reading this chapter closely. As a challenge to more advanced readers, I invite you to attempt to write better descriptions yourself—no doubt it will be an educational exercise for everyone.

## Understanding Security

All organisms have natural instincts to chart a course away from danger, defend against attacks, and aim toward whatever sanctuary they can find.

It is important to appreciate just how remarkable our innate sense of physical security is, when it works. By contrast, we have few genuine signals to work with in the virtual world—and fake signals are easily fabricated. Before we approach security from a technical perspective, let's consider a real-world story as an illustration of what humans are capable of. (As we'll see later, in the digital domain we need a whole new set of skills.)

The following is a true story from an auto salesman. After conducting a customer test drive, the salesman and customer returned to the lot. The salesman got out of the car and continued to chat with the customer while walking around to the front of the car. "When I looked him in the eyes," the salesman recounted, "That's when I said, 'Oh no. This guy's gonna try and steal this car.'" Events accelerated: the customer-turned-thief put the car in gear and sped away while the salesman hung on for the ride of his life *on the hood of the car*. The perpetrator drove violently in an unsuccessful attempt to throw him from the vehicle. (Fortunately, the salesman sustained no major injuries and the criminal was soon arrested, convicted, and ordered to pay restitution.)

A subtle risk calculation took place when those men locked eyes. Within fractions of a second, the salesman had processed complex visual signals, derived from the customer's facial expression and body language, distilling into a clear intention of a hostile action. Now imagine that the same salesman was the target of a *spear phishing* attack (a fraudulent email designed to fool a specific target, as opposed to a mass audience). In the digital realm, without the signals he detected when face-to-face with his attacker, he'd be much more easily tricked.

When it comes to information security, computers, networks, and software, we need to think analytically to assess the risks we face if we want to have any hope of securing digital systems. And we must do this despite being unable to directly see, smell, or hear bits or code. Whenever you're examining data online, you're using software to display information in human-readable fonts, and typically, there's a lot of code between you and the actual bits; in fact, it's potentially a hall of mirrors. So you must trust your tools and trust that you really are examining the data you think you are.

Software security centers on the protection of digital assets against an array of threats, an effort largely driven by a basic set of security principles that the rest of this chapter will discuss. By analyzing a system from these first principles, we can learn how vulnerabilities slip into software, as well as how to proactively avoid and mitigate problems. These foundational principles, along with other design techniques covered in subsequent chapters, apply not only to software but also to designing and operating bicycle locks, bank vaults, or prisons.

The term *information security* refers specifically to the protection of data and how access is granted. *Software security* is a broader term that focuses on the design, implementation, and operation of software systems that are trustworthy, including the reliable enforcement of information security.

## Trust

Trust is equally critical in the digital realm, yet too often taken for granted. Software security ultimately depends on trust, because you cannot control every part of a system, write all of your own software, or vet all suppliers of dependencies. Modern digital systems are so complex that not even the major tech giants can build a complete technology stack from scratch. From the silicon to the operating systems, networking, peripherals, and the numerous software layers that make it all work, the systems we rely on routinely are remarkable technical accomplishments of immense size and complexity. Since nobody can build these systems all by themselves, organizations rely on hardware and software products often chosen based on features or pricing—but it's important to remember that each dependency also involves a *trust decision*.

Security demands that we examine these trust relationships closely, even though nobody has the time or resources to investigate and verify everything. Failing to trust enough means doing a lot of needless work to protect a system when no real threat is likely. On the other hand, trusting too freely could mean getting blindsided later. Put bluntly, when you fully trust an entity, they are free to fail without consequences. Trust can be violated in two fundamentally different ways: by malice (cheating, lying, subterfuge) and by incompetence (mistakes, misunderstandings, negligence).

The need to make critical decisions in the face of incomplete information is precisely what trust is best suited for. But our innate sense of trust relies on subtle sensory inputs wholly unsuited to the digital realm. The following discussion begins with the concept of trust itself, dissects what trust as we experience it is, and then shifts to trust as it relates to software. As you read along, try to find the common threads and connect how you think about software to your intuitions about trust. Tapping into your existing trust skills is a powerful technique that over time gives you a gut feel for software security that is more effective than any amount of technical analysis.

## Feeling Trust

The best way to understand trust is to pay attention while experiencing what relying on trust actually feels like. Here's a thought experiment—or an exercise to try for real, with someone you *really trust*—that brings home exactly what trust means. Imagine walking along a busy thoroughfare with a friend, with traffic streaming by only a few feet away. Sighting a crosswalk up ahead, you explain that you would like them to guide you across the road, that you are relying on them to cross safely, and that you are closing your eyes and will obediently follow them. Holding hands, you and your friend proceed to the crosswalk, where they gently turn you to face the road, gesturing by touch that you should wait. Listening to the sounds of speeding cars, you know well that your friend (and now, guardian) is waiting until it is safe to cross, but your heartbeat has most likely also increased noticeably, and you may find yourself listening attentively for any sound of impending danger.

Now your friend unmistakably leads you forward, guiding you to step down from the curb. If you decide to step into the road with your eyes closed, what you are feeling is pure trust—or perhaps some degree of the lack thereof. Your mind keenly senses palpable risk, your senses strain to confirm safety directly, and something deep down is warning you not to do it. Your own internal security monitoring system has insufficient evidence and wants you to open your eyes before moving; what if your friend somehow misjudges the situation, or worse, is playing a deadly evil trick on you? Ultimately, it's the trust you have invested in your friend that allows you to override those instincts and cross the road.

Raise your own awareness of digital trust decisions, and help others see how important their impact is on security. Ideally, when you select a component or choose a vendor for a critical service, you'll be able to tap into the very same intuitions that guide trust decisions like in the exercise just described.

## You Cannot See Bits

All of this discussion is to emphasize the fact that when you think you are "looking directly at the data," you are actually looking at a distant representation. In fact, you are looking at pixels on a screen that you believe represent the contents of certain bytes whose physical location you don't know with any precision, and many millions of instructions were likely executed in order to map the data into the human-legible form on your display. Digital technology makes trust especially tricky, because it's so abstract, lightning fast, and hidden from direct view. Whenever you examine data, remember that there is a lot of software and hardware between the actual data in memory and the pixels that form characters that we interpret as the data value. If something in there were maliciously misrepresenting the actual data, how would you possibly know? Ground truth about digital information is extremely difficult to observe directly.

Consider the lock icon in the address bar of a web browser indicating a secure connection to the website. The appearance or absence of these distinctive pixels communicates a single bit to the user: safe or unsafe. Behind the scenes, there is a lot of data and considerable computation, as will be detailed in Chapter 11, all rolling up into a binary yes/no security indication. Even an expert developer would face a Herculean task attempting to manually confirm the validity of just one instance. So all we can do is trust the software—and there is every reason that we should trust it. The point here is to recognize how deep and pervasive that trust is, not just take it for granted.

## Competence and Imperfection

Most attacks begin by exploiting a software flaw or misconfiguration that resulted from the honest, good faith efforts of programmers and IT staff, who happen to be human, and hence imperfect. Since licenses routinely disavow essentially all liability, all software is used on a *caveat emptor* basis. If, as is routinely claimed, "all software has bugs," then a subset of those bugs will be exploitable, and eventually the attackers will find a few of those bugs and have an opportunity to use them maliciously. It's relatively rare for software professionals to fall victim to an attack due to misplaced trust in malicious software, enabling a direct attack.

Fortunately, making big trust decisions about operating systems and programming languages is usually easy. Many large corporations have extensive track records of providing and supporting quality hardware and software products, and it's quite reasonable to trust them. Trusting others with less of a track record might be riskier. While they likely have many skilled and motivated people working diligently, the industry's lack of transparency makes the security of their products difficult to judge. Open source provides transparency, but depends on the degree of supervision the project owners provide as a hedge against contributors slipping in code that is buggy or even outright malicious. Remarkably, no software company even attempts to distinguish itself by promising higher levels of security or indemnification in the event of an attack, so as customers we have no such options. Legal, regulatory, and business agreements all provide additional ways of mitigating the uncertainty around trust decisions.

Take trust decisions seriously, but recognize that nobody gets it right 100 percent of the time. The bad news is that these decisions will always be imperfect, because, as the US Securities and Exchange Commission warns us, "past performance does not guarantee future results." The good news is that people are highly evolved to gauge trust—though it works best face-to-face, decidedly not via digital media—and in the vast majority of cases we do make the right trust decisions, provided we have accurate information and act with intention.

## Trust Is a Spectrum

Trust is always granted in degrees, and trust assessments always have some uncertainty. At the far end of the spectrum, such as when undergoing major surgery, we may literally entrust our lives to medical professionals, willingly ceding not just control over our bodies but our very consciousness and ability to monitor the operation. In the worst case scenario, if they should fail us and we do not survive, we literally have no recourse whatsoever (legal rights of our estate aside). Everyday trust is much more limited: credit cards have limits to cap the bank's potential loss on nonpayment, while cars have valet keys so we can limit access to the trunk.

Since trust is a spectrum, a "trust but verify" policy is a useful tool that bridges the gap between full trust and complete distrust. In software, you can achieve this through the combination of authorization and diligent auditing. Typically, this involves a combination of *automated auditing* (to accurately check a large volume of mostly repetitive activity logs) and *manual auditing* (spot checking, handling exceptional cases, and having a human in the loop to make final decisions). We'll cover auditing in more detail later in this chapter.

## Trust Decisions

In software, you have a binary choice: to trust, or not to trust? While some systems do enforce a variety of permissions on applications, you still need to either allow or disallow each given permission. When in doubt, you can safely err on the side of distrusting, so long as at least one candidate solution reasonably gains your trust. If you are too demanding in your assessments, and no product can gain your trust, then you are stuck with the prospect of building the component yourself.

Think of making trust decisions as cutting branches off a decision tree that otherwise would be effectively infinite. When you can trust a service or computer to be secure, that saves you the effort of doing deeper analysis. On the other hand, if you are reluctant to trust, then you need to build and secure more parts of the system, including all subcomponents. Figure 1-1 illustrates an example of making a trust decision. If there is no available cloud storage service you would fully trust to store your data, then you must operate the service yourself, and this entails further trust decisions: to use a trusted hosting service or do it yourself, and to use existing database software that you trust or write it yourself. Note that when you don't trust a provider then more trust decisions are sure to follow since you cannot do everything.

For explicitly distrusted inputs—which should include virtually all inputs, especially anything from the public internet or any client—treat that data with suspicion and the highest levels of care (for more on this, see "Reluctance to Trust" on page 68 in Chapter 4). Even for trusted inputs, it can be risky to assume they are perfectly reliable. Consider opportunistically adding safety checks when it's easy to do so, if only to reduce the fragility of the overall system and to prevent the propagation of errors in the event of an innocent bug.

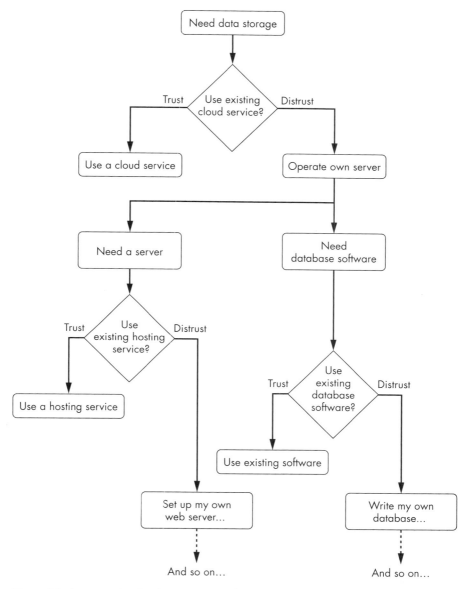

Figure 1-1: An example of a decision tree with trust decisions

## Implicitly Trusted Components

Every software project relies on an extensive stack of technology that is *implicitly trusted*, including hardware, operating systems, development tools, libraries, and other dependencies that are impractical to vet, so we trust them based on the reputation of the vendor. Nonetheless, you should maintain some sense of what is implicitly trusted, and give these decisions due consideration, especially before greatly expanding the scope of implicit trust.

There are no simple techniques for managing implicit trust, but here is an idea that can help: minimize the number of parties you trust. For example, if you are already committed to using Microsoft (or Apple, and so forth) operating systems, lean toward using their compilers, libraries, applications, and other products and services, so as to minimize your exposure. The reasoning is roughly that trusting additional companies increases the opportunities for any of these companies to let you down. Additionally, there is the practical aspect that one company's line of products tend to be more compatible and better tested when used together.

### Being Trustworthy

Finally, don't forget the flip side of making trust decisions, which is to *promote* trust when you offer products and services. Every software product must convince end users that it's trustworthy. Often, just presenting a solid professional image is all it takes, but if the product is fulfilling critical functions, it's crucial to give customers a solid basis for that trust.

Here are some suggestions of basic ways to enhance trust in your work:

- Transparency engenders trust. Working openly allows customers to assess the product.
- Involving a third party builds trust through their independence (for example, using hired auditors).
- Sometimes your product is the third party that integrates with other products. Trust grows because it's difficult for two parties with an arm's-length relationship to collude.
- When problems do arise, be open to feedback, act decisively, and publicly disclose the results of any investigation and steps taken to prevent recurrences.
- Specific features or design elements can make trust visible—for example, an archive solution that shows in real time how many backups have been saved and verified at distributed locations.

Actions beget trust, while empty claims, if anything, erode trust for savvy customers. Provide tangible evidence of being trustworthy, ideally in a way that customers can potentially verify for themselves. Even though few will actually vet the quality of open source code, knowing that they could (and assuming others likely are doing so) is nearly as convincing.

## Classic Principles

The guiding principles of information security originated in the early days of computing, when computers were emerging from special locked, air-conditioned, raised-floor rooms and starting to be connected in networks. These traditional models are the "Newtonian physics" of modern information security: a good and simple guide for many applications, but not the be-all and end-all. For example, information privacy is one of the more nuanced considerations for modern data protection and stewardship that traditional information security principles do not cover.

The foundational principles group nicely into two sets of three. The first three principles, which I will call *C-I-A*, define data access requirements; the other three, in turn, concern how access is controlled and monitored. We call these the *Gold Standard*. The two sets of principles are interdependent, and only as a whole do they protect data assets.

Beyond the prevention of unauthorized data access lies the question of who or what components and systems should be entrusted with access. This is a harder question of trust, and ultimately beyond the scope of information security, even though confronting it is unavoidable in order to secure any digital system.

## Information Security's C-I-A

We traditionally build software security on three basic principles of information security: *confidentiality*, *integrity*, and *availability*. Formulated around the fundamentals of data protection, the individual meanings of the three pillars are intuitive:

**Confidentiality**

Allow only authorized data access—don't leak information.

**Integrity**

Maintain data accurately—don't allow unauthorized modification or deletion.

**Availability**

Preserve the availability of data—don't allow significant delays or unauthorized shutdowns.

Each of these brief definitions describes the goal and defenses against its subversion. In reviewing designs, it's often helpful to think of ways one might undermine security, and work back to defensive measures.

All three components of C-I-A represent ideals, and it's crucial to avoid insisting on perfection. For example, an analysis of even solidly encrypted network traffic could allow a determined eavesdropper to deduce something about the communications between two endpoints, like the volume of data exchanged. Technically, this exchange of data weakens the confidentiality of interaction between the endpoints; but for practical purposes, we can't fix it without taking extreme measures, and usually the risk is minor enough to be safely ignored. (One way to conceal the fact of communication is for endpoints to always exchange a constant volume of data, adding dummy packets as needed when actual traffic is lower.) What activity corresponds to the traffic, and how might an adversary use that knowledge? The next chapter explains similar threat assessments in detail.

Notice that authorization is inherent in each component of C-I-A, which mandates only the right disclosures, modifications of data, or controls of availability. What constitutes "right" is an important detail, and an authorization policy needs to specify that, but it isn't part of these fundamental data protection primitive concepts. That part of the story will be discussed in "The Gold Standard" starting on page 14.

### Confidentiality

Maintaining confidentiality means disclosing private information in only an authorized manner. This sounds simple, but in practice it involves a number of complexities.

First, it's important to carefully identify what information to consider private. Design documents should make this distinction clear. While what counts as sensitive might sometimes seem obvious, it's actually surprising how people's opinions vary, and without an explicit specification, we risk misunderstanding. The safest assumption is to treat all externally collected information as private by default, until declared otherwise by an explicit policy that explains how and why the designation can be relaxed.

Here are some oft-overlooked reasons to treat data as private:

- An end user might naturally expect their data to be private, unless informed otherwise, even if revealing it isn't harmful.
- People might enter sensitive information into a text field intended for a different use.
- Information collection, handling, and storage might be subject to laws and regulations that many are unaware of. (For example, if Europeans browse your website, it may be subject to EU law, such as the General Data Protection Regulation.)

When handling private information, determine what constitutes proper access. Deciding when and how to disclose information is ultimately a trust decision, and it's worth not only spelling out the rules, but also explaining the subjective choices behind those rules.

Compromises of confidentiality happen on a spectrum. In a complete disclosure, attackers acquire an entire dataset, including metadata. At the lower end of the spectrum might be a minor disclosure of information, such as an internal error message or similar leak of no real consequence. As an example of a partial disclosure, consider the practice of assigning sequential numbers to new customers: a wily competitor can sign up as a new customer and get a new customer number from time to time, then compute the successive differences to learn the numbers of customers acquired during each interval. Any leakage of details about protected data is to some degree a confidentiality compromise.

It's so easy to underestimate the potential value of minor disclosures. Attackers might put data to use in a completely different way than the developers originally intended, and combining tiny bits of information can provide more powerful insights than any of the individual parts on their own. Learning someone's ZIP code might not tell you much, but if you also know their approximate age and that they're an MD, you could perhaps combine this information to identify the individual in a sparsely populated area—a process known as *deanonymization* or *reidentification*. By analyzing a supposedly anonymized dataset published by Netflix, researchers were able to match numerous user accounts to IMDb accounts: it turns out that your favorite movies are an effective means of unique personal identification.

### Integrity

Integrity, used in an information security context, is simply the authenticity and accuracy of data, kept safe from unauthorized tampering or removal. In addition to protecting against unauthorized modification, an accurate record of the *provenance* of data—the original source, and any authorized changes made—can be an important, and stronger, assurance of integrity.

One classic defense against many tampering attacks is to preserve versions of critical data and record their provenance. Simply put, keep good backups. Incremental backups can be excellent mitigations because they're simple and efficient to put in place and provide a series of snapshots that detail exactly what data changed, and when. However, the need for integrity goes far beyond the protection of data, and often includes ensuring the integrity of components, server logs, software source code and versions, and other forensic information necessary to determine the original source of tampering when problems occur. In addition to limited administrative access controls, secure digests (similar to checksums) and digital signatures are also strong integrity checks, as explained in Chapter 5.

Bear in mind that tampering can happen in many different ways, not necessarily by modifying data in storage. For instance, in a web application, tampering might happen on the client side, on the wire between the client and server, by tricking an authorized party into making a change, by modifying a script on the page, or in many other ways.

### Availability

Attacks on availability are a sad reality of the internet-connected world and can be among the most difficult to defend against. In the simplest cases, the attacker may just send an exceptionally heavy load of traffic to the server, overwhelming it with what looks like valid uses of the service. This principle implies that information is *temporarily* unavailable; while data that is permanently lost is also unavailable, this is generally considered to be fundamentally a compromise of integrity.

Anonymous denial-of-service (DoS) attacks, often for ransom, threaten any internet service, posing a difficult challenge. To best defend against these attacks, host on large-scale services with infrastructure that stands up to heavy loads, and maintain the flexibility to move infrastructure quickly in the event of problems. Nobody knows how common or costly DoS attacks really are, since many victims resolve these incidents privately. But without a doubt, you should create detailed plans in advance to prepare for such incidents.

Many other kinds of availability threats are possible as well. For a web server, a malformed request that triggers a bug, causing a crash or infinite loop, can devastate its service. Other attacks can also overload the storage, computation, or communication capacity of an application, or perhaps use patterns that break the effectiveness of caching, all of which pose serious issues. Unauthorized destruction of software, configuration, or data (even with backup, delays can result) also can adversely impact availability.

## The Gold Standard

If C-I-A is the goal of secure systems, the Gold Standard describes the means to that end. *Aurum* is Latin for gold, hence the chemical symbol "Au," and it just so happens that the three important principles of security enforcement start with those same two letters:

**Authentication**

High-assurance determination of the identity of a principal

**Authorization**

Reliably only allowing an action by an authenticated principal

**Auditing**

Maintaining a reliable record of actions by principals for inspection

**NOTE** *Jargon alert: because the words are so long and similar, you may encounter the handy abbreviations authN (for authentication) and authZ (for authorization) as short forms that plainly distinguish them.*

A *principal* is any reliably authenticated entity: a person, business or organization, government entity, application, service, device, or any other agent with the power to act.

*Authentication* is the process of reliably establishing the validity of the principal's credentials. Systems commonly allow registered users to authenticate by proving that they know the password associated with their user account, but authentication can be much broader. Credentials may be something the principal knows (a password) or possesses (a smart card), or something they are (biometric data); we'll talk more about credentials in the next section.

Data access for authenticated principals is subject to *authorization* decisions, either allowing or denying their actions according to prescribed rules. For example, filesystems with access control settings may make certain files read-only for specific users. In a banking system, clerks may record transactions up to a certain amount, but might require a manager to approve larger transactions.

If a service keeps a secure log that accurately records what principals do, including any failed attempts at performing some action, the administrators can perform a subsequent *audit* to inspect how the system performed and ensure that all actions are proper. Accurate audit logs are an important component of strong security, because they provide a reliable report of actual events. Detailed logs provide a record of what happened, shedding light on exactly what transpired when an unusual or suspicious event takes place. For example, if you discover that an important file is gone, the log should ideally provide details of who deleted it and when, providing a starting point for further investigation.

The Gold Standard acts as the enforcement mechanism that protects C-I-A. We defined confidentiality and integrity as protection against *unauthorized* disclosure or tampering, and availability is also subject to control by an authorized administrator. The only way to truly enforce authorization decisions is if the principals using the system are properly authenticated. Auditing completes the picture by providing a reliable log of who did what and when, subject to regular review for irregularities, and holding the acting parties responsible.

Secure designs should always explicitly separate authentication from authorization, because combining them leads to confusion, and audit trails are clearer when these stages are cleanly divided. These two real-world examples illustrate why the separation is important:

- "Why did you let that guy into the vault?" "I have no idea, but he looked legit!"
- "Why did you let that guy into the vault?" "His ID was valid for 'Sam Smith' and he had a written note from the branch manager."

The second response is much more complete than the first, which is of no help at all, other than proving that the guard is a nitwit. If the vault was compromised, the second response would give clear details to investigate: Did the branch manager have authority to grant vault access and write the note? If the guard retained a copy of the ID, then that information helps identify and find Sam Smith. By contrast, if the branch manager's note had just said, "let the bearer into the vault"—authorization without authentication—investigators would have had little idea what happened or who the intruder was after security was breached.

## Authentication

An authentication process tests a principal's claims of identity based on credentials that demonstrate they really are who they claim to be. Or the service might use a stronger form of credentials, such as a digital signature or a challenge, which proves that the principal possesses a private key associated with the identity, which is how browsers authenticate web servers via HTTPS. The digital signature is a better form of authentication because the principal can prove they know the secret without divulging it.

Evidence suitable for authentication falls into the following categories:

- *Something you know*, like a password
- *Something you have*, like a secure token, or in the analog world some kind of certificate, passport, or signed document that is unforgeable
- *Something you are*—that is, biometrics (fingerprint, iris pattern, and such)
- *Somewhere you are*—your verified location, such as a connection to a private network in a secure facility

Many of these methods are quite fallible. Something you know can be revealed, something you have can be stolen or copied, your location can be manipulated in various ways, and even something you are can potentially be faked (and if it's compromised, you can't later change what you are). On top of those concerns, in today's networked world, authentication almost always happens across a network, making the task more difficult than in-person authentication. On the web, for instance, the browser serves as a trust intermediary, locally authenticating and, only if successful, then passing along cryptographic credentials to the server. Systems commonly use multiple authentication factors to mitigate these concerns, and auditing these frequently is another important backstop. Two weak authentication factors are better than one (but not a lot better).

Before an organization can assign someone credentials, however, it has to address the gnarly question of how to determine a person's true identity when they join a company, sign up for an account, or call the helpdesk to reinstate access after forgetting their password.

For example, when I joined Google, all of us new employees gathered on a Monday morning opposite several IT admin folks, who checked our passports or other ID against a new employee roster. Only then did they give us our badges and company-issued laptops and have us establish our login passwords.

By checking whether the credentials we provided (our IDs) correctly identified us as the people we purported to be, the IT team confirmed our identities. The security of this identification depended on the integrity of the government-issued IDs and supporting documents (for example, birth certificates) we provided. How accurately were those issued? How difficult would they be to forge, or obtain fraudulently? Ideally, a chain of association from registration at birth would remain intact throughout our lifetimes to uniquely identify each of us authentically. Securely identifying people is challenging largely because the most effective techniques reek of authoritarianism and are socially unacceptable, so to preserve some privacy and freedom, we opt for weaker methods in daily life. The issue of how to determine a person's true identity is out of scope for this book, which will focus on the Gold Standard, not this harder problem of *identity management*.

Whenever feasible, rely on existing trustworthy authentication services, and do not reinvent the wheel unnecessarily. Even simple password authentication is quite difficult to do securely, and dealing securely with forgotten passwords is even harder. Generally speaking, the authentication process should examine credentials and provide either a pass or fail response. Avoid indicating partial success, since this could aid an attacker zeroing in on the credentials by trial and error. To mitigate the threat of brute-force guessing, a common strategy is to make authentication inherently computationally heavyweight, or to introduce increasing delay into the process (also see "Avoid Predictability" on page 61 in Chapter 4).

After authenticating the user, the system must find a way to securely bind the identity to the principal. Typically, an authentication module issues a token to the principal that they can use in lieu of full authentication for subsequent requests. The idea is that the principal, via an agent such as a web browser, presents the authentication token as shorthand assurance of who they claim to be, creating a *secure context* for future requests. This context binds the stored token for presentation with future requests on behalf of the authenticated principal. Websites often do this with a secure cookie associated with the browsing session, but there are many different techniques for other kinds of principals and interfaces.

The secure binding of an authenticated identity can be compromised in two fundamentally different ways. The obvious one is where an attacker usurps the victim's identity. Alternatively, the authenticated principal may collude and try to give away their identity or even foist it off on someone else. An example of the latter case is the sharing of a paid streaming subscription. The web does not afford very good ways of defending against this because the binding is loose and depends on the cooperation of the principal.

## Authorization

A decision to allow or deny critical actions should be based on the identity of the principal as established by authentication. Systems implement authorization in business logic, an access control list, or some other formal access policy.

Anonymous authorization (that is, authorization without authentication) can be useful in rare circumstances; a real-world example might be possession of the key to a public locker in a busy station. Access restrictions based on time (for example, database access restricted to business hours) are another common example.

A single guard should enforce authorization on a given resource. Authorization code scattered throughout a codebase is a nightmare to maintain and audit. Instead, authorization should rely on a common framework that grants access uniformly. A well-structured design can help the developers get it right. Use one of the many standard authorization models rather than confusing ad hoc logic wherever possible.

*Role-based access control (RBAC)* bridges the connection between authentication and authorization. RBAC grants access based on roles assigned to authenticated principals, simplifying access control with a uniform framework. For example, roles in a bank might include a clerk, manager, loan officer, security guard, financial auditor, and IT administrator. Instead of choosing access privileges for each person individually, RBAC designates one or more roles based on each person's responsibilities to automatically and uniformly assign them associated privileges. In more advanced models, one person might have multiple roles and explicitly select which role they choose to apply for a given access.

Authorization mechanisms can be much more granular than the simple read/write access control that operating systems traditionally provide. By designing more robust authorization mechanisms, you can strengthen security by limiting access without losing useful functionality. These more advanced authorization models include *attribute-based access control (ABAC)*, *policy-based access control (PBAC)*, and many more.

Consider a simple bank teller example to see how fine-grained authorization might tighten up policy:

**Rate-limited**

Tellers may do up to 20 transactions per hour, but more would be considered suspicious.

**Time of day**

Teller transactions must occur during business hours, when clocked in.

**No self-service**

Tellers are forbidden to do transactions with their personal accounts.

**Multiple principals**

Teller transactions over $10,000 require separate manager approval (eliminating the risk of one bad actor moving a lot of money at once).

Finally, even read-only access may be too high a level for certain data, like passwords. Systems usually check login passwords by comparing digests, which avoids any possibility of leaking the actual plaintext password. The username and password go to a frontend server that computes the digest of the password and passes it to an authentication service, quickly destroying any trace of the plaintext password. The authentication service cannot read the plaintext password from the credentials database, but it can read the digest, which it compares to what the frontend server provided. In this way, it checks the credentials, but the authentication service never has access to any passwords, so even if compromised, the service cannot leak them. Unless the design of interfaces affords these alternatives, they will miss these opportunities to mitigate the possibility of data leakage. We'll explore this further when we discuss the pattern of "Least Information" on page 57 in Chapter 4.

### Auditing

In order for an organization to audit system activity, the system must produce a reliable log of all events that are critical to maintaining security. These include authentication and authorization events, system startup and shutdown, software updates, administrative accesses, and so forth. Audit logs must also be tamper-resistant, and ideally even difficult for administrators to meddle with, to be considered fully reliable records. Auditing is a critical leg of the Gold Standard, because incidents do happen, and authentication and authorization policies can be flawed. Auditing can also provide necessary oversight to mitigate the risk of inside jobs in which authorized principals betray their trust.

If done properly, audit logs are essential for routine monitoring, measuring system activity level, detecting errors and suspicious activity, and, after an incident, determining when and how an attack actually happened and gauging the extent of the damage. Remember that completely protecting a digital system is not simply a matter of correctly enforcing policies; it's about being a responsible steward of information assets. Auditing ensures that trusted principals acted properly within the broad range of their authority.

In May 2018, Twitter disclosed an embarrassing bug: they had discovered that a code change had inadvertently caused raw login passwords to appear in internal logs. It's unlikely that this resulted in any abuse, but it certainly hurt customer confidence and should never have happened. Logs should record operational details but not store any actual private information so as to minimize the risk of disclosure, since many members of the technical staff may routinely view the logs. For a detailed treatment of this requirement, see the sample design document in Appendix A detailing a logging tool that addresses just this problem.

The system must also prevent anyone from tampering with the logs to conceal bad acts. If the attacker can modify logs, they'll just clean out all traces of their activity. For especially sensitive logs at high risk, an independent system under different administrative and operational controls should manage audit logs in order to prevent the perpetrators of inside jobs from covering their own tracks. This is difficult to do completely, but the mere presence of independent oversight often serves as a powerful disincentive to any funny business, just as a modest fence and conspicuous video surveillance camera can be an effective deterrent to trespassing.

Furthermore, any attempt to circumvent the system would seem highly suspicious, and any false move would result in serious repercussions for the offender. Once caught, they would have a hard time repudiating their guilt.

*Non-repudiability* is an important property of audit logs; if the log shows that a named administrator ran a certain command at a certain time and the system crashed immediately, it's hard to point fingers at others. By contrast, if an organization allowed multiple administrators to share the same account (a terrible idea), it would have no way of definitively knowing who actually did anything, providing plausible deniability to all.

Ultimately, audit logs are useful only if you monitor them, analyze unusual events carefully, and follow up, taking appropriate actions when necessary. To this end, it's important to log the right amount of detail by following the *Goldilocks principle*. Too much logging bloats the volume of data to oversee, and excessively noisy or disorganized logs make it difficult to glean useful information. On the other hand, sparse logging with insufficient detail might omit critical information, so finding the right balance is an ongoing challenge.

## Privacy

In addition to the foundations of information security—C-I-A and the Gold Standard—another fundamental topic I want to introduce is the related field of information privacy. The boundaries between security and privacy are difficult to clearly define, and they are at once closely related and quite different. In this book I would like to focus on the common points of intersection, not to attempt to unify them, but to incorporate both security and privacy into the process of building software.

To respect people's digital information privacy, we must extend the principle of confidentiality by taking into account additional human factors, including:

- Customer expectations regarding information collection and use
- Clear policies regarding appropriate information use and disclosure
- Legal and regulatory issues relating to the collection and use of various classes of information
- Political, cultural, and psychological aspects of processing personal information

As software becomes more pervasive in modern life, people use it in more intimate ways involving sensitive areas of their lives, resulting in many complex issues. Past accidents and abuses have raised the visibility of the risks, and as society grapples with new challenges through political and legal means, handling private information properly has become challenging.

In the context of software security, this means:

- Considering the customer and stakeholder consequences of all data collection and sharing
- Flagging all potential issues, and getting expert advice where necessary
- Establishing and following clear policies and guidelines regarding private information use
- Translating policy and guidance into software-enforced checks and balances
- Maintaining accurate records of data acquisition, use, sharing, and deletion
- Auditing data access authorizations and extraordinary access for compliance

Privacy work tends to be less well-defined than the relatively cut-and-dried security work of maintaining proper control of systems and providing appropriate access. Also, we're still working out privacy expectations and norms as society ventures deeper into a future with more data collection. Given these challenges, you would be wise to consider maximal transparency about data use, including keeping your policies simple enough to be understood by all, and to collect minimal data, especially personally identifiable information.

Collect information for a specific purpose only, and retain it only as long as it's useful. Unless the design envisions an authorized use, avoid collection in the first place. Frivolously collecting data for use "someday" is risky, and almost never a good idea. When the last authorized use of some data becomes unnecessary, the best protection is secure deletion. For especially sensitive data, or for maximal privacy protection, make that even stronger: delete data when the potential risk of disclosure exceeds the potential value of retaining it. Retaining many years' worth of emails might occasionally be handy for something, but probably not for any clear business need. Yet internal emails could represent a liability if leaked or disclosed, such as by power of subpoena. Rather than hang onto all that data indefinitely "just in case," the best policy is usually to delete it.

A complete treatment of information privacy is outside the scope of this book, but privacy and security are tightly bound facets of the design of any system that collects data about people—and people interact with almost all digital systems, in one way or another. Strong privacy protection is only possible when security is solid, so these words are an appeal for awareness to consider and incorporate privacy considerations into software by design.

For all its complexity, one best practice for privacy is well known: the necessity of clearly communicating privacy expectations. In contrast to security, a privacy policy potentially affords a lot of leeway as to how much an information service does or does not want to leverage the use of customer data. "We will reuse and sell your data" is one extreme of the privacy spectrum, but "some days we may not protect your data" is not a viable stance on security. Privacy failures arise when user expectations are out of joint with actual privacy policy, or when there is a clear policy and it is somehow violated. The former problem stems from not proactively explaining data handling to the user. The latter happens when the policy is unclear, or ignored by responsible staff, or subverted in a security breakdown.

**NOTE**   *See Appendix D for a cheat sheet summarizing the C-I-A and Gold Standard principles.*

# 2

## THREATS

*The threat is usually more terrifying than the thing itself.*
—Saul Alinsky

Threats are omnipresent, but you can live with them if you manage them. Software is no different, except that you don't have the benefit of millions of years of evolution to prepare yourself. That is why you need to adopt a software security mindset, which requires you to flip from the builder's perspective to that of the attackers. Understanding the potential threats to a system is the essential starting point in order to bake solid defenses and mitigations into your software designs. But to perceive these threats in the first place, you'll have to stop thinking about typical use cases and using the software as intended. Instead, you must simply see it for what it is: a bunch of code and components, with data flowing around and getting stored here and there.

For example, consider the paperclip: it's cleverly designed to hold sheets of paper together, but if you bend a paperclip just right, it's easily refashioned into a stiff wire. A security mindset discerns that you could insert this wire into the keyhole of a lock to manipulate the tumblers and open it without the key.

It's worth emphasizing that threats include all manner of ways in which harm occurs. Adversarial attacks conducted with intention are an important focus of the discussion, but this does not mean that you should exclude other threats due to software bugs, human error, accidents, hardware failures, and so on.

Threat modeling provides a perspective with which to guide any decisions that impact security throughout the software development process. The following treatment focuses on concepts and principles, rather than any of the many specific methodologies for doing threat modeling. Early threat modeling as first practiced at Microsoft in the early 2000s proved effective, but it required extensive training, as well as a considerable investment of effort. Fortunately, you can do threat modeling in any number of ways, and once you understand the concepts, it's easy to tailor your process to fit the time and effort available while still producing meaningful results.

Setting out to enumerate all the threats and identify all the points of vulnerability in a large software system is a daunting task. However, smart security work targets incrementally raising the bar, not shooting for perfection. Your first efforts may only find a fraction of all the potential issues, and only mitigate some of those: even so, that's a substantial improvement. Such an effort may just possibly avert a major security incident—a real accomplishment. Unfortunately, you almost never know about foiled attacks, and that absence of feedback can feel disappointing. The more you flex your security mindset muscles, the better you'll become at seeing threats.

Finally, it's important to understand that threat modeling can provide new levels of understanding of the target system beyond the scope of security. Through the process of examining the software in new ways, you may gain insights that suggest various improvements, efficiencies, simplifications, and new features unrelated to security.

## The Adversarial Perspective

*Exploits are the closest thing to "magic spells" we experience in the real world: Construct the right incantation, gain remote control over device.*

—Halvar Flake

Human perpetrators are the ultimate threat; security incidents don't just happen by themselves. Any concerted analysis of software security includes considering what hypothetical adversaries might try in order to anticipate and defend against potential attacks. Attackers are a motley group, from *script kiddies* (criminals without tech skills using automated malware) to sophisticated nation-state actors, and everything in between. To the extent you can think from an adversary's perspective, that's great, but don't fool yourself into believing you can accurately predict their every move or spend too much time trying to get inside their heads, like a master sleuth outsmarting a wily foe. It's helpful to understand the attacker's mindset, but for our purposes of building secure software, the details of actual techniques they might use to probe, penetrate, and exfiltrate data are unimportant.

Consider what the obvious targets within a system might be (sometimes, what's valuable to an adversary is less valuable to you, or vice versa) and ensure that those assets are robustly secured, but don't waste time attempting to read the minds of hypothetical attackers. Rather than expend unnecessary effort, they'll often focus on the weakest link to accomplish their goal (or they might be poking around aimlessly, which can be very hard to defend against since their actions will seem undirected and arbitrary). Bugs definitely attract attention because they suggest weakness, and attackers who stumble onto an apparent bug will try creative variations to see if they can really bust something. Errors or side effects that disclose details of the insides of the system (for example, detailed stack dumps) are prime fodder for attackers to jump on and run with.

Once attackers find a weakness, they're likely to focus more effort on it, because some small flaws have a way of expanding to produce larger consequences under concerted attack (as we shall see in Chapter 8 in detail). Often, it's possible to combine two tiny flaws that are of no concern individually to produce a major attack, so it's wise to take all vulnerabilities seriously. Skilled attackers definitely know about threat modeling, though they are working without inside information (at least until they manage some degree of penetration).

Even though we can never really anticipate what our adversaries will spend time on, it does make sense to consider the motivation of hypothetical attackers as a measure of the likelihood of diligent attacks. Basically, this amounts to a famous criminal's explanation of why he robbed banks: "Because that's where the money is." The point is, the greater the prospective gain from attacking a system, the higher the level of skill and resources you can expect potential attackers to apply. Speculative as this might be, the analysis is useful as a relative guide: powerful corporations and government, military, and financial institutions are big targets. Your cat photos are not.

In the end, as with all forms of violence, it's always far easier to attack and cause harm than to defend. Attackers get to choose their point of entry, and with determination they can try as many exploits as they like, because they only need to succeed once. All this amounts to more reasons why it's important to prioritize security work: the defenders need every advantage available.

## The Four Questions

Adam Shostack, who carried the threat modeling torch at Microsoft for years, boils the methodology down to Four Questions:

- What are we working on?
- What can go wrong?
- What are we going to do about it?
- Did we do a good job?

The first question aims to establish the project's context and scope. Answering it includes describing the project's requirements and design, its components and their interactions, as well as considering operational issues and use cases. Next, at the core of the method, the second question attempts to anticipate potential problems, while the third question explores mitigations to those problems we identify. (We'll look more closely at mitigations in Chapter 3, but first we will examine how they relate to threats.) Finally, the last question asks us to reflect on the entire process—what the software does, how it can go wrong, and how well we've mitigated the threats—in order to assess the risk reduction and confirm that the system will be sufficiently secure. Should unresolved issues remain, we go through the questions again to fill in the remaining gaps.

There is much more to threat modeling than this, but it's surprising how far simply working from the Four Questions can take you. Armed with these concepts, in conjunction with the other ideas and techniques in this book, you can significantly raise the security bar for the systems you build and operate.

## Threat Modeling

"What could possibly go wrong?"

We often ask this question to make a cynical joke. But when asked unironically, it succinctly expresses the point of departure for threat modeling. Responding to this question requires us to identify and assess threats; we can then prioritize these and work on mitigations that reduce the risk of the important threats.

Let's unpack that previous sentence. The following steps outline the basic threat modeling process:

1. Work from a model of the system to ensure that we consider everything in scope.

2. Identify *assets* (valuable data and resources) within the system that need protection.

3. Scour the system model for potential threats, component by component, identifying *attack surfaces* (places where an attack could originate), *trust boundaries* (interfaces bridging more-trusted parts of the system with the less-trusted parts), and different types of threats.

4. Analyze these potential threats, from the most concrete to the hypothetical.

5. Rank the threats, working from the most to least critical.

6. Propose mitigations to reduce risk for the most critical threats.

7. Add mitigations, starting from the most impactful and easiest, and working up to the point of diminishing returns.

8. Test the efficacy of the mitigations, starting with those for the most critical threats.

For complex systems, a complete inventory of all potential threats will be enormous, and a full analysis is almost certainly infeasible (just as enumerating every conceivable way of doing anything would never end if you got imaginative, which attackers often do). In practice, the first threat modeling pass should focus on the biggest and most likely threats to the high-value assets only. Once you've understood those threats and put first-line mitigations in place, you can evaluate the remaining risk by iteratively considering the remaining lesser threats that you've already identified. From that point, you can perform one or more additional threat modeling passes as needed, casting a wider net each time to include additional assets, deeper analysis, and more of the less likely or minor threats. The process stops when you've achieved a sufficiently thorough understanding of the most important threats, planned the necessary mitigations, and deemed the remaining known risk acceptable.

People intuitively do something akin to threat modeling in daily life, taking what we call common-sense precautions. To send a private message in a public place, most people type it instead of dictating it aloud to their phones. Using the language of threat modeling, we'd say the message content is the information asset, and disclosure is the threat. Speaking within earshot of others is the attack surface, and using a silent, alternative input method is a good mitigation. If a nosy stranger is watching, you could add an additional mitigation, like cupping the phone with your other hand to shield the screen from view. But while we do this sort of thing all the time quite naturally in the real world, applying these same techniques to complex software systems, where our familiar physical intuitions don't apply, requires much more discipline.

## Work from a Model

You'll need a rigorous approach in order to thoroughly identify threats. Traditionally, threat modeling uses data flow diagrams (DFDs) or Unified Modeling Language (UML) descriptions of the system, but you can use whatever model you like. Whatever high-level description of the system you choose, be it a DFD, UML, a design document, or an informal "whiteboard session," the idea is to look at an abstraction of the system, so long as it has enough granularity to capture the detail you need for analysis.

More formalized approaches tend to be more rigorous and produce more accurate results, but at the cost of additional time and effort. Over the years, the security community has invented a number of alternative methodologies that offer different trade-offs, in no small part because the full-blown threat modeling method (involving formal models like DFDs) is so costly and effort-intensive. Today, you can use specialized software to help with the process. The best ones automate significant parts of the work, although interpreting the results and making risk assessments will always require human judgment. This book tells you all you need to know in order to threat model on your own, without special diagrams or tools, so long as you understand the system well enough to thoroughly answer the Four Questions. You can work toward more advanced forms from there as you like.

Whatever model you work from, thoroughly cover the target system at the appropriate resolution. Choose the appropriate level of detail for the analysis by the Goldilocks principle: don't attempt too much detail or the work will be endless, and don't go too high-level or you'll omit important details. Completing the process quickly with little to show for it is a sure sign of insufficient granularity, just as making little headway after hours of work indicates your model may be too granular.

Let's consider what the right level of granularity would be for a generic web server. You're handed a model consisting of a block diagram showing "the internet" on the left, connected to a "frontend server" in the center, with a third component, "database," on the right. This isn't helpful, because nearly every web application ever devised fits this model. All the assets are presumably in the database, but what exactly are they? There must be a trust boundary between the system and the internet, but is that the only one? Clearly, this model operates at too high a level. At the other extreme would be a model showing a detailed breakdown of every library, all the dependencies of the framework, and the relationships of components far below the level of the application you want to analyze.

The Goldilocks version would fall somewhere between these extremes. The data stored in the database (assets) would be clumped into categories, each of which you could treat as a whole: say, customer data, inventory data, and system logs. The server component would be broken into parts granular enough to reveal multiple processes, including what privilege each runs at, perhaps an internal cache on the host machine, and descriptions of the communication channels and network used to talk to the internet and the database.

### Identify Assets

Working methodically through the model, identify assets and the potential threats to them. Assets are the entities in the system that you must protect. Most assets are data, but they could also include hardware, communication bandwidth, computational capacity, and physical resources, such as electricity.

Beginners at threat modeling naturally want to protect everything, which would be great in a perfect world. But in practice, you'll need to prioritize your assets. For example, consider any web application: anyone on the internet can access it using browsers or other software that you have no control over, so it's impossible to fully protect the client side. Also, you should always keep internal system logs private, but if the logs contain harmless details of no value to outsiders, it doesn't make sense to invest much energy in protecting them. This doesn't mean that you ignore such risks completely; just make sure that less important mitigations don't take away effort needed elsewhere. For example, it literally takes a minute to protect non-sensitive logs by setting permissions so that only administrators can read the contents, so that's effort well spent.

On the other hand, you could effectively treat data representing financial transactions as real money and prioritize it accordingly. Personal information is another increasingly sensitive category of asset, because knowledge of a person's location or other identifying details can compromise their privacy or even put them at risk.

Also, I generally advise against attempting to perform complex risk-assessment calculations. For example, avoid attempting to assign dollar values for the purpose of risk ranking. To do this, you would have to somehow come up with probabilities for many unknowables. How many attackers will target you, and how hard will they try, and to do what? How often will they succeed, and to what degree? How much money is the customer database even worth? (Note that its value to the company and the amount an attacker could sell it for often differ, as might the value that users would assign to their own data.) How many hours of work and other expenses will a hypothetical security incident incur?

Instead, a simple way to prioritize assets that's surprisingly effective is to rank them by "T-shirt sizes"—a simplification that I find useful, though it's not a standard industry practice. Assign "Large" to major assets you definitely protect, "Medium" to valuable assets that are less critical, and "Small" to lesser ones of minor consequence (usually not even listed). High-value systems may have "Extra-Large" assets that deserve extraordinary levels of protection, such as bank account balances at a financial institution, or private encryption keys that anchor the security of communications. In this simple scheme, protection and mitigation efforts focus first on Large assets, and then *opportunistically* on Medium ones. Opportunistic protection consists of low-effort work that has little downside. But even if you can secure Small assets very opportunistically, defend all Large assets before spending any time on these. Chapter 13 discusses ranking vulnerabilities in detail, and much of that is applicable to threat assessment as well.

The assets you choose to prioritize should probably include data such as customer resources, personal information, business documents, operational logs, and software internals, to name just a few possibilities. Prioritizing protection of data assets considers many factors, including information security (the C-I-A triad discussed in Chapter 1), because the harms of leaking, modification, and destruction of data may differ greatly. Information leaks, including partial disclosures of information (for example, the last four digits of a credit card number), are tricky to evaluate, because you must consider what an attacker could do with the information. Analysis becomes harder still when an attacker could join multiple shards of information into an approximation of the complete dataset.

If you lump assets together, you can simplify the analysis considerably, but beware of losing resolution in the process. For example, if you administer several of your databases together, grant access similarly, use them for data that originates from similar sources, and store them in the same location, treating them as one makes good sense. However, if any of these factors differs significantly, you would have sufficient reason to handle them separately. Make sure to consider these distinctions in your risk analysis, as well as for mitigation purposes.

Finally, always consider the value of assets from the perspectives of all parties involved. For instance, social media services manage all kinds of data: internal company plans, advertising data, and customer data. The value of each of these assets differs depending on if you are the company's CEO, an advertiser, a customer, or perhaps an attacker seeking financial gain or pursuing a political agenda. In fact, even among customers you'll likely find great differences in how they perceive the importance of privacy in their communications, or the value they place on their data. Good data stewardship principles suggest that your protection of customer and partner data should arguably exceed that of the company's own proprietary data (and I have heard of company executives actually stating this as policy).

Not all companies take this approach. Facebook's Beacon feature automatically posted the details of users' purchases to their news feeds, then quickly shut down following an immediate outpouring of customer outrage and some lawsuits. While Beacon never endangered Facebook (except by damaging the brand's reputation), it posed a real danger to customers. Threat modeling the consequences of information disclosure for customers would have quickly revealed that the unintended disclosure of purchases of Christmas or birthday presents, or worse, engagement rings, was likely to prove problematic.

## Identify Attack Surfaces

Pay special attention to attack surfaces, because these are the attacker's first point of entry. You should consider any opportunity to minimize the attack surface a big win, because doing so shuts off a potential source of trouble entirely. Many attacks potentially fan out across the system, so stopping them early can be a great defense. This is why secure government buildings have checkpoints with metal detectors just inside the single public entrance.

Software design is typically much more complex than the design of a physical building, so identifying the entire attack surface is not so simple. Unless you can embed a system in a trusted, secure environment, having some attack surface is inevitable. The internet always provides a huge point of exposure, since literally anyone anywhere can anonymously connect through it. While it might be tempting to consider an *intranet* (a private network) as trusted, you probably shouldn't, unless it has very high standards of both physical and IT security. At the very least, treat it as an attack surface with reduced risk. For devices or kiosk applications, consider the outside portion of the box, including screens and user interface buttons, an attack surface.

Note that attack surfaces exist outside the digital realm. Consider the kiosk, for example: a display in a public area could leak information via "shoulder surfing." An attacker could also perform even subtler *side-channel attacks* to deduce information about the internal state of a system by monitoring its electromagnetic emissions, heat, power consumption, keyboard sounds, and so forth.

## Identify Trust Boundaries

Next, identify the system's trust boundaries. Since trust and privilege are almost always paired, you can think in terms of privilege boundaries if that makes more sense. Human analogs of trust boundaries might be the interface between a manager (who is privy to more internal information) and an employee, or the door of your house, where you choose whom to let inside.

Consider a classic example of a trust boundary: an operating system's kernel-userland interface. This architecture became popular in a time when mainframe computers were the norm and machines were often shared by many users. The system booted up the kernel, which isolated applications in different userland process instances (corresponding to different user accounts) from interfering with each other or crashing the whole system. Whenever userland code calls into the kernel, execution crosses a trust boundary. Trust boundaries are important, because the transition into higher-privilege execution is an opportunity for bigger trouble.

---

### TRUST VERSUS PRIVILEGE

In this book I'll be talking about *high* and *low privilege* as well as *high* and *low trust*, and there is great potential for confusion since they are very closely related and difficult to separate cleanly. The inherent character of trust and privilege is such that they almost invariably correlate: where trust is high, privilege is also usually high, and vice versa. Beyond the scope of this book, it's common for people to use these expressions (trust versus privilege) interchangeably, and generously interpreting them however makes best sense to you without insisting on correcting others is usually the best practice.

---

The SSH secure shell daemon (sshd(8)) is a great example of secure design with trust boundaries. The SSH protocol allows authorized users to remotely log in to a host, then run a shell via a secure network channel over the internet. But the SSH daemon, which persistently listens for connections to initiate the protocol, requires very careful design because it crosses a trust boundary. The listener process typically needs superuser privileges, because when an authorized user presents valid credentials, it must be able to create processes for any user. Yet it must also listen to the public internet, exposing it to the world for attack.

To accept SSH login requests, the daemon must generate a secure channel for communication that's impervious to snooping or tampering, then handle and validate sensitive credentials. Only then can it instantiate a shell process on the host computer with the right privileges. This entire process involves a lot of code, running with the highest level of privilege (so it can create a process for any user account), that must operate perfectly or risk deeply compromising the system. Incoming requests can come from anywhere on the internet and are initially indistinguishable from attacks, so it's hard to imagine a more attractive target with higher stakes.

Given the large attack surface and the severity of any vulnerability, extensive efforts to mitigate risk are justified for the daemon process. Figure 2-1 shows a simplified view of how it is designed to protect this critical trust boundary.

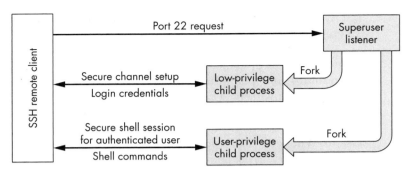

*Figure 2-1: How the design of the SSH daemon protects critical trust boundaries*

Working from the top, each incoming connection forks a low-privilege child process, which listens on the socket and communicates with the parent (superuser) process. This child process also sets up the protocol's complex secure-channel encryption and accepts login credentials that it passes to the privileged parent, which decides whether or not to trust the incoming request and grant it a shell. Forking a new child process for each request provides a strategic protection on the trust boundary; it isolates as much of the work as possible, and also minimizes the risk of unintentional side effects building up within the main daemon process. When a user successfully logs in, the daemon creates a new shell process with the privileges of the authenticated user account. When a login attempt fails to authenticate, the child process that handled the request terminates, so it can't adversely affect the system in the future.

As with assets, you'll decide when to lump together or split trust levels. In an operating system, the superuser is, of course, the highest level of trust, and some other administrative users may be close enough that you should consider them to be just as privileged. Authorized users typically rank next on the totem pole of trust. Some users may form a more trusted group with special privileges, but usually, there is no need to decide who you trust a little or more or less among them. Guest accounts typically rank lowest in trust, and you should probably emphasize protecting the system from them, rather than protecting their resources.

Web services need to resist malicious client users, so web frontend systems may validate incoming traffic and only forward well-formed requests for service, in effect straddling the trust boundary to the internet. Web servers often connect to more trusted databases and microservices behind a firewall. If money is involved (say, in a credit card processing service), a dedicated high-trust system should handle payments, ideally isolated in a fenced-off area of the datacenter. Authenticated users should be trusted to access their own account data, but you should treat them as very much untrusted beyond that, since anyone can typically create a login. Anonymous public web access represents an even lower trust level, and static public content could be served by machines unconnected to any private data services.

Always conduct transitions across trust boundaries through well-defined interfaces and protocols. You can think of these as analogous to checkpoints staffed by armed guards at international frontiers and ports of entry. Just as the border control agents ask for your passport (a form of authentication) and inspect your belongings (a form of input validation), you should treat the trust boundary as a rich opportunity to mitigate potential attacks.

The biggest risks usually hide in low-to-high trust transitions, like the SSH listener example, for obvious reasons. However, this doesn't mean you should ignore high-to-low trust transitions. Any time your system passes data to a less-trusted component, it's worth considering if you're disclosing information, and if doing so might be a problem. For example, even low-privilege processes can read the hostname of the computer they are running in, so don't name machines using sensitive information that might give attackers a hint if they attain a beachhead and get code running on the system. Additionally, whenever high-trust services work on behalf of low-trust requests, you risk a DoS attack if the userland requester manages to overtax the kernel.

## Identify Threats

Now we begin the work at the heart of threat modeling: identifying potential threats. Working from your model, pore over the parts of the system. The threats tend to cluster around assets and at trust boundaries, but could potentially lurk anywhere.

I recommend starting with a rough pass (say, from a 10,000-foot view of the system), then coming back later for a more thorough examination (at 1,000 feet) of the more fruitful or interesting parts. Keep an open mind, and be sure to include possibilities even if you cannot yet see exactly how to exploit them.

Identifying direct threats to your assets should be easy, as well as threats at trust boundaries, where attackers might easily trick trusted components into doing their bidding. Many examples of such threats in specific situations are given throughout this book. Yet you might also find threats that are indirect, perhaps because there is no asset immediately available to harm, or a trust boundary to cross. Don't immediately disregard these without considering how such threats might work as part of a chain of events—think of them as bank shots in billiards, or stepping stones that form a path. In order to do damage, an attacker would have to combine multiple indirect threats; or perhaps, paired with bugs or poorly designed functionality, the indirect threats afford openings that give attackers a foot in the door. Even lesser threats might be worth mitigating, depending on how promising they look and how critical the asset at risk may be.

### A Bank Vault Example

So far, these concepts may still seem rather abstract, so let's look at them in context by threat modeling an imaginary bank vault. While reading this walkthrough, focus on the concepts, and if you are paying attention, you should be able to expand on the points I raise (which, intentionally, are not exhaustive).

Picture a bank office in your hometown. Say it's an older building, with impressive Roman columns framing the heavy solid oak double doors in front.

Built back when labor and materials were inexpensive, the thick, reinforced concrete walls appear impenetrable. For the purpose of this example, let's focus solely on the large stock of gold stored in the secure vault at the heart of the bank building: this is the major asset we want to protect. We'll use the building's architectural drawings as the model, working from a floor plan with a 10-foot to 1-inch scale that provides an overview of the entire building's layout.

The major trust boundary is clearly at the vault door, but there's another one at the locked door to the employee-only area behind the counter, and a third at the bank's front door that separates the customer lobby from the exterior. For simplicity, we'll omit the back door from the model because it's very securely locked at all times and only opened rarely, when guards are present. This leaves the front door and easily-accessible customer lobby areas as the only significant attack surfaces.

All of this sets the stage for the real work of finding potential threats. Obviously, having the gold stolen is the top threat, but that's too vague to provide much insight into how to prevent it, so we continue looking for specifics. The attackers would need to gain unauthorized access to the vault in order to steal the gold. In order to do that, they'd need unauthorized access to the employee-only area where the vault is located. So far, we don't know *how* such abstract threats could occur, but we can break them down and get more specific. Here are just a few potential threats:

- Observe the vault combination covertly.
- Guess the vault combination.
- Impersonate the bank's president with makeup and a wig.

Admittedly, these made-up threats are fairly silly, but notice how we developed them from a model, and how we transitioned from abstract threats to concrete ones.

In a more detailed second pass, we now use a model that includes full architectural drawings, the electrical and plumbing layout, and vault design specifications. Armed with more detail, we can imagine specific attacks more easily. Take the first threat we just listed: the attacker observing the vault combination. This could happen in several ways. Let's look at three of them:

- An eagle-eyed robber loiters in the lobby to observe the opening of the vault.
- The vault combination is on a sticky note, visible to a customer at the counter.
- A confederate across the street can watch the vault combination dial through a scope.

Naturally, just knowing the vault combination does not get the intruders any gold. An outsider learning the combination is a major threat, but it's just one part of a complete attack that must include entering the employee-only area, entering the vault, and then escaping with the gold.

Now we can prioritize the enumerated threats and propose mitigations. Here are some straightforward mitigations to each potential attack we've identified:

- Lobby loiterer: put an opaque screen in front of the vault.
- Sticky-note leak: institute a policy prohibiting unsecured written copies.
- Scope spy: install opaque, translucent glass windows.

These are just a few of the many possible defensive mitigations. If these types of attacks had been considered during the building's design, perhaps the layout could have eliminated some of these threats in the first place (for example, by ensuring there was no direct line of sight from any exterior window to the vault area, avoiding the need to retrofit opaque glass).

Real bank security and financial risk management are of course far more complex, but this simplified example shows how the threat modeling process works, including how it propels analysis forward. Gold in a vault is about as simple an asset as it gets, but now you should be wondering, how exactly does one examine a model of a complex software system to be able to see the threats it faces?

## Categorizing Threats with STRIDE

In the late 1990s, Microsoft Windows dominated the personal computing landscape. As PCs became essential tools for both businesses and homes, many believed the company's sales would grow endlessly. But Microsoft had only begun to figure out how networking should work. The Internet (back then still usually spelled with a capital I) and this new thing called the World Wide Web were rapidly gaining popularity, and Microsoft's Internet Explorer web browser had aggressively gained market share from the pioneering Netscape Navigator. Now the company faced this new problem of security: Who knew what can of worms connecting all the world's computers might open up?

While a team of Microsoft testers worked creatively to find security flaws, the rest of the world appeared to be finding these flaws much faster. After a couple of years of reactive behavior, issuing patches for vulnerabilities that exposed customers over the network, the company formed a task force to get ahead of the curve. As part of this effort, I co-authored a paper with Praerit Garg that described a simple methodology to help developers see security flaws in their own products. Threat modeling based on the *STRIDE threat taxonomy* drove a massive education effort across all the company's product groups. More than 20 years later, researchers across the industry continue to use STRIDE and many independent derivatives to enumerate threats.

STRIDE focuses the process of identifying threats by giving you a checklist of specific kinds of threats to consider: What can be *spoofed (S), tampered (T)* with, or *repudiated (R)*? What *information (I)* can be disclosed? How could a *denial of service (D)* or *elevation of privilege (E)* happen? These categories are specific enough to focus your analysis, yet general enough that you can mentally flesh out details relevant to a particular design and dig in from there.

Though members of the security community often refer to STRIDE as a threat modeling methodology, this is a misuse of the term (to my mind, at least, as the one who concocted the acronym). STRIDE is simply a taxonomy of threats to software. The acronym provides an easy and memorable mnemonic to ensure that you haven't overlooked any category of threat. It's not a complete threat modeling methodology, which would have to include the many other components we've already explored in this chapter.

To see how STRIDE works, let's start with spoofing. Looking through the model, component by component, consider how secure operation depends on the identity of the user (or machine, or digital signature on code, and so on). What advantages might an attacker gain if they could spoof identity here? This thinking should give you lots of possible threads to pull on. By approaching each component in the context of the model from a threat perspective, you can more easily set aside thoughts of how it should work, and instead begin to perceive how it might be abused.

Here's a great technique I've used successfully many times: start your threat modeling session by writing the six threat names on a whiteboard. To get rolling, brainstorm a few of these abstract threats before digging into the details. The term "brainstorm" can mean different things, but the idea here is to move quickly, covering a lot of area, without overthinking it too much or judging ideas yet (you can skip the duds later on). This warm-up routine primes you for what to look out for, and also helps you switch into the necessary mindset. Even if you're familiar with these categories of threat, it's worth going through them all, and a couple that are less familiar and more technical bear careful explanation.

Table 2-1 lists six security objectives, their corresponding threat categories, and several examples of threats in each category. The security objective and threat category are two sides of the same coin, and sometimes it's easier to work from one or the other—on the defense (the objective) or the offense (the threat).

**Table 2-1:** Summary of STRIDE Threat Categories

| Objective | STRIDE threats | Examples |
|---|---|---|
| Authenticity | Spoofing | Phishing, stolen password, impersonation, replay attack, BGP hijacking |
| Integrity | Tampering | Unauthorized data modification and deletion, Superfish ad injection |
| Non-repudiability | Repudiation | Plausible deniability, insufficient logging, destruction of logs |
| Confidentiality | Information disclosure | Data leak, side channel attack, weak encryption, residual cached data, Spectre/Meltdown |
| Availability | Denial of service | Simultaneous requests swamp a web server, ransomware, memcrashed |
| Authorization | Elevation of privilege | SQL injection, xkcd's "Exploits of a Mom" |

Half of the STRIDE menagerie are direct threats to the information security fundamentals you learned about in Chapter 1: information disclosure is the enemy of confidentiality, tampering is the enemy of integrity, and denial of service compromises availability. The other half of STRIDE targets the Gold Standard. Spoofing subverts authenticity by assuming a false identity. Elevation of privilege subverts proper authorization. That leaves repudiation as the threat to auditing, which may not be immediately obvious and so is worth a closer look.

According to the Gold Standard, we should maintain accurate records of critical actions taken within the system and then audit those actions. Repudiation occurs when someone credibly denies that they took some action. In my years working in software security, I have never seen anyone directly repudiate anything (nobody has ever yelled "did so!" and "did not!" at each other in front of me). But what does happen is, say, a database suddenly disappears, and nobody knows why, because nothing was logged, and the lost data is gone without a trace. The organization might suspect that an intrusion occurred. Or it could have been a rogue insider, or possibly a regrettable blunder by an administrator. But without any evidence, nobody knows. That's a big problem, because if you cannot explain what happened after an incident, it's very hard to prevent it from happening again. In the physical world, such perfect crimes are rare because activities such as robbing a bank involve physical presence, which inherently leaves all kinds of traces. Software is different; unless you provide a means to reliably collect evidence and log events, no fingerprints or muddy boot tracks remain as evidence.

Typically, we mitigate the threat of repudiation by running systems in which administrators and users understand they are responsible for their actions, because they know an accurate audit trail exists. This is also one more good reason to avoid having admin passwords written on a sticky note that everyone shares. If you do that, when trouble happens, everyone can credibly claim someone else must have done it. This applies even if you fully trust everyone, because accidents happen, and the more evidence you have available when trouble arises, the easier it is to recover and remediate.

## STRIDE at the Movies

Just for fun (and to solidify these concepts), consider the STRIDE threats applied to the plot of the film *Ocean's Eleven*. This classic heist story nicely demonstrates threat modeling concepts, including the full complement of STRIDE categories, from the perspectives of both attacker and defender. Apologies for the simplification of the plot, which I've done for brevity and focus, as well as for spoilers.

Danny Ocean violates parole (an *elevation of privilege*), flies out to meet his old partner in crime, and heads for Vegas. He pitches an audacious heist to a wealthy casino insider, who fills him in on the casino's operational details (*information disclosure*), then gathers his gang of ex-cons. They plan their operation using a full-scale replica vault built for practice. On the fateful night, Danny appears at the casino and is predictably apprehended by security, creating the perfect alibi (*repudiation* of guilt). Soon he slips away through an air duct, and through various intrigues he and his accomplices extract half the money from the vault (*tampering* with its integrity), exfiltrating their haul with a remote-control van.

Threatening to blow up the remaining millions in the vault (a very expensive *denial of service*), the gang negotiates to keep the money in the van. The casino owner refuses and calls in the SWAT team, and in the ensuing chaos the gang destroys the vault's contents and gets away. After the smoke clears, the casino owner checks the vault, lamenting his total loss, then notices a minor detail that seems amiss. The owner confronts Danny—who is back in lockup, as if he had never left—and we learn that the SWAT team was, in fact, the gang (*spoofing* by impersonating the police), who walked out with the money hidden in their tactical equipment bags after the fake battle. The practice vault mock-up had provided video to make it only appear (*spoofing* of the location) that the real vault had been compromised, which didn't actually happen until the casino granted full access to the fake SWAT team (an *elevation of privilege* for the gang). Danny and the gang make a clean getaway with the money—a happy ending for the perpetrators that might have turned out quite differently had the casino hired a threat modeling consultant!

## Mitigate Threats

At this stage, you should have a collection of potential threats. Now you need to assess and prioritize them to best guide an effective defense. Since threats are, at best, educated guesses about future events, all of your assessments will contain some degree of subjectivity.

What exactly does it mean to understand threats? There is no easy answer to this question, but it involves refining what we know, and maintaining a healthy skepticism to avoid falling into the trap of thinking that we have it all figured out. In practice, this means quickly scanning to collect a bunch of mostly abstract threats, then poking into each one a little further to learn more. Perhaps we will see one or two fairly clear-cut attacks, or parts of what could constitute an attack. We elaborate until we run up against a wall of diminishing returns.

At this point, we can deal with the threats we've identified in one of four ways:

- *Mitigate* the risk by either redesigning or adding defenses to reduce its occurrence or lower the degree of harm to an acceptable level.

- *Remove* a threatened asset if it isn't necessary, or, if removal isn't possible, seek to reduce its exposure or limit optional features that increase the threat.

- *Transfer* the risk by offloading responsibility to a third party, usually in exchange for compensation. (Insurance, for example, is a common form of risk transfer, or the processing of sensitive data could be outsourced to a service with a duty to protect confidentiality.)

- *Accept* the risk, once it is well understood, as reasonable to incur.

Always attempt to mitigate any significant threats, but recognize that results are often mixed. In practice, the best possible solution isn't always feasible, for many reasons: a major change might be too costly, or you may be stuck using an external dependency beyond your control. Other code might also depend on vulnerable functionality, such that a fix might break things. In these cases, mitigation means doing anything that reduces the threat. Any kind of edge for defense helps, even a small one.

Here are some examples of ways to do partial mitigation:

**Make harm less likely to occur**

Make it so the attack only works a fraction of the time.

**Make harm less severe**

Make it so only a small part of the data can be destroyed.

**Make it possible to undo the harm**

Ensure that you can easily restore any lost data from a backup.

**Make it obvious that harm occurred**

Use tamper-evident packaging that makes it easy to detect a modified product, protecting consumers. (In software, good logging helps here.)

Much of the remainder of the book is about mitigation: how to design software to minimize threats, and what strategies and secure software patterns are useful for devising mitigations of various sorts.

## Privacy Considerations

Privacy threats are just as real as security threats, and they require separate consideration in a full assessment of threats to a system, because they add a human element to the risk of information disclosure. In addition to possible regulatory and legal considerations, personal information handling may involve ethical concerns, and it's important to honor stakeholder expectations.

If you're collecting personal data of any kind, you should take privacy seriously as a baseline stance. Think of yourself as a steward of people's private information. Strive to stay mindful of your users' perspectives, including careful consideration of the wide range of privacy concerns they might have, and err on the side of care. It's easy for builders of software to discount how sensitive personal data can be when they're immersed in the logic of system building. What in code looks like yet another field in a database schema could be information that, if leaked, has real consequences for an actual person. As modern life increasingly goes digital, and mobile computing becomes ubiquitous, privacy will depend more and more on code, potentially in new ways that are difficult to imagine. All this is to say that you would be smart to stay well ahead of the curve by exercising extreme vigilance now.

A few very general considerations for minimizing privacy threats include the following:

- Assess privacy by modeling scenarios of actual use cases, not thinking in the abstract.
- Learn what privacy policies or legal requirements apply, and follow the terms rigorously.
- Restrict the collection of data to only what is necessary.
- Be sensitive to the possibility of seeming creepy.
- Never collect or store private information without a clear intention for its use.
- When information already collected is no longer used or useful, proactively delete it.
- Minimize information sharing with third parties (which, if it occurs, should be well documented).
- Minimize disclosure of sensitive information—ideally this should be done only on a need-to-know basis.
- Be transparent, and help end users understand your data protection practices.

## Threat Modeling Everywhere

The threat modeling process described here is a formalization of how we navigate in the world; we manage risk by balancing it against opportunities. In a dangerous environment, all living organisms make decisions based on these same basic principles. Once you start looking for it, you can find instances of threat modeling everywhere.

When expecting a visit from friends with a young child, we always take a few minutes to make special preparations. Alex, an active three-year-old, has an inquisitive mind, so we go through the house "child-proofing." This is pure threat modeling, as we imagine the threats by categories—what could hurt Alex, what might get broken, what's better kept out of view of a youngster—then look for assets that fit these patterns. Typical threats include a metal letter opener, which he could stick in a wall socket; a fragile antique vase that he might easily break; or perhaps a coffee table book of photography that contains images inappropriate for children. The attack surface is any place reachable by an active toddler. Mitigations generally consist of removing, reducing, or eliminating points of exposure or vulnerability: we could replace the fragile vase with a plastic one that contains just dried flowers, or move it up onto a mantelpiece. People with children know how difficult it is to anticipate what they might do. For instance, did we anticipate Alex might stack up enough books to climb up and reach a shelf that we thought was out of reach? This is what threat modeling looks like outside of software, and it illustrates why preemptive mitigation can be well worth the effort.

Here are a few other examples of threat modeling you may have noticed in daily life:

- Stores design return policies specifically to mitigate abuses such as shoplifting and then returning the product for store credit, or wearing new apparel once and then returning it for a refund.

- Website terms of use agreements attempt to prevent various ways that users might maliciously abuse the site.

- Traffic safety laws, speed limits, driver licensing, and mandatory auto insurance requirements are all mitigation mechanisms to make driving safer.

- Libraries design loan policies to mitigate theft, hoarding, and damage to the collection.

You can probably think of lots of ways that you apply these techniques, too. For most of us, when we can draw on our physical intuitions about the world, threat modeling is remarkably easy to do. Once you recognize that software threat modeling works the same way as your already well-honed skills in other contexts, you can begin to apply your natural capabilities to software security analysis, and quickly raise your skills to the next level.

**NOTE** *See Appendix D for a cheat sheet summarizing the Four Questions and STRIDE as a handy reference for threat modeling.*

# 3

## MITIGATION

*Everything is possible to mitigate through art and diligence.*
—Gaius Plinius Caecilius Secundus (Pliny the Younger)

This chapter focuses on the third of the Four Questions from Chapter 2: "What are we going to do about it?" Anticipating threats, then protecting against potential vulnerabilities, is how security thinking turns into effective action. This proactive response is called *mitigation*—reducing the severity, extent, or impact of problems—and as you saw in the previous chapter, it's something we all do all the time. Bibs to catch the inevitable spills when feeding an infant, seat belts, speed limits, fire alarms, food safety practices, public health measures, and industrial safety regulations are just a few examples of mitigations. The common thread among these is that they take proactive measures to avoid, or lessen, anticipated harms in the face of risk. This is much of what we do to make software more secure.

It's important to bear in mind that mitigations reduce risk but don't eliminate it. To be clear, if you can eliminate a risk somehow—say, by removing a legacy feature that is known to be insecure—by all means do that, but I would not call it a mitigation. Instead, mitigations focus on making attacks less likely, more difficult, or less harmful when they do occur. Even measures that make exploits more detectable are mitigations, analogous to tamper-evident packaging, if they lead to a faster response and remediation. Every small effort ratchets up the security of the system as a whole, and even modest wins can collectively add up to significantly better protection.

This chapter begins with a conceptual discussion of mitigation, and from there presents a number of general techniques. The focus here is on structural mitigations based on the perspective gained through threat modeling that can be useful for securing almost any system design. Subsequent chapters will build on these ideas to provide more detailed methods, drilling down into specific technologies and threats.

The rest of the chapter provides guidance for recurrent security challenges encountered in software design: instituting an access policy and access controls, designing interfaces, and protecting communications and storage. Together, these discussions form a playbook for addressing common security needs that will be fleshed out over the remainder of the book.

## Addressing Threats

Threat modeling reveals what can go wrong, and in doing so, focuses our security attention where it counts. But believing we can always eliminate vulnerabilities would be naive. Points of risk—critical events or decision thresholds—are great opportunities for mitigation.

As you learned in the previous chapter, you should always address the biggest threats first, limiting them as best you can. For systems that process sensitive personal information, as one example, the threat of unauthorized disclosure inevitably looms large. For this major risk, consider any or all of the following: minimizing access to the data, reducing the amount of information collected, actively deleting old data when no longer needed, auditing for early detection in the event of compromise, and taking measures to reduce an attacker's ability to exfiltrate data. After securing the highest-priority risks, opportunistically mitigate lesser risks where it is easy to do so without adding much overhead or complexity to the design.

A good example of a smart mitigation is the best practice of checking the password submitted with each login attempt against a salted hash, instead of the actual password in plaintext. Protecting passwords is critical because disclosure threatens the fundamental authentication mechanism. Comparing hashes only requires slightly more work than comparing directly, yet it's a big win as it eliminates the need to store plaintext passwords. This means that even if attackers somehow breach the system, they won't learn actual passwords as easily.

This example illustrates the idea of harm reduction but is quite specific to password checking. Now let's consider mitigation strategies that are more widely applicable.

# Structural Mitigation Strategies

Mitigations often amount to common sense: reducing risk where there are opportunities to do so. Threat modeling helps us see potential vulnerabilities in terms of attack surfaces, trust boundaries, and assets (targets needing protection). *Structural mitigations* generally apply to these very features of the model, but their realization depends on the specifics of the design. The subsections that follow discuss techniques that should be widely applicable because they operate at the model level of abstraction.

## Minimize Attack Surfaces

Once you have identified the attack surfaces of a system, you know where exploits are most likely to originate, so anything you can do to harden the system's "outer shell" will be a significant win. A good way to think about attack surface reduction is in terms of how much code and data are touched downstream of each point of entry. Systems that provide multiple interfaces to perform the same function may benefit from unifying these interfaces because that means less code that might contain vulnerabilities. Here are a few examples of this commonly used technique:

- In a client/server system, you can reduce the attack surface of the server by pushing functionality out to the client. Any operation that requires a server request represents an additional attack surface that a malformed request or forged credentials might be able to exploit. By contrast, if the necessary information and compute power exist on the client side, that reduces both the load on and the attack surface of the server.

- Moving functionality from a publicly exposed API that anyone can invoke anonymously to an authenticated API can effectively reduce your attack surface. The added friction of account creation slows down attacks, and also helps trace attackers and enforce rate limiting.

- Libraries and drivers that use kernel services can reduce the attack surface by minimizing interfaces to, and code within, the kernel. Not only are there fewer kernel transitions to attack that way, but userland code will be incapable of doing as much damage even if an attack is successful.

- Deployment and operations offer many attack surface reduction opportunities. For an enterprise network, moving anything you can behind a firewall is an easy win.

- A configuration setting that enables remote administration over the network is another good example: this feature may be convenient, but if it's rarely used, consider disabling it and use wired access instead when necessary.

These are just some of the most common scenarios where attack surface reduction works. For particular systems, you might find much more creative customized opportunities. Keep thinking of ways to reduce external access, minimize functionality and interfaces, and protect any services that are needlessly exposed. The better you understand where and how a feature is actually used, the more of these mitigations you'll be able to find.

## Narrow Windows of Vulnerability

This mitigation technique is similar to attack surface reduction, but instead of metaphorical surface area, it reduces the effective time interval in which a vulnerability can occur. Also based on common sense, this is why hunters only disengage the safety just before firing and reengage it soon after.

We usually apply this mitigation to trust boundaries, where low-trust data or requests interact with high-trust code. To best isolate the high-trust code, minimize the processing that it needs to do. For example, when possible, perform error checking ahead of invoking the high-trust code so it can do its work and exit quickly.

*Code Access Security (CAS)*, a security model that is rarely used today, is a perfect illustration of this mitigation because it provides fine-grained control over code's effective privileges. (Full disclosure: I was the program manager for security in .NET Framework version 1.0, which prominently featured CAS as a major security feature.)

The CAS runtime grants different permissions to different units of code based on trust. The following pseudocode example illustrates a common idiom for a generic *permission*, which could grant access to certain files, to the clipboard, and so on. In effect, CAS ensures that high-trust code inherits the lower privileges of the code invoking it, but when necessary, it can temporarily assert its higher privileges. Here's how such an assertion of privilege works:

```
Worker(parameters) {
    // When invoked from a low-trust caller, privileges are reduced.
    DoSetup();
    permission.Assert();
    // Following assertion, the designated permission can now be used.
    DoWorkRequiringPrivilege();
    CodeAccessPermission.RevertAssert();
    // Reverting the assertion undoes its effect.
    DoCleanup();
}
```

The code in this example has powerful privileges, but it may be called by less-trusted code. When invoked by low-trust code, this code initially runs with the reduced privileges of the caller. Technically, the effective privileges are the intersection (that is, the minimum) of the privileges granted to the code, its caller, and its caller's caller, and so on all the way up the stack. Some of what the Worker method does requires higher privileges than its callers may have, so after doing the setup, it asserts the necessary permission before invoking DoWorkRequiringPrivilege, which must also have that permission. Having done that portion of its work, it immediately drops the special permission by calling RevertAssert, before doing whatever is left that needs no special permissions and returning. In the CAS model, time window minimization provides for such assertions of privilege to be used when necessary and reverted as soon as they are no longer needed.

Consider this application of narrowing windows of vulnerability in a different way. Online banking offers convenience and speed, and mobile devices allow us to bank from anywhere. But storing your banking credentials in your phone is risky—you don't want someone emptying out your bank account if you lose it, which is much more likely with a mobile device. A great mitigation that I would like to see implemented across the banking industry would be the ability to configure the privilege level you are comfortable with for each device. A cautious customer might restrict the mobile app to checking balances and a modest daily transaction dollar limit. The customer would then be able to bank by phone with confidence. Further useful limits might include windows of time, geolocation, domestic currency only, and so on. All of these mitigations help because they limit the worst-case scenario in the event of any kind of compromise.

## Minimize Data Exposure

Another structural mitigation to data disclosure risk is limiting the lifetime of sensitive data in memory. This is much like the preceding technique, but here you're minimizing the duration for which sensitive data is accessible and potentially exposed instead of the duration for which code is running at high privilege. Recall that intraprocess access is hard to control, so the mere presence of data in memory puts it at risk. When the stakes are high, such as handling extremely sensitive data, you can think of it as "the meter is running." For the most critical information—data such as private encryption keys, or authentication credentials such as passwords—it may be worth overwriting any in-memory copies as soon as they are no longer needed. This reduces the time during which a leak is conceivably possible through any means. As we shall see in Chapter 9, the Heartbleed vulnerability threatened security for much of the web, exposing all kinds of sensitive data lying around in memory. Limiting how long such data was retained probably would have been a useful mitigation ("stanching the blood flow," if you will), even without foreknowledge of the exploit.

You can apply this technique to data storage design as well. When a user deletes their account in the system, that typically causes their data to be destroyed, but the system often offers a provision for a manual restore of the account in case of accidental or malicious closure. The easy way to implement this is to mark closed accounts as to-be-deleted but keep the data in place for, say, 30 days (after the manual restore period has passed) before the system finally deletes everything. To make this work, lots of code needs to check if the account is scheduled for deletion, lest it accidentally access the account data that the user directed to be destroyed. If a bulk mail job forgets to check, it could errantly send the user some notice that, to the user, would appear to be a violation of their intentions after they closed the account. This mitigation suggests a better option: after the user deletes the account, the system should push its contents to an offline backup and promptly delete the data. The rare case where a manual restore is needed can still be accomplished using the backup data, and now there is no way for a bug to possibly result in that kind of error.

Generally speaking, proactively wiping copies of data is an extreme measure that's appropriate only for the most sensitive data, or important actions such as account closure. Some languages and libraries help do this automatically, and except where performance is a concern, a simple wrapper function can wipe the contents of memory clean before it is recycled.

## Access Policy and Access Controls

Standard operating system permissions provide very rudimentary file access controls. These control *read* (confidentiality) or *write* (integrity) access on an all-or-nothing basis for individual files based on the user and group ownership of a process. Given this functionality, it's all too easy to think in the same limited terms when designing protections for assets and resources—but the right access policy might be more granular and depend on many other factors.

First, consider how ill-suited traditional access controls are for many modern systems. Web services and microservices are designed to work on behalf of principals that usually do not correspond to the process owner. In this case, one process services all authenticated requests, requiring permission to access all client data all the time. This means that in the presence of a vulnerability, all client data is potentially at risk.

Defining an efficacious access policy is an important mitigation, as it closes the gap between what accesses should be allowed and what access controls the system happens to offer. Rather than start with the available operating system access controls, think through the needs of the various principals acting through the system and define an ideal access policy that expresses an accurate description of what constitutes proper access. A granular access policy potentially offers a wealth of options: you can cap the number of accesses per minute or hour or day, or enforce a maximum data volume, time-based limits corresponding to working hours, or variable access limits based on activity by peers or historical rates (to name a few obvious mechanisms).

Determining safe access limitations is hard work but worthwhile because it helps you understand the application's security requirements. Even if the policy is not fully implemented in code, it will at least provide guidance for effective auditing. Given the right set of controls, you can start with lenient restrictions to gauge what real usage looks like and then, over time, narrow the policy as you learn how the system is used in practice.

For example, consider a hypothetical system that serves a team of customer service agents. Agents need access to the records of any customer who might contact them, but they only interact with a limited number of customers on a given day. A reasonable access policy might limit each agent to no more than 100 different customer records in one shift. With access to all records all the time, a dishonest agent could leak a copy of all customer data, whereas the limited policy greatly limits the worst-case daily damage.

Once you have a fine-grained access policy, you face the challenge of setting the right limits. This can be difficult when you must avoid impeding rightful use in extreme edge cases. In the customer service example, for instance, you might restrict agents to accessing the records of up to 100 customers per shift as a way of accommodating seasonal peak demand, even though, on most days, needing even 50 records would be unusual. Why? It would be impractical to adjust the policy configuration throughout the year, and you want to allow for leeway so the limit never impedes work. Also, defining a more specific and detailed policy based on fixed dates might not work well, as there could be unexpected surges in activity at any time.

But is there a way to narrow the gap between normal circumstances and the rare highest-demand case that the system should allow? One great tool to handle this tricky situation is a policy provision for self-declared exceptions to be used in extraordinary circumstances. Such an option allows individual agents to bump up their own limits for a short period of time by providing a rationale. With this kind of "relief valve" in place, the basic access policy can be tightly constrained. When needed, once agents hit the access limit, they can file a quick notice—stating, for example, "high call volume today, I'm working late to finish up"—and receive additional access authorization. Such notices can be audited, and if they become commonplace, management could bump the policy up with the knowledge that demand has legitimately grown and an understanding of why. Such flexible techniques enable you to create access policies with softer limits, rather than hard-and-fast restrictions that tend to be arbitrary.

## Interfaces

Software designs consist of components that correspond to functional parts of the system. You can visualize these designs as block diagrams, with lines representing the connections between the parts. These connections denote *interfaces*, which are a major focus of security analysis—not only because they reveal data and control flows, but also because they serve as well-defined chokepoints where you can add mitigations. In particular, where there is a trust boundary, the main security focus is on the flow of data and control from the lower- to the higher-trust component, so that is where defensive measures are often needed.

In large systems, there are typically interfaces between networks, between processes, and within processes. Network interfaces provide the strongest isolation because it's virtually certain that any interactions between the endpoints will occur over the wire, but with the other kinds of interfaces it's more complicated. Operating systems provide strong isolation at process boundaries, so interprocess communication interfaces are nearly as trustworthy as network interfaces. In both of these cases, it's generally impossible to go around these channels and interact in some other way. The attack surface is cleanly constrained, and hence this is where most of the important trust boundaries are. As a consequence, interprocess communication and network interfaces are the major focal points of threat modeling.

Interfaces also exist within processes, where interaction is relatively unconstrained. Well-written software can still create meaningful security boundaries within a process, but these are only effective if all the code plays together well and stays within the lines. From the attacker's perspective, intraprocess boundaries are much easier to penetrate. However, since attackers may only gain a limited degree of control via a given vulnerability, any protection you can provide is better than none. By analogy, think of a robber who only has a few seconds to act: even a weak precaution might be enough to prevent a loss.

Any large software design faces the delicate task of structuring components to minimize regions of highly privileged access, as well as restricting sensitive information flow in order to reduce security risk. To the extent that the design restricts information access to a minimal set of components that are well isolated, attackers will have a much harder time getting access to sensitive data. By contrast, in weaker designs, all kinds of data flow all over the place, resulting in greater exposure from a vulnerability anywhere within the component. The architecture of interfaces is a major factor that determines the success systems have at protecting assets.

## Communication

Modern networked systems are so common that standalone computers, detached from any network, have become rare exceptions. The cloud computing model, combined with mobile connectivity, makes network access ubiquitous. As a result, communication is fundamental to almost every software system in use today, be it through internet connections, private networks, or peripheral connections via Bluetooth, USB, and the like.

In order to protect these communications, the channel must be physically secured against wiretapping and snooping, or else the data must be encrypted to ensure its integrity and confidentiality. Reliance on physical security is typically fragile in the sense that if attackers bypass it, they usually gain access to the full data flow, and such incursions are difficult to detect. Modern processors are fast enough that the computational overhead of encryption is usually acceptable, so there is rarely a good reason not to encrypt communications. I cover basic encryption in Chapter 5, and HTTPS for the web specifically in Chapter 11.

Even the best encryption is not a magic bullet, though. One remaining threat is that encryption cannot conceal the *fact of communication*. In other words, if attackers can read the raw data in the channel, even if they're unable to decipher its contents, they can still see that data is being sent and received on the wire, and roughly estimate the amount of data flow. Furthermore, if attackers can tamper with the communication channel, they might be able to delay or block the transmission entirely.

# Storage

The security of data storage is much like the security of communications, because storing data is analogous to sending it into the future, at which point you will retrieve it for some purpose. Viewed in this way, just as data that is being communicated is vulnerable on the wire, stored data is vulnerable at rest on the storage medium. Protecting data at rest from potential tampering or disclosure requires either physical security or encryption. Likewise, availability depends on the existence of backup copies or successful physical protection.

Storage is so ubiquitous in system designs that it's easy to defer the details of data security for operations to deal with, but doing so misses good opportunities for proactively mitigating data loss in the design. For instance, data backup requirements are an important part of software designs, because the demands are by no means obvious, and there are many trade-offs. You could plan for redundant storage systems, designed to protect against data loss in the event of failure, but these can be expensive and incur performance costs. Your backups might be copies of the whole dataset, or they could be incremental, recording transactions that, cumulatively, can be used to rebuild an accurate copy. Either way, they should be reliably stored independently and with specific frequency, within acceptable limits of latency. Cloud architectures can provide redundant data replication in near real-time for perhaps the best continuous backup solution, but at a cost.

All data at rest, including backup copies, is at risk of exposure to unauthorized access, so you must physically secure or encrypt it for protection. The more backup copies you make, the greater the risk is of a leak due to having so many copies. Considering the potential extremes makes this point clear. Photographs are precious memories and irreplaceable pieces of every family's history, so keeping multiple backup copies is wise—if you don't have any copies and the original files are lost, damaged, or corrupted, the loss could be devastating. To guard against this, you might send copies of your family photos to as many relatives as possible for safekeeping. But this has a downside too, as it raises the chances that one of them might have the data stolen (via malware, or perhaps a stolen laptop). This could also be catastrophic, as these are private memories, and it would be a violation of privacy to see all those photos publicly spread all over the web (and potentially a greater threat if it allowed strangers to identify children in a way that could lead to exploitation). This is a fundamental trade-off that requires you to weigh the risks of data loss against the risk of leaks—you cannot minimize both at once, but you can balance these concerns to a degree in a few ways.

As a compromise between these threats, you could send your relatives encrypted photos. (This means they would not be able to view them, of course.) However, now you are responsible for keeping the key that you chose not to entrust them with, and if you lose the key, the encrypted copies are worthless.

Preserving photos also raises an important aspect of backing up data, which is the problem of media lifetime and obsolescence. Physical media (such as hard disks or DVDs) inevitably degrade over time, and support for legacy media fades away as new hardware evolves (this author recalls long ago personally moving data from dozens of floppy disks, which only antiquated computers can use, onto one USB memory stick, now copied to the cloud). Even if the media and devices still work, new software tends to drop support for older data formats. The choice of data format is thus important, with widely used open standards highly preferred, because proprietary formats must be reverse-engineered once they are officially retired. Over longer time spans, it might be necessary to convert file formats, as software standards evolve and application support for older formats becomes deprecated.

The examples mentioned throughout this chapter have been simplified for explanatory purposes, and while we've covered many techniques that can be used to mitigate identified threats, these are just the tip of the iceberg of possibilities. Adapt specific mitigations to the needs of each application, ideally by making them integral to the design. While this sounds simple, effective mitigations are challenging in practice because a panoply of threats must be considered in the context of each system, and you can only do so much. The next chapter presents major patterns with useful security properties, as well as anti-patterns to watch out for, that are useful in crafting these mitigations as part of secure design.

# 4

## PATTERNS

*Art is pattern informed by sensibility.*
—Herbert Read

 Architects have long used design patterns to envision new buildings, an approach just as useful for guiding software design. This chapter introduces many of the most useful patterns promoting secure design. Several of these patterns derive from ancient wisdom; the trick is knowing how to apply them to software and how they enhance security.

These patterns either mitigate or avoid various security vulnerabilities, forming an important toolbox to address potential threats. Many are simple, but others are harder to understand and best explained by example. Don't underestimate the simpler ones, as they can be widely applicable and are among the most effective. Still, other concepts may be easier to grasp as anti-patterns describing what *not* to do. I present these patterns in groups based on shared characteristics that you can think of as sections of the toolbox (Figure 4-1).

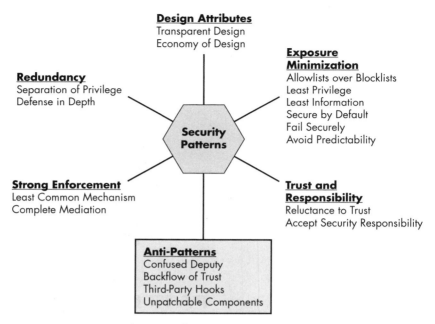

Figure 4-1: Groupings of secure software patterns this chapter covers

When and where to apply these patterns requires judgment. Let necessity and simplicity guide your design decisions. As powerful as these patterns are, don't overdo it; just as you don't need seven deadbolts and chains on your doors, you don't need to apply every possible design pattern to fix a problem. Where several patterns are applicable, choose the best one or two, or maybe more for critical security demands. Overuse can be counterproductive because the diminishing returns of increased complexity and overhead quickly outweigh additional security gains.

## Design Attributes

The first group of patterns describe at a high level what secure design looks like: simple and transparent. These derive from the adages "keep it simple" and "you should have nothing to hide." As basic and perhaps obvious as these patterns may be, they can be applied widely and are very powerful.

### Economy of Design

Designs should be as simple as possible.

*Economy of Design* raises the security bar because simpler designs likely have fewer bugs, and thus fewer undetected vulnerabilities. Though developers claim that "all software has bugs," we know that simple programs certainly can be bug-free. Prefer the simplest of competing designs for security mechanisms, and be wary of complicated designs that perform critical security functions.

LEGO bricks are a great example of this pattern. Once the design and manufacture of the standard building element is perfected, it enables building a countless array of creative designs. A similar system composed of a number of less universally useful pieces would be more difficult to build with; any particular design would require a larger inventory of parts and involve other technical challenges.

You can find many examples of Economy of Design in the system architecture of large web services built to run in massive datacenters. For reliability at scale, these designs decompose functionality into smaller, self-contained components that collectively perform complicated operations. Often, a basic frontend terminates the HTTPS request, parsing and validating the incoming data into an internal data structure. That data structure gets sent on for processing by a number of subservices, which in turn use microservices to perform various functions.

In the case of an application such as web search, different machines may independently build different parts of the response in parallel, then yet another machine blends them into the complete response. It's much easier to build many small services to do separate parts of the whole task—query parsing, spelling correction, text search, image search, results ranking, and page layout—than to do everything in one massive program.

Economy of Design is not an absolute mandate that everything must always be simple. Rather, it highlights the great advantages of simplicity, and says that you should only embrace complexity when it adds significant value. Consider the differences between the design of access control lists (ACLs) in *nix and Windows. The former is simple, specifying read/write/execute permissions by user or user group, or for everybody. The latter is much more involved, including an arbitrary number of both allow and deny access control entries as well as an inheritance feature; notably, evaluation is dependent on the ordering of entries within the list. (These simplified descriptions are to make a point about design, and are not intended as complete.) This pattern correctly shows that the simpler *nix permissions are easier to correctly enforce, and beyond that, it's easier for users of the system to correctly understand how ACLs work and therefore to use them correctly. However, if the Windows ACL provides just the right protection for a given application and can be accurately configured, then it may be a fine solution.

The Economy of Design pattern does not say that the simpler option is unequivocally better, or that the more complex one is necessarily problematic. In this example, *nix ACLs are not inherently better, and Windows ACLs are not necessarily buggy. However, Windows ACLs do represent more of a learning curve for developers and users, and using their more complicated features can easily confuse people as well as invite unintended consequences. The key design choice here, which I will not weigh in on, is to what extent the ACL designs best fit the needs of users. Perhaps *nix ACLs are too simplistic and fail to meet real demands; on the other hand, perhaps Windows ACLs are overly feature-bound and cumbersome in typical use patterns. These are difficult questions we must each answer for our own purposes, but for which this design pattern provides insight.

### Transparent Design

Strong protection should never rely on secrecy.

Perhaps the most famous example of a design that failed to follow the pattern of *Transparent Design* is the Death Star in *Star Wars*, whose thermal exhaust port afforded a straight shot at the heart of the battle station. Had Darth Vader held his architects accountable to this principle as severely as he did Admiral Motti, the story would have turned out very differently. Revealing the design of a well-built system should have the effect of dissuading attackers by showing its invincibility. It shouldn't make the task easier for them. The corresponding anti-pattern may be better known: we call it *Security by Obscurity*.

This pattern specifically warns against a *reliance* on the secrecy of a design. It doesn't mean that publicly disclosing designs is mandatory, or that there is anything wrong with secret information. If full transparency about a design weakens it, you should fix the design, not rely on keeping it secret. This in no way applies to legitimately secret information, such as cryptographic keys or user identities, which actually would compromise security if leaked. That's why the name of the pattern is Transparent *Design*, not Absolute Transparency. Full disclosure of the design of an encryption method—the key size, message format, cryptographic algorithms, and so forth—shouldn't weaken security at all. The anti-pattern should be a big red flag: for instance, distrust any self-anointed "experts" who claim to invent amazing encryption algorithms that are so great that they cannot publish the details. Without exception, these are bogus.

The problem with Security by Obscurity is that while it may help forestall adversaries temporarily, it's extremely fragile. For example, imagine that a design used an outdated cryptographic algorithm: if the attackers ever found out that the software was still using, say, DES (a legacy symmetric encryption algorithm from the 1970s), they could easily crack it within a day. Instead, do the work necessary to get to a solid security footing so that there is nothing to hide, whether or not the design details are public.

## Exposure Minimization

The largest group of patterns call for caution: think "err on the safe side." These are expressions of basic risk/reward strategies where you play it safe unless there is an important reason to do otherwise.

### Least Privilege

It's always safest to use just enough privilege for the job.

Never clean a loaded gun. Unplug power saws when changing blades. These commonplace safety practices are examples of the *Least Privilege* pattern, which aims to reduce the risk of making mistakes when performing a task. This pattern is the reason that administrators of important systems should not be randomly browsing the internet while logged in at work; if they visit a malicious website and get compromised, the attack could easily do serious harm.

The *nix sudo(1) command performs exactly this purpose. User accounts with high privilege (known as *sudoers*) need to be careful not to inadvertently use their extraordinary power by accident or if compromised. To provide this protection, the user must prefix superuser commands with sudo, which may prompt the user for a password, in order to run them. Under this system, most commands (those that do not require sudo) will affect only the user's own account, and cannot impact the entire system. This is akin to the "IN CASE OF EMERGENCY BREAK GLASS" cover on a fire alarm switch to prevent accidental activation, in that this forces an explicit step (corresponding to the sudo prefix) before activating the switch. With the glass cover, nobody can claim to have accidentally pulled the fire alarm, just as a competent administrator would never type sudo and a command that breaks the system all by accident.

This pattern is important for the simple reason that when vulnerabilities are exploited, it's better for the attacker to have minimal privileges to use as leverage. Use all-powerful authorizations such as superuser privileges only when strictly necessary, and for the minimum possible duration. Even Superman practiced Least Privilege by only wearing his uniform when there was a job to do, and then, after saving the world, immediately changing back into his Clark Kent persona.

In practice, it does take more effort to selectively and sparingly use elevated privileges. Just as unplugging power tools to work on them requires more effort, discretion when using permissions requires discipline, but doing it right is always safer. In the case of an exploit, it means the difference between a minor incursion and total system compromise. Practicing Least Privilege can also mitigate damage done by bugs and human error.

Like all rules of thumb, use this pattern with a sense of balance to avoid overcomplication. Least Privilege does not mean the system should always grant literally the minimum level of authorization (for instance, creating code that, in order to write file X, is given write access to only that one file). You may wonder, why not always apply this excellent pattern to the max? In addition to maintaining a general sense of balance and recognizing diminishing returns for any mitigation, a big factor here is the granularity of the mechanism that controls authorization, and the cost incurred while adjusting privileges up and down. For instance, in a *nix process, permissions are conferred based on user and group ID access control lists. Beyond the flexibility of changing between effective and real IDs (which is what sudo does), there is no easy way to temporarily drop unneeded privileges without forking a process. Code should operate with lower ambient privileges where it can, using higher privileges in the necessary sections and transitioning at natural decision points.

### Least Information

It's always safest to collect and access the minimum amount of private information needed for the job.

The *Least Information* pattern, the data privacy analog of Least Privilege, helps to minimize unintended disclosure risks. Avoid providing more private information than necessary when calling a subroutine, requesting a service, or responding to a request, and at every opportunity curtail unnecessary information flow. Implementing this pattern can be challenging in practice because software tends to pass data around in standard containers not optimized for purpose, so extra data often is included that isn't really needed.

All too often, software fails this pattern because the design of interfaces evolves over time to serve a number of purposes, and it's convenient to reuse the same parameters or data structure for consistency. As a result, data that isn't strictly necessary gets sent along as extra baggage that seems harmless enough. The problem arises, of course, when this needless data flowing through the system creates additional opportunities for attack.

For example, imagine a large customer relationship management (CRM) system used by various workers in an enterprise. Different workers use the system for a wide variety of purposes, including sales, production, shipping, support, maintenance, R&D, and accounting. Depending on their roles, each has a different authorization for access to subsets of this information. To practice Least Information, the applications in this enterprise should request only the minimum amount of data needed to perform a specific task. Consider a customer support representative responding to a phone call: if the system uses Caller ID to look up the customer record, the support person doesn't need to know their phone number, just their purchase history. Contrast this with a more basic design that either allows or disallows the lookup of customer records that include all data fields. Ideally, even if the representative has more access, they should be able to request the minimum needed for a given task and work with that, thereby minimizing the risk of disclosure.

At the implementation level, Least Information design includes wiping locally cached information when no longer needed, or perhaps displaying a subset of available data on the screen until the user explicitly requests to see certain details. The common practice of displaying passwords as ******** uses this pattern to mitigate the risk of shoulder surfing.

It's particularly important to apply this pattern at design time, as it can be extremely difficult to implement later on because both sides of the interface need to change together. If you design independent components suited to specific tasks that require different sets of data, you're more likely to get this right. APIs handling sensitive data should provide flexibility to allow callers to specify subsets of data they need in order to minimize information exposure (Table 4-1).

**Table 4-1:** How Least Information Changes API Design

| Least Information non-compliant API | Least Information compliant API |
| --- | --- |
| `RequestCustomerData(id='12345')` | `RequestCustomerData(id='12345', items=['name', 'zip'])` |
| `{'id': '12345', 'name': 'Jane Doe', 'phone': '888-555-1212', 'zip': '01010', ...}` | `{'name': 'Jane Doe', 'zip': '01010'}` |

The `RequestCustomerData` API in the left column ignores the Least Information pattern because the caller has no option but to request the complete data record by ID. They don't need the phone number, so there is no need to request it, and even ignoring it still expands the attack surface for an attacker trying to get it. The right column has a version of the same API that allows callers to specify what fields they need and delivers only those, which minimizes the flow of private information.

Considering the Secure by Default pattern as well, the default for the items parameter should be a minimal set of fields, provided that callers can request exactly what they need to minimize information flow.

## Secure by Default

Software should always be secure "out of the box."

Design your software to be *Secure by Default*, including in its initial state, so that inaction by the operator does not represent a risk. This applies to the overall system configuration, as well as configuration options for components and API parameters. Databases or routers with default passwords notoriously violate this pattern, and to this day, this design flaw remains surprisingly widespread.

If you are serious about security, never configure an insecure state with the intention of making it secure later, because this creates an interval of vulnerability and is too often forgotten. If you must use equipment with a default password, for example, first configure it safely on a private network behind a firewall before deploying it in the network. A pioneer in this area, the state of California has mandated this pattern by law; its Senate Bill No. 327 (2018) outlaws default passwords on connected devices.

Secure by Default applies to any setting or configuration that could have a detrimental security impact, not just to default passwords. Permissions should default to more restrictive settings; users should have to explicitly change them to less restrictive ones if needed, and only if it's safe to do so. Disable all potentially dangerous options by default. Conversely, enable features that provide security protection by default so they are functioning from the start. And of course, keeping the software fully up-to-date is important; don't start out with an old version (possibly one with known vulnerabilities) and hope that, at some point, it gets updated.

Ideally, you shouldn't ever need to have insecure options. Carefully consider proposed configurable options, because it may be simple to provide an insecure option that will become a booby trap for others thereafter. Also remember that each new option increases the number of possible combinations, and the task of ensuring that all of those combinations of settings are actually useful and safe becomes more difficult as the number of options increases. Whenever you must provide unsafe configurations, make a point of proactively explaining the risk to the administrator.

Secure by Default applies much more broadly than to configuration options, though. Defaults for unspecified API parameters should be secure choices. A browser accepting a URL entered into the address bar without any protocol specified should assume the site uses HTTPS, and fall back to HTTP only if the former fails to connect. Two peers negotiating a new HTTPS connection should default to accepting the more secure cipher suite choices first.

## Allowlists over Blocklists

Prefer allowlists over blocklists when designing a security mechanism. *Allowlists* are enumerations of what's safe, so they are inherently finite. By contrast, *blocklists* attempt to enumerate all that isn't safe, and in doing so implicitly allow an infinite set of things you *hope* are safe. It's clear which approach is riskier.

First, here's a non-software example to make sure you understand what the allowlist versus blocklist alternative means, and why allowlists are always the way to go. During the early months of the COVID-19 stay-at-home emergency order, the governor of my state ordered the beaches closed with the following provisos, presented here in simplified form:

> No person shall sit, stand, lie down, lounge, sunbathe, or loiter
> on any beach except when "running, jogging, or walking on the
> beach, so long as social distancing requirements are maintained"
> (crossing the beach to surf is also allowed).

The first clause is a blocklist, because it lists what activities are not allowed, and the second exception clause is an allowlist, because it grants permission to the activities listed. Due to legal issues, there may well be good reasons for this language, but from a strictly logical perspective, I think it leaves much to be desired.

First let's consider the blocklist: I'm confident that there are other risky activities people could do at the beach that the first clause fails to prohibit. If the intention of the order was to keep people moving, it omitted many— kneeling, for example, as well as yoga and living statue performances. The problem with blocklists is that any omissions become flaws, so unless you can completely enumerate every possible bad case, it's an insecure system.

Now consider the allowlist of allowable beach activities. While it, too, is incomplete—who would contest that skipping is also fine?—this won't cause a big security problem. Perhaps a fraction of a percent of beach skippers will be unfairly punished, but the harm is minor, and more importantly, an incomplete enumeration doesn't open up a hole that allows a risky activity. Additional safe items initially omitted can easily be added to the allowlist as needed.

More generally, think of a continuum, ranging from disallowed on the left, then shading to allowed on the right. Somewhere in the middle is a dividing line. The goal is to allow the good stuff on the right of the line while disallowing the bad on the left. Allowlists draw the line from the right side, then gradually move it to the left, including more parts of the continuum as the list of what to allow grows. If you omit something good from the allowlist, you're still on the safe side of the elusive line that's the true divide. You may never get to the precise point that allows all safe actions, at which point any addition to the list would be too much, but using this technique makes it easy to stay on the safe side. Contrast that to the blocklist approach: unless you enumerate everything to the left of the true divide, you're allowing something you shouldn't. The safest blocklist will be one that includes just about everything, and that's likely to be overly restrictive, so it doesn't work well either way.

Often, the use of an allowlist is so glaringly obvious we don't notice it as a pattern. For example, a bank would reasonably authorize a small set of trusted managers to approve high-value transactions. Nobody would dream of maintaining a blocklist of all the employees *not* authorized, tacitly allowing any other employee such privilege. Yet sloppy coders might attempt to do input validation by checking that the value did not contain any of a list of invalid characters, and in the process easily forget about characters like NUL (ASCII 0) or perhaps DEL (ASCII 127).

Ironically, perhaps the biggest-selling consumer security product, antivirus software, attempts to block all known malware. Modern antivirus products are much more sophisticated than the old-school versions, which relied on comparing a digest against a database of known malware, but still, they all appear to work based on a blocklist to some extent. (A great example of Security by Obscurity, most commercial antivirus software is proprietary, so we can only speculate.) It makes sense that they're stuck with blocklist techniques because they know how to collect examples of malware, and the prospect of somehow allowlisting all good software in the world before it's released seems to be a nonstarter. My point isn't about any particular product or an assessment of its worth, but about the design choice of protection by virtue of a blocklist, and why that's inevitably risky.

## Avoid Predictability

Any data (or behavior) that is predictable cannot be kept private, since attackers can learn it by guessing.

Predictability of data in software design can lead to serious flaws because it can result in the leakage of information. For instance, consider the simple example of assigning new customer account IDs. When a new customer signs up on a website, the system needs a unique ID to designate the account. One obvious and easy way to do this is to name the first account 1, the second account 2, and so on. This works, but from the point of view of an attacker, what does it give away?

New account IDs now provide an attacker an easy way of learning the number of user accounts created so far. For example, if the attacker periodically creates a new, throwaway account, they have an accurate metric for how many customer accounts the website has at a given time—information that most businesses would be loathe to disclose to a competitor. Many other pitfalls are possible, depending on the specifics of the system. Another consequence of this poor design is that attackers can easily guess the account ID assigned to the next new account created, and armed with this knowledge, they might be able to interfere with the new account setup by claiming to be the new account and confusing the registration system.

The problem of predictability takes many guises, and different types of leakage can occur with different designs. For example, an account ID that includes several letters of the account holder's name or ZIP code would needlessly leak clues about the account owner's identity. Of course, this same problem applies to IDs for web pages, events, and more. The simplest mitigation against these issues is that if the purpose of an ID is to be a unique handle, you should make it just that—never a count of users, the email of the user, or based on other identifying information.

The easy way to avoid these problems is to use *securely random* IDs. Truly random values cannot be guessed, so they do not leak information. (Strictly speaking, the length of IDs leaks the maximum number of possible IDs, but this usually isn't sensitive information.) A standard system facility, random number generators come in two flavors: pseudorandom number generators and secure random number generators. You should use the secure option, which is slower, unless you're certain that predictability is harmless. See Chapter 5 for more about secure random number generators.

## *Fail Securely*

If a problem occurs, be sure to end up in a secure state.

In the physical world, this pattern is common sense itself. An old-fashioned electric fuse is a great example: if too much current flows through it, the heat melts the metal, opening the circuit. The laws of physics make it impossible to fail in a way that maintains excessive current flow. This pattern perhaps may seem like the most obvious one, but software being what it is (we don't have the laws of physics on our side), it's easily disregarded.

Many software coding tasks that at first seem almost trivial often grow in complexity due to error handling. The normal program flow can be simple, but when a connection is broken, memory allocation fails, inputs are invalid, or any number of other potential problems arise, the code needs to proceed if possible, or back out gracefully if not. When writing code, you might feel as though you spend more time dealing with all these distractions than with the task at hand, and it's easy to quickly dismiss error-handling code as unimportant, making this a common source of vulnerabilities. Attackers will intentionally trigger these error cases if they can, in hopes that there is a vulnerability they can exploit.

Error cases are often tedious to test thoroughly, especially when combinations of multiple errors can compound into new code paths, so this can be fertile ground for attack. Ensure that each error is either safely handled, or leads to full rejection of the request. For example, when someone uploads an image to a photo sharing service, immediately check that it is well formed (because malformed images are often used maliciously), and if not, then promptly remove the data from storage to prevent its further use.

# Strong Enforcement

These patterns concern how to ensure that code behaves by enforcing the rules thoroughly. Loopholes are the bane of any laws and regulations, so these patterns show how to avoid creating ways of gaming the system. Rather than write code and reason that you don't think it will do something, it's better to structurally design it so that forbidden operations cannot possibly occur.

## Complete Mediation

Protect all access paths, enforcing the same access, without exception.

An obscure term for an obvious idea, *Complete Mediation* means securely checking all accesses to a protected asset consistently. If there are multiple access methods to a resource, they must all be subject to the same authorization check, with no shortcuts that afford a free pass or looser policy.

For example, suppose a financial investment firm's information system policy declares that regular employees cannot look up the tax IDs of customers without manager approval, so the system provides them with a reduced view of customer records omitting that field. Managers can access the full record, and in the rare instance that a non-manager has a legitimate need, they can ask a manager to look it up. Employees help customers in many ways, one of which is providing replacement tax documents if, for some reason, customers did not receive theirs in the mail. After confirming the customer's identity, the employee requests a duplicate form (a PDF), which they print out and mail to the customer. The problem with this system is that the customer's tax ID, which the employee should not have access to, appears on the tax form: that's a failure of Complete Mediation. A dishonest employee could request any customer's tax form, as if for a replacement, just to learn their tax ID, defeating the policy preventing disclosure to employees.

The best way to honor this pattern is, wherever possible, to have a single point where a particular security decision occurs. This is often known as a *guard* or, informally, a *bottleneck*. The idea is that all accesses to a given asset must go through one gate. Alternatively, if that is infeasible and multiple pathways need guards, then all checks for the same access should be functionally equivalent and ideally implemented as identical code.

In practice, this pattern can be challenging to accomplish consistently. There are different degrees of compliance, depending on the guards in place:

**High compliance**

> Resource access only allowed via one common routine (bottleneck guard)

**Medium compliance**

> Resource access in various places, each guarded by an identical authorization check (common multiple guards)

**Low compliance**

> Resource access in various places, variously guarded by inconsistent authorization checks (incomplete mediation)

A counter-example demonstrates why designs with simple authorization policies that concentrate authorization checks in a single bottleneck code path for a given resource are the best way to get this pattern right. A Reddit user recently reported a case of how easy it is to get it wrong:

> I saw that my 8-year-old sister was on her iPhone 6 on iOS 12.4.6 using YouTube past her screen time limit. Turns out, she discovered a bug with screen time in messages that allows the user to use apps that are available in the iMessage App Store.

Apple designed iMessage to include its own apps, making it possible to invoke the YouTube app in multiple ways, but it didn't implement the screen-time check on this alternate path to video watching—a classic failure of Complete Mediation.

Avoid having multiple paths for accessing the same resource, each with custom code that potentially works slightly differently, because any discrepancies could mean weaker guards on some paths than on others. Multiple guards would require implementing the same essential check multiple times, and would be more difficult to maintain because you'd need to make matching changes in several places. The use of multiple guards incurs more chances of making an error and more work to thoroughly test.

### Least Common Mechanism

Maintain isolation between independent processes by minimizing shared mechanisms.

To best appreciate what this means and how it helps, let's consider an example. The kernel of a multiuser operating system manages system resources for processes running in different user contexts. The design of the kernel fundamentally ensures the isolation of processes unless they explicitly share a resource or a communication channel. Under the covers, the kernel maintains various data structures necessary to service requests from all user processes. This pattern points out that the common mechanism of these structures could inadvertently bridge processes, and therefore it's best to minimize such opportunities. For example, if some functionality can be implemented in userland code, where the process boundary necessarily isolates it to the process, the functionality will be less likely to somehow bridge user processes. Here, the term *bridge* specifically means either leaking information, or allowing one process to influence another without authorization.

If that still feels abstract, consider this non-software analogy. You visit your accountant to review your tax return the day before the filing deadline. Piles of papers and folders cover the accountant's desk like miniature skyscrapers. After shuffling through the chaotic mess, they pull out your paperwork and start the meeting. While waiting, you can see tax forms and bank statements with other people's names and tax IDs in plain sight. Perhaps your accountant accidentally jots a quick note about your taxes in someone else's file by mistake. This is exactly the kind of bridge between independent parties, created because the accountant uses the desktop as a common workspace, that the Least Common Mechanism strives to avoid.

Next year, you hire a different accountant, and when you meet with them, they pull your file out of a cabinet. They open it on their desk, which is neat, with no other clients' paperwork in sight. That's how to do Least Common Mechanism right, with minimal risk of mix-ups or nosy clients seeing other documents.

In the realm of software, apply this pattern by designing services that interface to independent processes or different users. Instead of a monolithic database with everyone's data in it, can you provide each user with a separate database or otherwise scope access according to the context? There may be good reasons to put all the data in one place, but when you choose not to follow this pattern, be alert to the added risk and explicitly enforce the necessary separation. Web cookies are a great example of using this pattern because each client stores its own cookie data independently.

# Redundancy

*Redundancy* is a core strategy for safety in engineering that's reflected in many common-sense practices, such as spare tires for cars. These patterns show how to apply it to make software more secure.

## Defense in Depth

Combining independent layers of protection makes for a stronger overall defense that is often synergistically far more effective than any single layer.

This powerful technique is one of the most important patterns we have for making inevitably bug-ridden software systems more secure than their components. Visualize a room that you want to convert to a darkroom by putting plywood over the window. You have plenty of plywood, but somebody has randomly drilled several small holes in every sheet. Nail up just one sheet, and numerous pinholes ruin the darkness. Nail a second sheet on top of that, and unless two holes just happen to align, you now have a completely dark room. A security checkpoint that utilizes both a metal detector and a pat-down is another example of this pattern.

In the realm of software design, deploy *Defense in Depth* by layering two or more independent protection mechanisms to enforce a particularly critical security decision. Like the holey plywood, there might be flaws in each of the implementations, but the likelihood that any given attack will penetrate both is minuscule, akin to having two plywood holes just happen to line up and let light through. Since two independent checks require double the effort and take twice as long, you should use this technique sparingly.

A great example of this technique that balances the effort and overhead against the benefit is the implementation of a *sandbox*, a container in which untrusted arbitrary code can run safely. (Modern web browsers run

WebAssembly in a secure sandbox.) Running untrusted code in your system could have disastrous consequences if anything goes wrong, justifying the overhead of multiple layers of protection (Figure 4-2).

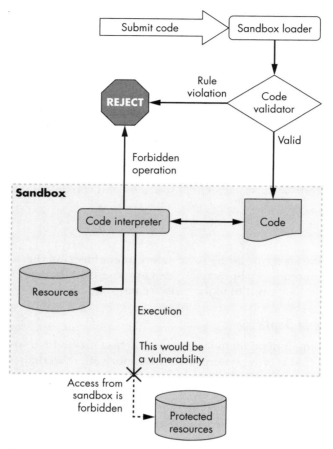

Figure 4-2: An example of a sandbox as the Defense in Depth pattern

Code for sandbox execution first gets scanned by an analyzer (defense layer one), which examines it against a set of rules. If any violation occurs, the system rejects the code completely. For example, one rule might forbid the use of calls into the kernel; another rule might forbid the use of specific privileged machine instructions. If and only if the code passes the scanner, it then gets loaded into an interpreter that runs the code while also enforcing a number of restrictions intended to prevent the same kinds of overprivileged operations. For an attacker to break this system, they must first get past the scanner's rule checking and also trick the interpreter into executing the forbidden operation. This example is especially effective because code scanning and interpretation are fundamentally different, so the chances of the same flaw appearing in both layers is low, especially if they're developed independently. Even if there is a one-in-a-million chance that the scanner misses a particular attack technique, and the same goes for the interpreter, once they're combined, the total system has about a one-in-a-trillion chance of actually failing. That's the power of this pattern.

## Separation of Privilege

Two parties are more trustworthy than one.

Also known as *Separation of Duty*, the *Separation of Privilege* pattern refers to the indisputable fact that two locks are stronger than one when those locks have different keys entrusted to two different people. While it's possible that those two people may be in cahoots, that rarely happens; plus, there are good ways to minimize that risk, and in any case it's way better than relying entirely on one individual.

For example, safe deposit boxes are designed such that a bank maintains the security of the vault that contains all the boxes, and each box holder has a separate key that opens their box. Bankers cannot get into any of the boxes without brute-forcing them, such as by drilling the locks, yet no customer knows the combination that opens the vault. Only when a customer gains access from the bank and then uses their own key can their box be opened.

Apply this pattern when there are distinct overlapping responsibilities for a protected resource. Securing a datacenter is a classic case: the datacenter has a system administrator (or a team of them for a big operation) responsible for operating the machines with superuser access. In addition, security guards control physical access to the facility. These separate duties, paired with corresponding controls of the respective credentials and access keys, should belong to employees who report to different executives in the organization, making collusion less likely and preventing one boss from ordering an extraordinary action in violation of protocol. Specifically, the admins who work remotely shouldn't have physical access to the machines in the datacenter, and the people physically in the datacenter shouldn't know any of the access codes to log in to the machines, or the keys needed to decrypt any of the storage units. It would take two people colluding, one from each domain of control, to gain both physical and admin access in order to fully compromise security. In large organizations, different groups might be responsible for various datasets managed within the datacenter as an additional degree of separation.

The other use of this pattern, typically reserved for the most critical functions, is to split one responsibility into multiple duties to avoid any serious consequences as a result of a single actor's mistake or malicious intent. As extra protection against a backup copy of data possibly leaking, you could encrypt it twice with different keys entrusted separately, so that it can be used only with the help of both parties. An extreme example, triggering a nuclear missile launch, requires two keys turned simultaneously in locks 10 feet apart, ensuring that no individual acting alone could possibly actuate it.

Secure your audit logs by Separation of Privilege, with one team responsible for the recording and reviewing of events and another for initiating the events. This means that the admins can audit user activity, but a separate group needs to audit the admins. Otherwise, a bad actor could block the recording of their own corrupt activity or tamper with the audit log to cover their tracks.

You can't achieve Separation of Privilege within a single computer because an administrator with superuser rights has full control, but there are still many ways to approximate it to good effect. Implementing a design with multiple independent components can still be valuable as a mitigation, even though an administrator can ultimately defeat it, because it makes subversion more complicated; any attack will take longer and the attacker is more likely to make mistakes in the process, increasing their likelihood of being caught. Strong Separation of Privilege for administrators could be designed by forcing the admin to work via a special ssh gateway under separate control that logged their session in full detail and possibly imposed other restrictions.

Insider threats are difficult, or in some cases impossible, to eliminate, but that doesn't mean mitigations are a waste of time. Simply knowing that somebody is watching is, in itself, a large deterrent. Such precautions are not just about distrust: honest staff should welcome any Separation of Privilege that adds accountability and reduces the risk posed by their own mistakes. Forcing a rogue insider to work hard to cleanly cover their tracks slows them down and raises the odds of their being caught red-handed. Fortunately, human beings have well-evolved trust systems for face-to-face encounters with coworkers, and as a result, insider duplicity is extremely rare in practice.

## Trust and Responsibility

Trust and responsibility are the glue that makes cooperation work. Software systems are increasingly interconnected and interdependent, so these patterns are important guideposts.

### Reluctance to Trust

Trust should be always be an explicit choice, informed by solid evidence.

This pattern acknowledges that trust is precious, and so urges skepticism. Before there was software, criminals exploited people's natural inclination to trust others, dressing up as workmen to gain access, selling snake oil, or perpetrating an endless variety of other scams. *Reluctance to Trust* tells us not to assume that a person in a uniform is necessarily legit, and to consider that the caller who says they're with the FBI may be a trickster. In software, this pattern applies to checking the authenticity of code before installing it, and requiring strong authentication before authorization.

The use of HTTP cookies is a great example of this pattern, as Chapter 11 explains in detail. Web servers set cookies in their response to the client, expecting clients to send back those cookies with future requests. But since clients are under no actual obligation to comply, servers should always take cookies with a grain of salt, and it's a huge risk to absolutely trust that clients will always faithfully perform this task.

Reluctance to Trust is important even in the absence of malice. For example, in a critical system, it's vital to ensure that all components are up to the same high standards of quality and security so as not to compromise the whole. Poor trust decisions, such using code from an anonymous developer (which might contain malware, or simply be buggy) for a critical function quickly undermines security. This pattern is straightforward and rational, yet can be challenging in practice because people are naturally trusting and it can feel paranoid to withhold trust.

## Accept Security Responsibility

All software professionals have a clear duty to take responsibility for security; they should reflect that attitude in the software they produce.

For example, a designer should include security requirements when vetting external components to incorporate into the system. And at the interface between two systems, both sides should explicitly take on certain responsibilities they will honor, as well as confirm any guarantees they depend on the caller to uphold.

The anti-pattern that you don't want is to someday encounter a problem and have two developers say to each other, "I thought you were handling security, so I didn't have to." In a large system, both sides can easily find themselves pointing the finger at the other. Consider a situation where component A accepts untrusted input (for example, a web frontend server receiving an anonymous internet request) and passes it through, possibly with some processing or reformatting, to business logic in component B. Component A could take no security responsibility at all and blindly pass through all inputs, assuming B will handle the untrusted input safely with suitable validation and error checking. From component B's perspective, it's easy to assume that the frontend validates all requests and only passes safe requests on to B, so there is no need for B to worry about this. The right way to handle this situation is by explicit agreement; decide who validates requests and what guarantees to provide downstream, if any. For maximum safety, use Defense in Depth, where both components independently validate the input.

Consider another all-too-common case, where the responsibility gap occurs between the designer and user of the software. Recall the example of configuration settings from our discussion of the Secure by Default pattern, specifically when an insecure option is given. If the designer knows a configurable option to be less secure, they should carefully consider whether providing that option is truly necessary. That is, don't just give users an option because it's easy to do, or because "someone, someday, might want this." That's tantamount to setting a trap that someone will eventually fall into unwittingly. When valid reasons for a potentially risky configuration exist, first consider methods of changing the design to allow a safe way of solving the problem. Barring that, if the requirement is inherently unsafe, the designer should advise the user and protect them from configuring the option when unaware of the consequences. Not only is it important to document the risks and suggest possible mitigations to offset the vulnerability, but users should also receive clear feedback—ideally, something better than the responsibility-ditching "Are you sure? (Learn more: *<link>*)" dialog.

## WHAT'S WRONG WITH THE "ARE YOU SURE" DIALOG?

This author personally considers "Are you sure?" dialogs and their ilk to almost always be a failure of design, and one that also often compromises security. I have yet to come across an example in which such a dialog is the best possible solution to the problem. When there are security consequences, this practice runs afoul of the Accept Security Responsibility pattern, in that the designer is foisting responsibility on to the user, who may well not be "sure" but has run out of options. To be clear, in these remarks I would not include normal confirmations, such as rm(1) command interactive prompts or other operations where it's important to avoid accidental operation.

These dialogs can fall victim to the *dialog fatigue* phenomenon, in which people trying to get something done reflexively dismiss dialogs, almost universally considering them hindrances rather than help. As security conscious as I am, when presented with these dialogs I, too, wonder, "How else can I do what I want to do?" My choices are to either give up on what I want to do or proceed at my own considerable risk—and I can only guess at exactly what that risk is, since even if there is a "learn more" text provided, it never seems to provide a good solution. At this point, "Are you sure?" only signals to me that I'm about to do something I'll potentially regret, without explaining exactly what might happen and implying there likely is no going back.

I'd like to see a new third option added to these dialogs—"No, I'm not sure but proceed anyway"—and have that logged as a severe error because the software has failed the user. For any situation where security is critical, scrutinize examples of this sort of responsibility offloading and treat them as significant bugs to be eventually resolved. Exactly how to eliminate these will depend on the particulars, but there are some general approaches to accepting responsibility. Be clear as to precisely what is about to happen and why. Keep the wording concise, but provide a link or equivalent reference to a complete explanation and good documentation. Avoid vague wording ("Are you sure you want to do this?") and show exactly what the target of the action will be (don't let the dialog box obscure important information). Never use double negatives or confusing phrasing ("Are you sure you want to go back?" where answering "No" selects the action). If possible, provide an undo option; a good pattern, seen more these days, is passively offering an undo following any major action. If there is no way to undo, then in the linked documentation, offer a workaround, or suggest backing up data beforehand if unsure. Let's strive to reduce these Hobson's choices in quantity, and ideally confine them to use by professional administrators who have the know-how to accept responsibility.

# Anti-Patterns

*Learn to see in another's calamity the ills which you should avoid.*

—Publilius Syrus

Some skills are best learned by observing how a master works, but another important kind of learning comes from avoiding the past mistakes of others. Beginning chemists learn to always dilute acid by adding the acid to a container of water—never the reverse, because in the presence of a large amount of acid, the first drop of water reacts suddenly, producing a lot of heat that could instantly boil the water, expelling water and acid explosively. Nobody wants to learn this lesson by imitation, and in that spirit, I present here several anti-patterns best avoided in the interests of security.

The following short sections list a few software security anti-patterns. These patterns may generally carry security risks, so they are best avoided, but they are not actual vulnerabilities. In contrast to the named patterns covered in the previous sections, which are generally recognizable terms, some of these don't have well-established names, so I have chosen descriptive monikers here for convenience.

## Confused Deputy

The *Confused Deputy* problem is a fundamental security challenge that is at the core of many software vulnerabilities. One could say that this is the mother of all anti-patterns. To explain the name and what it means, a short story is a good starting point. Suppose a judge issues a warrant, instructing their deputy to arrest Norman Bates. The deputy looks up Norman's address, and arrests the man living there. The man insists there is a mistake, but the deputy has heard that excuse before. The plot twist of our story (which has nothing to do with *Psycho*) is that Norman anticipated getting caught and for years has used a false address. The deputy, confused by this subterfuge, used their arrest authority wrongly; you could say that Norman played them, managing to direct the deputy's duly granted authority to his own malevolent purposes. (The despicable crime of swatting—falsely reporting an emergency to direct police forces against innocent victims—is a perfect example of the Confused Deputy problem, but I didn't want to tell one of those sad stories in detail.)

Common examples of confused deputies include the kernel when called by userland code, or a web server when invoked from the internet. The callee is a *deputy* because the higher-privilege code is invoked to do things on behalf of the lower-privilege caller. This risk derives directly from the trust boundary crossing, which is why those are of such acute interest in threat modeling. In later chapters, numerous ways of confusing a deputy will be covered, including buffer overflows, poor input validation, and cross-site request forgery (CSRF) attacks, just to name a few. Unlike human deputies, who can rely on instinct, past experience, and other cues (including common sense), software is trivially tricked into doing things it wasn't intended to, unless it's designed and implemented with all necessary precautions fully anticipated.

**Intention and Malice**

To recap from Chapter 1, for software to be trustworthy, there are two requirements: it must be built by people you can trust are both honest and competent to deliver a quality product. The difference between the two conditions is intention. The problem with arresting Norman Bates wasn't that the deputy was crooked; it was failing to properly ID the arrestee. Of course, code doesn't disobey or get lazy, but poorly-written code can easily work in ways other than how it was intended. While many gullible computer users and occasionally even technically adept software professionals do get tricked into trusting malicious software, many attacks work by exploiting a Confused Deputy in software that is duly trusted but happens to be flawed.

Often, Confused Deputy vulnerabilities arise when the context of the original request gets lost earlier in the code—for example, if the requester's identity is no longer available. This sort of confusion is especially likely in common code shared by both high- and low-privilege invocations. Figure 4-3 shows what such an invocation looks like.

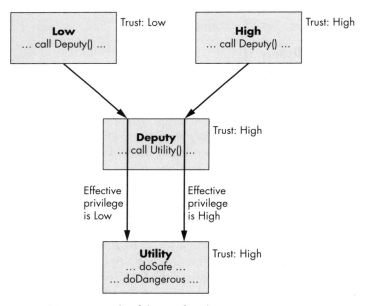

*Figure 4-3: An example of the Confused Deputy anti-pattern*

The Deputy code in the center performs work for both low- and high-privilege code. When invoked from High on the right, it may do potentially dangerous operations in service of its trusted caller. Invocation from Low represents a trust boundary crossing, so Deputy should only do safe operations appropriate for low-privilege callers. Within the implementation, Deputy uses a subcomponent, Utility, to do its work. Code within Utility has no notion of high- and low-privilege callers, and hence is liable to mistakenly do potentially dangerous operations on behalf of Deputy that low-privilege callers should not be able to do.

**Trustworthy Deputy**

Let's break down how to be a trustworthy deputy, beginning with a consideration of where the danger lies. Recall that trust boundaries are where the potential for confusion begins, because the goal in attacking a Confused Deputy is to leverage its higher privilege. So long as the deputy understands the request and who is requesting it, and the appropriate authorization checks happen, everything should be fine.

Recall the previous example involving the Deputy code, where the problem occurred in the underlying Utility code that did not contend with the trust boundary when called from Low. In a sense, Deputy unwittingly made Utility a Confused Deputy. If Utility was not intended to defend against low-privilege callers, then either Deputy needs to thoroughly shield it from being tricked, or Utility may require modification to be aware of low-privilege invocations.

Another common Confused Deputy failing occurs in the actions taken on behalf of the request. *Data hiding* is a fundamental design pattern where the implementation hides the mechanisms it uses behind an abstraction, and the deputy works directly on the mechanism though the requester cannot. For example, the deputy might log information as a side effect of a request, but the requester has no access to the log. By causing the deputy to write the log, the requester is leveraging the deputy's privilege, so it's important to beware of unintended side effects. If the requester can present a malformed string to the deputy that flows into the log with the effect of damaging the data and making it illegible, that's a Confused Deputy attack that effectively wipes the log. In this case, the defense begins by noting that a string from the requester can flow into the log and, considering the potential impact that might have, requiring input validation, for example.

The Code Access Security model, mentioned in Chapter 3, is designed specifically to prevent Confused Deputy vulnerabilities from arising. When low-privilege code calls high-privilege deputy code, the effective permissions are reduced accordingly. When the deputy needs its greater privileges, it must assert them explicitly, acknowledging that it is working at the behest of lower-privilege code.

In summary, at trust boundaries, handle lower-trust data and lower-privilege invocations with care so as not to become a Confused Deputy. Keep the context associated with requests throughout the process of performing the task so that authorization can be fully checked as needed. Beware that side effects do not allow requesters to exceed their authority.

## Backflow of Trust

*Backflow of Trust* is present whenever a lower-trust component controls a higher-trust component. An example of this is when a system administrator uses their personal computer to remotely administer an enterprise system. While the person is duly authorized and trusted, their home computer isn't within the enterprise regime and shouldn't be hosting sessions using admin rights. In essence, you can think of this as a structural Elevation of Privilege just waiting to happen.

While nobody in their right mind would fall into this anti-pattern in real life, it's surprisingly easy to miss in an information system. Remember that what counts here is not the trust you *give* components, but how much trust the components *merit*. Threat modeling can surface potential problems of this variety through an explicit look at trust boundaries.

### Third-Party Hooks

Another form of the Backflow of Trust anti-pattern is when hooks in a component within your system provide a third party undue access. Consider a critical business system that includes a proprietary component performing some specialized process within the system. Perhaps it uses advanced AI to predict future business trends, consuming confidential sales metrics and updating forecasts daily. The AI component is cutting-edge, and so the company that makes it must tend to it daily. To make it work like a turnkey system, it needs a direct tunnel through the firewall to access the administrative interface.

This also is a perverse trust relationship because this third party has direct access into the heart of the enterprise system, completely outside the purview of the administrators. If the AI provider were dishonest, or compromised, they could easily exfiltrate internal company data, or worse, and there would be no way of knowing. Note that a limited type of hook may not have this problem and would be acceptable. For example, if the hook implements an auto-update mechanism and is only capable of downloading and installing new versions of the software, it may be fine, given a suitable level of trust.

### Unpatchable Components

It's almost invariably a matter of when, not if, someone will discover a vulnerability in any given popular component. Once such a vulnerability becomes public knowledge, unless it is completely disconnected from any attack surface, it needs patching promptly. Any component in a system that you cannot patch will eventually become a permanent liability.

Hardware components with preinstalled software are often unpatchable, but for all intents and purposes, so is any software whose publisher has ceased supporting it or gone out of business. In practice, there are many other categories of effectively unpatchable software: unsupported software provided in binary form only; code built with an obsolete compiler or other dependency; code retired by a management decision; code that becomes embroiled in a lawsuit; code lost to ransomware compromise; and, remarkably enough, code written in a language such as COBOL that is so old that, these days, experienced programmers are in short supply. Major operating system providers typically provide support and upgrades for a certain time period, after which the software becomes effectively unpatchable. Even software that is updatable may effectively be no better if the maker fails to provide timely releases. Don't tempt fate by using anything you are not confident you can update quickly when needed.

**NOTE** *See Appendix D for a cheat sheet listing the secure design patterns and anti-patterns presented in this chapter.*

# 5

## CRYPTOGRAPHY

*Cryptography is typically bypassed, not penetrated.*
—Adi Shamir

Back in high school, I nearly failed driver's education. This was long ago, when public schools had funding to teach driving and when gasoline contained lead (nobody had threat modeled that brilliant idea). My first attempts at driving had not gone well. I specifically recall the day I first got behind the wheel of the Volkswagen Beetle, a manual transmission car, and the considerable trepidation on the stony face of the PE coach riding shotgun. I soon learned that pushing in the clutch while going downhill caused the car to speed up, not slow down as I'd intended. But from that mistake onward, something clicked, and suddenly I could drive. The coach expressed unguarded surprise, and relief, at this unlikely turn of events. With hindsight, I believe that my breakthrough was due to the hands-on feel of driving stick, which gave me a more direct connection to the vehicle, enabling me to drive by instinct for the first time.

Just as driver's ed teaches students how to drive a car safely, but not how to design or do major repairs, this chapter introduces the basic toolset of cryptography by discussing how to use it properly, without going into the nuts and bolts of how it works. To make crypto comprehensible to the less mathematically inclined, this chapter eschews the math, except in one instance, whose inclusion I couldn't resist because it's so clever.

This is an unconventional approach to the topic, but also an important one. Crypto tools are underutilized precisely because cryptography has come to be seen as the domain of experts with a high barrier of entry. Modern libraries provide cryptographic functionality, but developers need to know how to use these (and how to use them correctly) for them to be effective. I hope that this chapter serves as a springboard to provide useful intuitions about the potential uses of crypto. You should supplement this with further research as needed for your specific uses.

## Crypto Tools

At its core, much of modern crypto derives from pure mathematics, so when used properly, it really works. This doesn't mean the algorithms are provably impenetrable, but that it will take major breakthroughs in mathematics to crack them.

Crypto provides a rich array of security tools, but for them to be effective, you must use them thoughtfully. As this book repeatedly recommends, rely on high-quality libraries of code that provide complete solutions. It's important to choose a library that provides an interface at the right level of abstraction, so you fully understand what it is doing.

The history of cryptography and the mathematics behind it are fascinating, but for the purposes of creating secure software, the modern toolbox consists of a modest collection of basic tools. The following list enumerates the basic crypto security functions and describes what each does, as well as what the security of each depends on:

- *Random numbers* are useful as padding and nonces, but only if they are unpredictable.
- *Message digests* (or *hash functions*) serve as a fingerprint of data, but only if impervious to collisions.
- *Symmetric encryption* conceals data based on a secret key the parties share.
- *Asymmetric encryption* conceals data based on a secret the recipient knows.
- *Digital signatures* authenticate data based on a secret only the signer knows.
- *Digital certificates* authenticate signers based on trust in a root certificate.
- *Key exchange* allows two parties to establish a shared secret over an open channel, despite eavesdropping.

The rest of this chapter will cover these tools and their uses in more detail.

# Random Numbers

Human minds struggle to grasp the concept of randomness. For security purposes, we can focus on *unpredictability* as the most important attribute of random numbers. As we shall see, these are critical in cases where we must prevent attackers from guessing correctly, in the same way that a predictable password would be weak. Applications for random numbers include authentication, hashing, encryption, and key generation, each of which depends on unpredictability. The following subsections describe the two classes of random numbers available to software, how they differ in predictability, and when to use which kind.

## Pseudo-Random Numbers

*Pseudo-random number generators (PRNGs)* use deterministic computations to produce what looks like an infinite sequence of random numbers. The outputs they generate can easily exceed our human capacity for pattern detection, but analysis and adversarial software may easily learn to mimic a PRNG, disqualifying these from use in security contexts because they are predictable.

However, since calculating pseudo-random numbers is very fast, they're ideal for a broad range of non-security uses. If you want to run a Monte Carlo simulation or randomly assign variant web page designs for A/B testing, for example, a PRNG is the way to go, because even in the unlikely event that someone predicts the algorithm, there's no real threat.

Taking a look at an example of a pseudo-random number may help solidify your understanding of why it is not truly random. Consider this digit sequence:

---

9465764078951269468398352595709825822620522489407726719 4782684826

---

Is this sequence random? There happen to be relatively few 1s and 3s, and disproportionally many 2s, but it wouldn't be unreasonable to find these deviations from a flat distribution in a truly random number. Yet as random as this sequence appears, it's easy to predict the next digits if you know the trick. And as the pattern of Transparent Design cautions us, it's risky to assume we can keep our methods secret. In fact, if you entered this string of digits in a simple web search, you would learn that they are the digits of pi 200 decimals out, and that the next few digits will be 0147.

As the decimals of an irrational number, the digits of pi have a statistically normal distribution and are, in a colloquial sense, entirely random. On the other hand, as an easily computed and well-known number, this sequence is completely predictable, and hence unsuitable for security purposes.

## Cryptographically Secure Pseudo-Random Numbers

Modern operating systems provide *cryptographically secure pseudo-random number generator (CSPRNG)* functions to address the shortcomings of PRNGs when you need random bits for security. You may also see this written as

CSRNG or CRNG; the important part is the "C," which means it's secure for crypto. The inclusion of "pseudo" is an admission that these, too, may fall short of perfect randomness, but experts have deemed them unpredictable enough to be secure for all practical purposes.

Use this kind of random number generator when security is at stake. In other words, if the hypothetical ability to predict the value of a supposedly random number weakens your security, use a CSPRNG. This applies to every security use of random numbers mentioned in this book.

Truly random data, by definition, isn't generated by an algorithm, but comes from an unpredictable physical process. A Geiger counter could be such a *hardware random number generator (HRNG)*, also known as an *entropy source*, because the timing of radioactive decay events is random. HRNGs are built into many modern processors, or you can buy a hardware add-on. Software can also contribute entropy, usually by deriving it from the timing of events such as disk accesses, keyboard and mouse input events, and network transmissions that depend on complex interactions with external entities.

One major internet tech company uses an array of lava lamps to colorfully generate random inputs. But consider a threat model of this technique: because the company chooses to display these lava lamps in its corporate office, and in the reception area no less, potential attackers might be able to observe the state of this input and make an educated guess about the entropy source. In practice, however, the lava lamps merely add entropy to a (presumably) more conventional entropy source behind the scenes, mitigating the risk that this display will lead to an easy compromise of the company's systems.

Entropy sources need time to produce randomness, and a CSPRNG will slow down to a crawl if you demand too many bits too fast. This is the cost of secure randomness, and why PRNGs have an important purpose as a reliably fast alternative. Use CSPRNGs sparingly unless you have a fast HRNG, and where throughput is an issue, test that it won't become a bottleneck.

## Message Authentication Codes

A message *digest* (also called a *hash*) is a fixed-length value computed from a message using a one-way function. This means that each unique message will have a specific digest, and any tampering will result in a different digest value. Being one-way is important because it means the digest computation is irreversible, so it won't be possible for an attacker to find a different message that happens to have the same digest result. If you know that the digest matches, then you know that the message content has not been tampered with.

If two different messages produce the same digest, we call this a *collision*. Since digests map large chunks of data to fixed-length values, collisions are inevitable because there are more possible messages than there are digest values. The defining feature of a good digest function is that collisions are extremely difficult to find. A *collision attack* succeeds if an attacker finds two different inputs that produce the same digest value. The most devastating kind of attack on a digest function is a *preimage attack*, where, given a specific digest value, the attacker can find an input that produces it.

Cryptographically secure digest algorithms are strong one-way functions that make collisions so unlikely that you can assume they never happen. This assumption is necessary to leverage the power of digests because it means that by comparing two digests for equality, you are essentially comparing the full messages. Think of this as comparing two fingerprints (which is also an informal term for a digest) to determine if they were made by the same finger.

If everyone used the same digest function for everything, then attackers could intensively study and analyze it, and they might eventually find a few collisions or other weaknesses. One way to guard against this is to use *keyed hash functions*, which take an extra secret key parameter that transforms the digest computation. In effect, a keyed hash function that takes a 256-bit key is a class of $2^{256}$ different functions. These functions are also called *message authentication codes (MACs)*, because so long as the hash function key is secret, attackers cannot forge them. That is, by using a unique key, you get a customized digest function of your very own.

## Using MACs to Prevent Tampering

MACs are often used to prevent attackers from tampering with data. Suppose Alice wants to send a message to Bob over a public channel. The two of them have privately shared a certain secret key; they don't care about eavesdropping, so they don't need to encrypt their data, but fake messages would be a problem if undetected. Say the evil Mallory is able to tamper with communications on the wire, but she does not know the key. Alice uses the key to compute and send a MAC along with each message. When Bob receives a communication, he computes the MAC of the received message and compares it to the accompanying MAC that Alice sent; if they don't match, he ignores it as bogus.

How secure is this arrangement at defending against the clever Mallory? First, let's consider the obvious attacks:

- If Mallory tampers with the message, its MAC will not match the message digest (and Bob will ignore it).
- If Mallory tampers with the MAC, it won't match the message digest (and Bob will ignore it).
- If Mallory concocts a brand-new message, she will have no way to compute the MAC (and Bob will ignore it).

However, there is one more case that we need to protect against. Can you spot another opening for Mallory, and how you might defend against it?

## Replay Attacks

There is a remaining problem with the MAC communication scheme described previously, and it should give you an idea of how tricky using crypto tools against a determined attacker is. Suppose that Alice sends daily orders to Bob indicating how many widgets she wants delivered the next day. Mallory observes this traffic and collects message and MAC pairs that Alice sends: she orders three widgets the first day, then five the next. On the third day, Alice orders 10 widgets. At this point, Mallory gets an idea of how to tamper with Alice's messages. Mallory intercepts Alice's message and replaces it with a copy of the first day's message (specifying three widgets), complete with the corresponding MAC that Alice has helpfully computed already and which Mallory recorded earlier. Of course, this fools Bob.

This is a *replay attack*, and secure communications protocols need to address it. The problem isn't that the cryptography is weak, it's that it wasn't used properly. In this case, the root problem is that authentic messages ordering three widgets are identical, which is fundamentally a predictability problem.

## Secure MAC Communications

There are a number of ways to fix Alice and Bob's protocol and defeat replay attacks, and they all depend on ensuring that messages are always unique and unpredictable. A simple fix might be for Alice to include a timestamp in the message, with the understanding that Bob should ignore messages with old timestamps. Now if Mallory replays Monday's order of three widgets on Wednesday, Bob will notice when he compares the timestamps and detect the fraud. However, if the messages are frequent or there's a lot of network latency, then timestamps might not work well.

A more secure solution to the threat of replay attacks would be for Bob to send Alice a *nonce*—a random number for one-time use—before Alice sends each message. Then Alice can send back a message along with Bob's nonce and a MAC of the message and nonce combined. This shuts down replay attacks because the nonce varies with every exchange. Mallory could intercept and change the nonce Bob sends, but Bob would notice if a different nonce came back.

Another problem with this simple example is that the messages are short, consisting of just a number of widgets. Setting aside the danger of replay attacks, very short messages are vulnerable to brute-force attacks. The time required to compute a keyed hash function is typically proportional to the message data length, and for just a few bits that computation is going to be fast. The faster Mallory can try different possible hash function keys, the easier it is to guess the right key to match the MAC of an authentic message. Knowing the key, Mallory can now impersonate Alice sending messages.

You can mitigate short message vulnerabilities by padding the messages with random bits until they reach a suitable minimum length. Computing the MACs for these longer messages takes time, but that's good as it slows down Mallory's brute-force attack to the point of being infeasible. In fact, it's desirable for hash functions to be expensive computations for just this reason. This is a situation where it's important for the padding to be random (as opposed to predictably pseudo-random) to make Mallory work as hard as possible.

# Symmetric Encryption

All encryption conceals messages by transforming the *plaintext*, or original message, into an unrecognizable form called the *ciphertext*. Symmetric encryption algorithms use a secret key to customize the message's transformation for the private use of the communicants, who must agree on a key in advance. The decryption algorithm uses the same secret key to convert ciphertext back to plaintext. We call this reversible transformation *symmetric cryptography* because knowledge of the secret key allows you to both encrypt and decrypt.

This section introduces a couple of these symmetric encryption algorithms to illustrate their security properties, and explains some of the precautions necessary to use them safely.

## One-Time Pad

Cryptographers long ago discovered the ideal encryption algorithm, and even though, as we shall see, it is almost never actually used, it's a great starting point for discussing encryption due to its utter simplicity. Known as the *one-time pad*, this algorithm requires the communicants to agree on a secret, random string of bits as the encryption key in advance. In order to encrypt a message, the sender exclusive-ors the message with the key, creating the ciphertext. The recipient then exclusive-ors the ciphertext with the same corresponding key bits to recover the plaintext message. Recall that in the exclusive-or ($\oplus$) operation, if the key bit is a zero, then the corresponding message bit is unchanged; if the key bit is a one, then the message bit is inverted. Figure 5-1 graphically illustrates a simple example of one-time pad encryption and decryption.

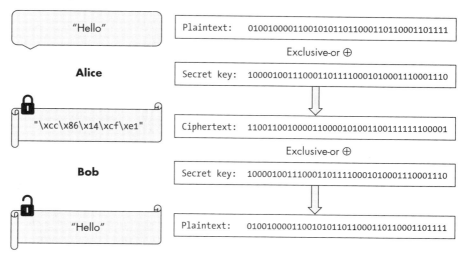

*Figure 5-1: Alice and Bob using one-time pad encryption*

Subsequent messages are encrypted using bits further along in the secret key bit string. When the key is exhausted, the communicants need to somehow agree on a new secret key. There are good reasons it's a *one-time* key, as I will explain shortly. Assuming that the key is random, the message bits either randomly invert or stay the same, so there is no way for attackers to discern the original message without knowing the key. Flipping half the bits randomly is the perfect disguise for a message, since either showing or inverting a large majority of the bits would partially reveal the plaintext. Impervious to attack by analysis as this may be, it's easy to see why this method is rarely used: the key length limits the message length.

Let's consider the prohibition against reusing one-time pad keys. Suppose that Alice and Bob use the same secret key K to encrypt two distinct plaintext messages, M1 and M2. Mallory intercepts both ciphertexts: M1 ⊕ K and M2 ⊕ K. If Mallory exclusive-ors the two encrypted ciphertexts, the key cancels out, because when you exclusive-or any number with itself the result is zero (the ones invert to zeros, while the zeros are unchanged). The result is a weakly encrypted version of the two messages:

(M1 ⊕ K) ⊕ (M2 ⊕ K) = (M1 ⊕ M2) ⊕ (K ⊕ K) = M1 ⊕ M2

While this doesn't directly disclose the plaintext, it begins to leak information. Having stripped away the key bits, analysis could reveal clues about patterns within the messages. For example, if either message contains a sequence of zero bits, then the corresponding bits of the other message will leak through.

The one-time key use limitation is a showstopper for most applications: Alice and Bob may not know how much data they want to encrypt in advance, making it infeasible to decide on how long the key will need to be.

## Advanced Encryption Standard

The *Advanced Encryption Standard (AES)* is a frequently used modern symmetric encryption block cipher algorithm. In a *block cipher*, long messages are broken up into block-sized chunks, and shorter messages are padded with random bits to fill out the remainder of the block. AES encrypts 128-bit blocks of data using a secret key that is typically 256 bits long. Alice uses the same agreed-upon secret key to encrypt data that Bob uses to decrypt.

Let's consider some possible weaknesses. If Alice sends identical message blocks to Bob over time, these will result in identical ciphertext, and clever Mallory will notice these repetitions. Even if Mallory can't decipher the meaning of these messages, this represents a significant information leak that requires mitigation. The communication is also vulnerable to a replay attack because if Alice can resend the same ciphertext to convey the same plaintext message, then Mallory could do that, too.

Encrypting the same message in the same way is known as *electronic code book (ECB) mode*. Because of the vulnerability to replay attacks, this is usually a poor choice. To avoid this problem, you can use other modes that introduce feedback or other differences into subsequent blocks, so that the resulting ciphertext depends on the contents of preceding blocks or the position in the sequence. This ensures that even if the plaintext blocks are identical, the ciphertext results will be completely different. However, while chained encryption of data streams in blocks is advantageous, it does impose obligations on the communicants to maintain context of the ordering to encrypt and decrypt correctly. The choice of encryption modes thus often depends on the particular needs of the application.

### Using Symmetric Cryptography

Symmetric crypto is the workhorse for modern encryption because it's fast and secure when applied properly. Encryption protects data communicated over an insecure channel, as well as data at rest in storage. When using symmetric crypto, it's important to consider some fundamental limitations:

**Key establishment**

Crypto algorithms depend on the prearrangement of secret keys, but do not specify how these keys should be established.

**Key secrecy**

The effectiveness of the encryption entirely depends on maintaining the secrecy of the keys while still having the keys available when needed.

**Key size**

Larger secret keys are stronger (with a one-time pad being the ideal in theory), but managing large keys becomes costly and unwieldy.

Symmetric encryption inherently depends on shared secret keys, and unless Alice and Bob can meet directly for a trusted exchange, it's challenging to set up. To address this limitation, *asymmetric encryption* offers some surprisingly useful new capabilities that fit the needs of an internet-connected world.

# Asymmetric Encryption

Asymmetric cryptography is a deeply counterintuitive form of encryption, and therein lies its power. With symmetric encryption Alice and Bob can both encrypt and decrypt messages using the same key, but with asymmetric encryption Bob can send secret messages to Alice that he is unable to decrypt. Thus, for Bob encryption is a one-way function, while only Alice knows the secret that enables her to invert the function (that is, to decrypt the message).

Asymmetric cryptography uses a pair of keys: a *public key* for encryption and a *private key* for decryption. I will describe how Bob, or anyone in the world for that matter, sends encrypted messages to Alice; for a two-way conversation, Alice would reply using the same process with Bob's entirely separate key pair. The transformations made using the two keys are inverse functions, yet knowing only one of the keys does not help to figure out the other; so if you keep one key secret, then only you can perform that computation. As a result of this asymmetry, Alice can create a key pair and then publish one key for the world to see (her public key), enabling anyone to encrypt messages that only she can decrypt using her corresponding private key. This is revolutionary, because it grants Alice a unique capability based on knowing a secret. We shall see in the following pages all that this makes possible.

There are many asymmetric encryption algorithms, but the mathematical details of these are unimportant to understanding using them as crypto tools—what's important is that you understand the security implications. We'll focus on RSA, as it's the least mathematically complicated progenitor.

## The RSA Cryptosystem

At MIT, I had the great fortune of working with two of the inventors of the RSA cryptosystem, and my bachelor's thesis explored how asymmetric cryptography could improve security. The following simplified discussion follows the original RSA paper, though (for various technical reasons that we don't need to go into here) modern implementations are more involved.

The core idea of RSA is that it's easy to multiply two large prime numbers together, but given that product, it's infeasible to factor it into the constituent primes. To get started, choose a pair of random large prime numbers, which you will keep secret. Next, multiply the pair of primes together. From the result, which we'll call N, you can compute a unique key pair. Each of these keys, together with N, allows you compute two functions D and E that are inverse functions. That is, for any positive integer $x < N$, $D(E(x))$ is $x$, and $E(D(x))$ is also $x$. Finally, choose one of the keys of the key pair as your private key, and publicize to the world the other as the corresponding public key, along with N. So long as you keep the private key and the original two primes secret, only you can efficiently compute the function D.

Here's how Bob encrypts a message for Alice, and how she decrypts it. Here the functions $E_A$ and $D_A$ are based on Alice's public and private keys, respectively, along with N:

- Bob encrypts a ciphertext C from message M for Alice using her public key: $C = E_A(M)$.
- Alice decrypts message M from Bob's ciphertext C using her private key: $M = D_A(C)$.

Since the public key is not a secret, we assume that the attacker Mallory knows it, and this does raise a new concern particular to public key crypto. If an eavesdropper can guess a predictable message, they can encrypt various likely messages themselves using the public key and compare the results to the ciphertext transmitted on the wire. If they ever see matching ciphertext transmitted, they know the plaintext that produced it. Such a *chosen plaintext attack* is easily foiled by padding messages with a suitable number of random bits to make guessing impractical.

RSA was not the first published asymmetric cryptosystem, but it made a big splash because cracking it (that is, deducing someone's private key from their public key) requires solving the well-known hard problem of factoring the product of large prime numbers. Since I was collaborating in a modest way with the inventors of RSA at the time of its public debut, I can offer a historical note that may be of interest about its significance then versus now. The algorithm was too compute-intensive for the computers of its day, so its use required expensive custom hardware. As a result, we envisioned it being used only by large financial institutions or military intelligence agencies. We knew about Moore's law, which proposed that computational power increases exponentially over time—but nobody imagined then that 40 years later everyday people would routinely use connected mobile smartphones with processors capable of doing the necessary number crunching!

Today, RSA is being replaced by newer methods such as *elliptic curve algorithms*. These algorithms, which rely on different mathematics to achieve similar capabilities, offer more "bang for the buck," producing strong encryption with less computation. Since asymmetric crypto is typically more computationally expensive than symmetric crypto, encryption is usually handled by choosing a random secret key, asymmetrically encrypting that, and then symmetrically encrypting the message itself.

## Digital Signatures

Public key cryptography can also be used to create digital signatures, giving the receiving party assurance of authenticity. Independent of message encryption, Alice's signature assures Bob that a message is really from her. It also serves as evidence of the communication, should Alice deny having sent it. As you'll recall from Chapter 2, authenticity and non-repudiability are two of the most important security properties for communication, after confidentiality.

Let's walk through an example to illustrate exactly how this works. Alice creates digital signatures using the same key pair that makes public key encryption possible. Because only Alice knows the private key, only she can compute the signature function $S_A$. Bob, or anyone with the public key (and N), can verify Alice's signature by checking it using the function $V_A$. In other words:

- Alice signs message M to produce a signature $S = S_A(M)$.
- Bob verifies that the message M is from Alice by checking if $M = V_A(S)$.

There are a few more details to explain so you fully understand how digital signatures work. Since verification only relies on the public key, Bob can prove to a third party that Alice signed a message without compromising Alice's private key. Also, signing and encrypting messages are independent: you can do one, the other, or both as appropriate for the application. We won't tackle the underlying math of RSA in this book, but you should know that the signature and decryption functions (both require the private key) are in fact the same computation, as are the verification and encryption functions (using the public key). To avoid confusion, it's best to call them by different names according to their purpose.

Figure 5-2 summarizes the fundamental differences between symmetric encryption on the left, and asymmetric on the right. With symmetric encryption, signing isn't possible because both communicants know the secret key. The security of asymmetric encryption depends on a private key known only to one communicant, so they alone can use it for signatures. Since verification only requires the public key, no secrets are disclosed in the process.

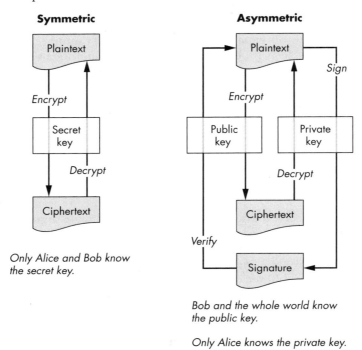

Figure 5-2: A comparison of symmetric and asymmetric cryptography

Digital signatures are widely used to sign digital certificates (the subject of the next section), emails, application code, and legal documents, and to secure cryptocurrencies such as Bitcoin. By convention, digests of messages are signed as a convenience so that one signing operation covers an entire document. Now you can appreciate why a successful preimage attack on a digest function is very bad. If Mallory can concoct a payment agreement with the same message digest, Bob's promissory note also serves as a valid signature for it.

## Digital Certificates

When I was first learning about the RSA algorithm from the inventors, we brainstormed at MIT about possible future applications. The defining advantage of public key crypto was the convenience it offered. It let you use one key for all of your correspondence, rather than managing separate keys for each correspondent, so long as you could announce your public key to the world for anyone to use. But how would one do that?

I came up with an answer in my thesis research and the idea has since been widely implemented. To promote the new phenomenon of digital public key crypto, we needed a new kind of organization, called a *certificate authority (CA)*. To get started, a new CA would widely publish its public key. In time, operating systems and browsers would preinstall a trustworthy set of CA *root certificates*, which are self-signed with their respective public keys.

The CAs collect public keys from applicants, usually for a fee, and then publish a digital certificate for each that lists their name (such as "Alice") and other details about them, along with their public key. The CA signs a digest of the digital certificate to ensure its authenticity. In theory, an important part of the CA's service would involve reviewing the application to ensure that it really came from Alice, and people would choose to trust a CA only if it performed this reliably. In practice, it's very hard to verify identities, especially over the internet, and this has proven problematic.

Once Alice has a digital certificate, she can send people a copy of it whenever she wants to communicate with them. If they trust the CA that issued it, then they have its public key and can validate the digital certificate signature that provides the public key that belongs to "Alice." The digital certificate is basically a signed message from the CA stating that "Alice's public key is X." At that point, the recipient can immediately start encrypting messages for Alice, typically by first sending their own digital certificate in a signed message to assure Alice that her message got to the right person.

This simplified explanation of digital certificates focuses on how trusted CAs authenticate the association of a name with a public key. In practice, there is more to it; people do not always have unique names, names change, corporations in different states may have the same name, and so on. (Chapter 11 digs into some of these complicating issues in the context of web security.) Today, digital certificates are used to bind keys to various identities, including web server domain names and email addresses, and for a number of specific purposes, such as code signing.

## Key Exchange

Whitfield Diffie and Martin Hellman developed a practical key exchange algorithm shortly before the invention of RSA. To understand the miracle of key exchange, imagine that Alice and Bob have somehow established a communication channel, but they have no prior arrangement of a secret key, or even a CA to trust as a source of public keys. Incredibly, key exchange allows them to establish a secret over an open channel while Mallory observes everything. The fact that this is possible is so counterintuitive that in this case I want to show the math so you can see for yourself how it works.

Fortunately, the math is simple enough and, for small numbers, easy to compute. The only notation that might be unfamiliar to some readers is the suffix *(mod p)*, which means to divide by the integer $p$ to yield the remainder of division. For example, $2^7$ (mod 103) is 25, because $128 - 103 = 25$.

This is the basis of the Diffie–Hellman key exchange algorithm:

1. Alice and Bob openly agree on a prime number $p$ and a random number $g$ *(1 < g < p)*.
2. Alice picks a random natural number $a$ *(1 < a < p)*, and sends $g^a$ *(mod p)* to Bob.
3. Bob picks a random natural number $b$ *(1 < b < p)*, and sends $g^b$ *(mod p)* to Alice.
4. Alice computes $S = (g^b)^a$ *(mod p)* as their shared secret $S$.
5. Bob computes $S = (g^a)^b$ *(mod p)*, getting the same shared secret $S$ as Alice.

Figure 5-3 illustrates a toy example using small numbers to show that this actually works. This example isn't secure, because an exhaustive search of about 60 possibilities is easy to do. However, the same math works for big numbers, and at the scale of a few hundred digits, it's wildly infeasible to do such an exhaustive search.

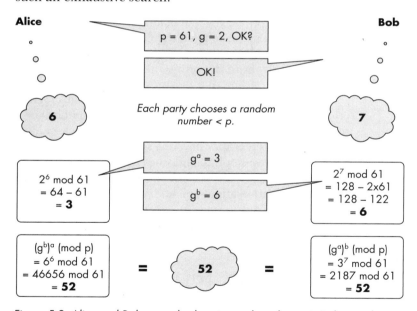

Figure 5-3: Alice and Bob securely choosing a shared secret via key exchange

In this example, chosen to keep the numbers small, by coincidence Alice chooses 6, which happens to equal Bob's result ($g^b$). That wouldn't happen in practice, but of course the algorithm still works and only Alice would notice the coincidence.

It's important that both parties actually choose secure random numbers from a CSPRNG in order to prevent Mallory from possibly guessing their choices. For example, if Bob used a formula to compute his choice from $p$ and $g$, Mallory might deduce that by observing many key exchanges and eventually mimic it, breaking the secrecy of the key exchange.

Key exchange is basically a magic trick that doesn't require any deception. Alice and Bob walk in from the wings of the stage with Mallory standing right in the middle. Alice calls out numbers, Bob answers, and after two back-and-forth exchanges Mallory is still clueless. Alice and Bob write their shared secret numbers on large cards, and at a signal hold up their cards to reveal identical numbers representing the agreed secret.

Today, key exchange is critical to establishing a secure communication channel over the internet between any two endpoints. Most applications use elliptic curve key exchange because those algorithms are more performant, but the concept is much the same. Key exchange is particularly handy in setting up secure communication channels (such as with the TLS protocol) on the internet. The two endpoints first use a TCP channel—traffic that Mallory may be observing—then do key exchange to negotiate a secret with the as-yet-unconfirmed opposite communicant. Once they have a shared secret, encrypted communication enables a secure private channel. This is how any pair of communicants can bootstrap a secure channel without a prearranged secret.

## Using Crypto

This chapter explained the tools in the crypto toolbox at the "driver's ed" level. Cryptographically secure random numbers add unpredictability to thwart attacks based on guessing. Digests are a secure way of distilling the uniqueness of data to a corresponding token for integrity checking. Encryption, available in both symmetric and asymmetric forms, protects confidentiality. Digital signatures are a way of authenticating messages. Digital certificates make it easy to share authentic public keys by leveraging trust in CAs. And key exchange rounds out the crypto toolbox, allowing remote parties to securely agree on a secret key via a public network connection.

The comic in Figure 5-4 illustrates the point made by the epigraph that opens this chapter: that well-built cryptography is so strong, the major threat is that it will be circumvented. Perhaps the most important takeaway from this chapter is that it's crucial to use crypto correctly so you don't inadvertently provide just such an opening for attack.

Crypto can help with many security challenges that arise in the design of your software, or which you identify by threat modeling. If your system must send data over the internet to a partner datacenter, encrypt it (for confidentiality) and digitally sign it (for integrity)—or you could do it the easy way with a TLS secure channel that authenticates the endpoints. Secure digests provide a nifty way to test for data equality, including as MACs, without you needing to store a complete copy of the data. Typically, you will use existing crypto services rather than building your own, and this chapter gives you an idea of when and how to use them, as well as some of the challenges involved in using the technology securely.

Figure 5-4: Security versus the $5 wrench (courtesy of Randall Munroe, xkcd.com/538)

Financial account balances and credit card information are clear examples of data you absolutely must protect. This kind of sensitive data flows through a larger distributed system, and even with limited access to the facility, you don't want someone to be able to physically plug in a network tap and siphon off sensitive data. One powerful mitigation would be to encrypt all incoming sensitive data immediately when it first hits the frontend web servers. Immediately encrypting credit card numbers with a public key enables you to pass around the encrypted data as opaque blobs while processing the transaction. Eventually, this data reaches the highly protected financial processing machine, which knows the private key and can decrypt the data and reconcile the transaction with the banking system. This approach allows most application code to safely pass along sensitive data for subsequent processing without risking disclosure itself.

Another common technique is storing symmetrically encrypted data and the secret key in separate locations. For example, consider an enterprise that wants to outsource long-term data storage for backup to a third party. They would hand over encrypted data for safekeeping while keeping the key in their own vault for use, should they need to restore from a backup. In terms of threats, the data storage service is being entrusted to protect integrity (because they could lose the data), but as long as the key is safe and the crypto was done right, there is no risk to confidentiality.

These are just a few common usages, and you will find many more ways to use these tools. (Cryptocurrency is one particularly clever application.) Modern operating systems and libraries provide mature implementations of a number of currently viable algorithms so you never have to even think about implementing the actual computations yourself.

Encryption is not a panacea, however, and if attackers can observe the frequency and volume of encrypted data or other metadata, you may disclose some information to them. For example, consider a cloud-based security camera system that captures images when it detects motion in the house. When the family is away, there is no motion, and hence no transmission from the cameras. Even if the images were encrypted, an attacker able to monitor the home network could easily infer the family's daily patterns and confirm when the house was unoccupied by the drop in camera traffic.

The security of cryptography rests on the known limits of mathematics and the state of the art of digital hardware technology, and both of these are inexorably progressing. Great fame awaits the mathematician who may someday find more efficient computational methods that undermine modern algorithms. Additionally, the prospect of a different kind of computing technology, such as quantum physics, is another potential threat. It is even possible that some powerful nation-state has already achieved such a breakthrough, and is currently using it discreetly, so as not to tip their hand. Like all mitigations, crypto inherently includes trade-offs and unknown risks, but it's still a great set of tools well worth using.

# PART II

## DESIGN

# 6

## SECURE DESIGN

*Overload, clutter, and confusion are not attributes of
information, they are failures of design.*
—Edward Tufte

Once you have a solid understanding of
security principles, patterns, and mitigations, the practice of integrating security
into your software designs becomes relatively
straightforward. As you discern threats to your design,
you can apply these tools as needed and explore better design alternatives that reduce risk organically.

   This chapter focuses on secure software design. It serves as a companion to Chapter 7, which covers security design reviews. These two topics are
aspects of the same activity, viewed from different perspectives. Software
designers should be considering the concepts discussed in this chapter
and applying these methods throughout the design process; they shouldn't
leave the system's security for a reviewer to patch up later. In turn, reviewers should look at designs through the lens of threats and mitigations as an
additional layer of security assessment. The secure design process is integra-
tive, and the security design review is analytic—used synergistically, they
produce better designs with security baked in.

Software design is an art, and this chapter focuses on just the security aspect. Whether you design according to a formal process or do it all in your head, you don't have to change how you work to incorporate the ideas presented here. Threat modeling and a security perspective do not need to drive design, but they should inform it.

The secure design practice described here follows a process typical of a large enterprise, but you can adapt these techniques to however you work. Smaller organizations will operate much more informally, and the designer and reviewer may be the same person. The techniques presented approach the problem in a general way so as to be easily applicable to however you like to do software design.

---

**A SAMPLE DESIGN DOCUMENT THAT INTEGRATES SECURITY**

Design is a creative process that's not reducible to "how to" steps, so I wanted to provide a complete example of a design document to demonstrate how to apply the concepts presented in this book. The sample in Appendix A illustrates how to bake in security right from the start. It's not intended to be a perfect example of masterful design, but rather a first draft of a work in progress with enough meat on its bones for you to get a feel for the end result. For brevity, parts of the design unimportant to our purposes are omitted and parts are presented unpolished, with some warts and rough spots, because most real designs are like that.

The sample design document envisions a logging tool designed to facilitate auditing while minimizing disclosure of private information, and the intention is that this might be a useful component to actually use. This kind of tool could be a practical mitigation in the context of a larger system processing sensitive data, and you're welcome to flesh out the design and build it if you like. Regardless, I strongly recommend that you take a look at this example, as seeing how the guidance in this chapter actually materializes in a design document will help you better understand how secure design works.

---

## Integrating Security in Design

*I will contend that conceptual integrity is the most important consideration in system design.*

—Fred Brooks (from *The Mythical Man-Month*)

The design stage provides a golden opportunity for building security principles and patterns into a software project. During this early phase, you can easily explore alternatives before investing in an implementation and getting tied down by past decisions.

In the design stage, developers should create *design documents* to capture the important high-level characteristics of a software project, analogous to architectural blueprint drawings for structures. I highly recommend investing effort into documenting your designs because it helps ensure rigor and also creates a valuable artifact that allows others to understand the decisions you've made—especially when it comes to balancing threats with mitigations and the trade-offs involved.

Design documents typically consist of a *functional description* (how the software works when viewed from the outside) and a *technical specification* (how it works when viewed from the inside). More formal designs are especially valuable when there are competing stakeholders, when coordinating a larger effort, when the designs must comply with a formal requirements specification or strict compatibility demands, when faced with difficult trade-offs, and so forth.

When you look at a prospective software design, put on your "security hat." Then, before coding begins, you can threat model, identify attack surfaces, map out data flows, and more. If the proposed design makes securing the system structurally challenging, now is the perfect time to consider alternatives that would be inherently more secure. You should also point out important security mitigations in the design document so that implementers will see the need for these in advance.

More experienced designers will incorporate security into the design from the start. If this seems daunting, it's fine to start with a "feature-complete" draft design and make a second pass through it with a focus on security, but that's a lot more work. Major changes are most easily made if caught earlier in the process, avoiding the wasted effort of redoing after the fact. Explore new architectures and play with basic requirements sooner rather than later, when it's more easily done. As Josh Bloch once quipped: "A week of coding can often save an hour of thought."

### Making Design Assumptions Explicit

In the mid-1980s, I worked for a company that designed and built what was then a powerful computer from the ground up: both the hardware and the software. After years of development, the work of both teams came together when the operating system was loaded into the prototype hardware at last. . . and immediately tanked. It turned out that the hardware team had largely come from IBM, where they use big-endian architecture, and the software team mostly came from HP, which traditionally used little-endian, so "bit 0" meant the high-order bit on the hardware but the low-order bit on the software. Throughout years of planning and meetings and prototyping, everybody had just assumed the endianness of the company culture they came from. (And of course, it was the software team that had to make the necessary changes once they figured this out.)

Unwritten assumptions can undermine the effectiveness of security design reviews, so designers should endeavor to document them (and reviewers should ask about anything that is unclear). A good place to capture these explicit assumptions is in a "background" section of the design document, preceding the body of the design itself.

One way to think about documenting assumptions is to anticipate serious misunderstandings, so you never hear anyone say, "But I thought. . ." Here is a list of some common assumptions that are important to document, but easily omitted in designs:

- Budget, resource, and time constraints limiting the design space
- Whether the system is likely to be a target of attack
- Non-negotiable requirements, such as compatibility with legacy systems
- Expectations about the level of security to which the system must perform
- Sensitivity of data and the importance of protecting it securely
- Anticipated needs for future changes to the system
- Specific performance or efficiency benchmarks the system must achieve

Clarification of assumptions is important to security because misunderstandings are often the root cause of a weak interface design or mismatched interaction between components that attackers can exploit. In addition, it ensures that the design reviewer has a clear and consistent view of the project.

Often within an enterprise, or any set of related projects, many of these assumptions will remain the same across a set of designs, in which case you can compile a list in a shared document that provides common background. Individual designs then need only reference this common base and detail any exceptions where the applicable assumptions vary. For example, a billing system may be subject to higher security standards and need to conform with specific financial regulations for a credit card processing component than the rest of the enterprise applications.

## Defining the Scope

It's impossible to do a good review of the security of a design if there is uncertainty about the scope of the review. Clarifying the scope is also vital to answering the first of the Four Questions from Chapter 2: "What are we working on?" To see why this is, consider the design for a new customer billing system. Does the design include the web app used for collecting reports of billable hours, or is that a separate design? What about the existing databases it relies on—is the security of those systems in scope or not? And should the review include the design of the new web-based API you'll be using to report to the corporate accounting system?

Usually, the designer makes a strategic decision about how to define the scope, choosing how much to bite off. When it's defined by others, the designer must understand the prescribed scope and the reasons for it. You can define the scope of the design as the code running in a process, specific components of a system represented in a block diagram, the code in a library, a division of a source repository, or whatever else makes the most sense, so long as it's clear to everyone involved. The billing system design I mentioned in the previous paragraph probably should include the new API, since it's an extension of the same design. Conversely, the existing databases are probably out of scope, provided they aren't being used in a fundamentally new way and have already received sufficient security attention.

If the scope of a design is vague, the reviewer might assume some important aspect of security is out of scope, while the designer might be unaware of the issue. By omission, it could fall through the cracks. For example, nearly every software design will involve some storage of data. Unless the data is expendable, which is rare, maintaining good backups is an obvious mitigation to the possible loss of integrity due to various threats (both malicious and accidental). Designers often omit such self-evident points, but without a clear statement of design scope, everyone might assume someone else regularly performs backups for all storage in the production system, resulting in this task falling by the wayside—until the first instance of failure, when the lesson is learned all too painfully.

Don't let excluding part of the design's ecosystem from the scope result in it falling between the cracks. When you have inherited a legacy system, your first efforts to understand it should focus on its most sensitive parts, those most fundamental to security, or perhaps the most obvious target of attack. Then judiciously undertake reviews of additional parts of the system that constitute independent components until you have covered everything.

You can handle design iterations, sprints, and major revisions of existing systems by defining a narrow scope that corresponds to where redesign happens. Once you have carved out boundaries for the new design work, there are clear preconditions defined by the design that are outside that scope, and you are free to redo everything anew on the inside. Existing design documentation makes this work much easier and more reliable, and the updated design should drive tracked changes to the document.

It's common, and often a good thing, for redesign to creep outside of its intended bounds, and when it does, you should adjust the scope as needed. For example, an incremental design change may require the modification of existing interfaces or data formats, and if the change involves handling more sensitive data, you may need to make changes on the other side of the interface due to the new security assumptions.

Few software designs exist in a vacuum; they depend on existing systems, processes, and components. Ensuring that the design works well with its dependencies is critical. In particular, matching security expectations is key, because you cannot build a secure application out of insecure components. And it's important to note that secure/insecure is not a binary choice; it's a continuum, where the assumptions and expectations need to align. Read up on security design review reports for peer systems and dependencies to substantiate your security expectations for them.

## Setting Security Requirements

Security requirements largely derive from the second of the Four Questions: "What can go wrong?" The C-I-A triad is a useful starting point: describe the need to protect private data from unauthorized disclosure (confidentiality), the importance of securing and backing up data (integrity), and the extent to which the system needs to be robust and reliable (availability). The security requirements of many software systems are straightforward, but it's still well worth detailing them for completeness and to convey priorities. What may be entirely obvious to you may not be to others, so it's a good idea to articulate the desired security stance.

One extreme to note is when security doesn't matter—or at least, when someone thinks it doesn't. That's an important assumption to call out, because someone else on the team might be thinking that it certainly does matter (and you can imagine the circumstances under which such mismatched expectations will eventually come to light). If you are designing a prototype to process artificial dummy data, you can skip the security review, but document it so the code isn't repurposed and used later with personal information. Another example of a low-security application might be the collection of weather data shared by several research groups: temperatures and other atmospheric conditions are free for anyone to measure, and disclosure is harmless.

At the other extreme, security-critical software deserves extra attention and a careful enumeration of its security-related requirements. These will provide a focus for threat modeling, security review, and testing to ensure the highest level of quality. See the sample design document (Appendix A) for a basic example of how security requirements inform the design. Large systems subject to complex regulations may have tightly prescribed security requirements to ensure high levels of compliance, but that's a specialized undertaking, out of scope for our purposes.

For software designs with critical or unusual security requirements, consider the following general guidelines:

- Express security requirements as end goals without dictating "how to."
- Consider all stakeholder needs. In particular, where these may be in conflict, it will be necessary to find a good balance.
- Acknowledge acceptable costs and trade-offs for critical mitigations.
- When there are unusual requirements, explain the motivation for them as well as their goals.
- Set security goals that are achievable, not mandates for perfection.

The following extreme examples illustrate what requirements statements for systems with significant security needs might look like:

**At the National Security Agency, to protect the nation's most sensitive secrets**

System administrators will have extraordinary access to an enormous trove of top-secret documents, and given the threat to national security this represents, we must mitigate insider attacks to the highest degree possible. Specifically, an administrator capable of impersonating high-ranking officers with broad access authority could potentially exfiltrate many files, covering their tracks by making it look like numerous independent access events by many different principals. (Unofficial accounts of Edward Snowden's tactics for exfiltrating NSA internal documents suggest that he used this sort of technique.)

### The authentication server for a large financial institution

Compromise of the server's private encryption key would completely undermine the security of all our internet-facing systems. While insider attacks are unlikely, operations personnel must *not* have plausible deniability. Requirements might include storing the key in a tamper-evident hardware device kept in a physically guarded location, and formal ceremonies for the creation and rotation of keys, with all accesses attended by at least two trusted persons. (Note: this includes "how to" as the most direct way of illustrating distribution of trust and the combination of overlapping physical and logical security.)

### Data integrity for an expensive scientific experiment

We plan to do this experiment only once, and the funding required for it will not likely be available again for years, so we cannot afford to lose the information our instruments collect. Streaming data must be instantly replicated and stored redundantly on different storage media, while simultaneously being communicated over two distinct networks to physically separated remote storage systems as additional backup.

## Threat Modeling

One of the best ways to improve the security of your software architecture is to incorporate threat modeling into the design process. Designing software involves creatively juggling competing requirements and strategies, iteratively deciding on some aspects of the system, and, at times, reversing course to progress toward a complete vision. Viewing the process through the lens of threat modeling can illuminate design trade-offs, so it has great potential to lead the designer in the right direction—but figuring out exactly how to achieve improved outcomes requires some trial and error.

First, there is the simplistic method for integrating threat modeling into software design. This involves concocting a series of potential designs, threat modeling each one in turn, scoring them by some kind of summary assessment, and then choosing the best one. In practice, these security-focused assessments inform other important factors, including usability, performance, and development cost. But since the effort involved in producing multiple designs and then threat modeling each one individually is prohibitive, designers often need to intuit which trade-offs offer promising possibilities, then compare the design alternatives by analyzing their differences rather than reassessing each from scratch.

In the early stages of software system design, pay careful attention to trust boundaries and attack surfaces, as these are critical for establishing an architecture amenable to security. Data flows of sensitive information should, as much as possible, be kept away from the most exposed parts of the topology. For example, consider an application for traveling sales staff who need offline access to customer contact information in order to make sales calls on the road. Putting the entire customer database in each mobile device would represent a huge risk of exposure, yet arguably would be necessary if staff travel to remote locations without good connectivity. Threat modeling would highlight this risk, spurring you to evaluate alternatives. Perhaps only regional subsets of the database would suffice, dynamically updated as the reps change location or based on travel schedule; or, instead of supplying customer phone numbers, each salesperson might get a code for each customer that they can use together with a unique PIN to place calls via a forwarding service, so there is no need for them to have access to the phone numbers at all.

Designers should also consider the *essential threat model* of the software they are building as a kind of baseline from which to gauge alternative designs. By this I mean a model of the security risk inherent in the idealized design, no matter how it's built. For example, if a client/server system is collecting personally identifiable information (PII) from the client, there is an unavoidable security risk of that information being exposed by the client, in transit, or on the server that processes the data. No design magic will make any of those risks disappear, though they often call for suitable mitigations.

When the inherent security risk is high, designers should consider alternatives whenever possible. Continuing with the PII example, is it really necessary to collect all (or any) of that information for all use cases? If not, then it may well be worth the effort of supporting subcases that avoid some of the information collection at the source.

Another way that an essential threat model guides design is by highlighting sources of additional risk that arise out of design decisions. An example of such an effect might be choosing to add a caching layer for sensitive data in an attempt to improve response time. The additional storing of data (potentially an asset that attackers would target) necessarily adds new risk, especially if the cache store is near an attack surface. This illustrates how changes to the design always modify the threat model—for better or for worse—and with an understanding of the security impact, designers can weigh the merits of alternatives wisely.

Good software design, in the end, depends on subjective judgments. These balance the various factors involved to find, if not the best, then at least a satisfactory result. As important as security is, it isn't everything, so difficult decisions are inevitable. Over the years I have found that, as scary as it may be at times, it's much more productive to remain open to discussions of compromise rather than declare security concerns preeminent.

When the costs of maximizing security are low, it's easy to push for doing so—but this isn't always the case. When compromise is necessary, here are some good strategies to keep in mind:

- Design for flexibility so that adding security protections later will be easy to do (that is, don't paint yourself into an insecure corner).

- If there are specific attacks that are of special concern, instrument the system to facilitate monitoring for instances of attempted abuse.

- When usability conflicts with security, explore user interface alternatives. Also, prototype and measure usability under realistic situations; sometimes usability concerns are imaginary and do not manifest in practice.

- Explain security risks with potential scenarios (derived from threat models) that illustrate major possible downsides of certain designs, and use these to demonstrate the cost of not implementing mitigations.

# Building in Mitigations

After you've defined the software system's scope and security requirements, answering the first two of the Four Questions, it's time to consider the third: "What are we going to do about it?" This question guides the designer to incorporate the needed protections and mitigations into the design. In the following subsections we will examine how to do this for interfaces and for data, two of the most common recurring themes in software design. The discussion and examples that follow only scratch the surface of possibilities for mitigations in design. All of the ideas in the preceding three chapters can be applied according to the needs of a particular design.

## *Designing Interfaces*

Interfaces define the boundaries of the system, delineating the limits of the design or of its constituent components. They may include system calls, libraries, networks (client/server or peer-to-peer), inter- and intraprocess APIs, shared data structures in common datastores, and more. Complex interfaces, such as secure communication protocols, often deserve their own design.

Define all interfaces within the scope of the design, making sure you have a clear understanding of the security responsibilities of the components that share it. Document whether inputs are reliably validated or should be treated as untrusted data. If there is a trust boundary, explain how to handle authentication and authorization for crossing it.

Interfaces to external components (those scoped outside of the design) should conform to the existing design specifications for those components. If no such information is available, either document your assumptions or consider defensive tactics to compensate for the uncertainty. For example, assume untrusted inputs if you cannot ascertain whether the input is being validated.

To design secure interfaces, begin with a solid description of how they work, including their necessary security properties (that is, C-I-A, Gold Standard, or privacy requirements). Reviewing the security of the interfaces amounts to verifying that they will function properly and remain robust against potential threats. Unless the designer is clear about the security requirements, the security reviewer (and developers using the interface later) will have to guess at the designer's intentions, and there will be confusion if they either under- or overestimate the requirements.

Sometimes, you are stuck using existing components that weren't designed with security in mind or are not sufficiently secure for your requirements—or you just don't know how secure the components are. Flag this as an issue if you have no choice in the matter and, if possible, do research to find out what you can about the components' security properties (this might include trying to attack a test mock-up). Another option in some cases is to wrap the interface to add security protection. For example, given a storage component that is vulnerable to data leaks, you could design an extra layer of software that provides encryption and decryption, ensuring that the component stores only encrypted data, which is harmless if disclosed.

### Designing Data Handling

Data handling is central to virtually all designs, so securing it is an important step. A good starting point for secure data handling is outlining your data protection goals. When a particular subset of data requires extra protection, make that explicit, and ensure it's handled consistently throughout the design. For example, in an online shopping application, apply additional safeguards to credit card information.

Limit the need to move sensitive data around. This is a key opportunity to reduce your risk exposure in a significant way at the design level (see the "Least Information" pattern in Chapter 4) that often isn't possible to do later in implementation. One way to reduce the need to pass data around is to associate it with an opaque identifier, then use the identifier as a handle that, when necessary, you can convert into the actual data. For example, as in the sample design in Appendix A, you can log transactions using such an identifier to keep customer details out of system logs. In the rare case that a log entry needs investigation, an auditor can look up those details.

Identify public information, or data otherwise exempt from any confidentiality requirement. This forms an important exception to data handling requirements, allowing you to relax protections where that makes sense. In applying such an approach, remember that data is context-sensitive, so public data paired with other information might well be sensitive. For example, the addresses of most businesses and the names of their chief executives are usually public information. However, exactly when named persons are on the premises should be kept private.

Always treat personal information as sensitive in the absence of an explicit decision otherwise, and only collect such data in the first place if there is a specific use for it. Storing sensitive data indefinitely creates an endless obligation to protect it. You can best avoid this by destroying disused information when possible (after a number of years of inactivity, for example). Designs should anticipate the need to eventually remove private data from the system when no longer needed and specify what conditions will trigger deletion, including of backup copies.

# Integrating Privacy into Design

Failures to protect private information make headlines routinely. I believe that integrating information privacy considerations into software design is an important way companies can do better. Privacy issues concern the human implications of data protection, involving not only legal and regulatory issues, but also customer expectations and the potential impact of unauthorized disclosures. Getting this right requires special expertise and subjective judgment. But part of the problem hinges on granting third parties the authorization to use data, which requires allowing access. To that extent, good software design can institute controls to minimize missteps.

As a starting point, designers should be familiar with all applicable private policies and understand how these relate to the design. Ask questions and ideally get answers in writing from the privacy policy owner so that the requirements are clear. This includes any third-party privacy policy obligations that might apply to data acquired via partners. These privacy policies govern data collection, use, storage, and sharing, so if these activities happen within the design, the policy stipulations imply requirements. If the public-facing privacy policy is short on details, consider developing an internal version that describes necessary details.

Privacy lapses tend to happen when people or processes misinterpret the promises in the policy, or simply fail to consider them. Data security protections offer opportunities to build limitations into a design to ensure compliance. Start by considering clear promises the privacy policy makes, then ensure that the design enforces them if possible. For example, if the policy says, "We do not share your data," then be wary of using a cloud storage service that makes sharing easy unless other provisions are in place to ensure that misconfigurations won't expose the data.

Auditing is an important tool for privacy stewardship, if only to reliably document proper access to sensitive data. With careful monitoring of accesses, problematic access and use can be detected and remedied early. In the aftermath of a leak, if there is no record of who had access to the data in question, it's very difficult to respond effectively.

Design explicit privacy protections wherever possible. In instances where you cannot make the judgment about privacy compliance, get the officer responsible for the privacy policy to sign off on the design. Some common techniques for integrating privacy in software design include:

- Identify the collection of new types of data, and ensure its privacy policy compliance.
- Confirm that policy allows you to use the data for the purpose you intend.
- If the design potentially enables unlimited data use, consider limiting access only to staff that are familiar with privacy policy constraints and how to audit for compliance.
- If the policy limits the term of data retention, design a system that ensures timely deletion.

- As the design evolves, if a field in a database becomes disused, consider deleting it in order to reduce the risk of disclosure.
- Consider building in an approval process for data sharing to ensure the receiving parties have management approval.

## Planning for the Full Software Life Cycle

Too many software designs implicitly assume that the system will last forever, ignoring the reality that the lifetime of all software is finite. Many aspects of a system's eventual lifetime—from its first release and deployment, through updates and maintenance, to its eventual decommissioning—have important security implications that are easily missed later on. As wonderful as any software design might be, whether it takes off or fizzles out, it will undergo changes as its environment evolves. The impacts of these changes are best anticipated during the design process and addressed then, or at least noted for posterity. Within an enterprise, many of these issues are generic, and a general treatment of them should cover most systems, with exceptions specified as needed in individual designs.

The end of a system's life is difficult to imagine when the new design is being created, but most of the implications should be clear, and any design should at least consider the long-term disposition of data. Specific legal or business reasons may require you to retain data for a certain period of time, but you should destroy it when it is no longer needed, including backup copies. Some systems need to go through specific stages when approaching end of life, and good design can make this easy to get right by having suitable structure and configuration options in place from the start. For example, a purchasing system might stop accepting orders but need to continue providing data for payroll and record-keeping purposes for another year, then archive transaction records for long-term retention.

## Making Trade-offs

Balancing trade-offs when there are no easy choices requires a lot of engineering judgment, while weighing many other considerations. Implementing more security mitigations reduces risk, but only up to the point that complexity leads to more bugs overall—and you should always be wary of increased development effort with diminishing returns. This book will repeatedly advise designers to compromise between competing priorities, but this is easier said than done. This section covers some rules of thumb for striking these important balances.

Anticipate the worst-case scenario: How bad would it be if you were to fail to protect the confidentiality, integrity, or availability of a particular system asset? For each scenario there are degrees of catastrophe to consider: How much of the data could potentially be affected? At what point does a period of unavailability become a serious issue? Major mitigations usually limit the worst case; for example, hourly backups should ensure that at most one hour of transaction data is at risk of loss. Note that a loss of confidentiality in the worst case is particularly difficult to cap, because once data has been purloined, there usually is no conceivable way to undo the disclosure (the 2017 Equifax breach is a striking example).

Most design work happens within an enterprise or project community where the level of security needed is usually consistent across a wide range of projects. Where a particular design might deviate—requiring either a higher or lower level of security—that assumption is well worth calling out in the design preface. Some examples will clarify this important point. An online store website should consider setting a higher security bar for the software that handles credit card processing, which is an obvious target of attack and is subject to special requirements because of the enormous financial liability. On the flip side, a web design company might put up an entire website that showcases examples of its design; since this would be for informational purposes only and never collect actual end user data, securing it would reasonably be less important.

The design phase represents the best opportunity to strike the right balance between competing demands on software. To be frank, rarely if ever is security fully supported as a top priority when there are schedule deadlines, constraints of budget and headcount, legacy compatibility issues, and the usual lengthy list of features to deal with—which is to say, nearly always. Designers are in the best position to consider many alternatives, including radical ones, and make foundational changes that would be infeasible to attempt later on.

Striking the right balance between these idealized principles and the pragmatic demands of building a real-world system is at the heart of secure software design. Perfect security is never the goal, and there is a limit to the benefits of additional mitigations. Exactly where the sweet spot lies is never easy to determine, but software designs that make these trade-offs explicit have better chances of finding a sensible compromise.

## Design Simplicity

*Simplicity is the ultimate sophistication.*

—Leonardo da Vinci

Ironically, as the da Vinci quote suggests, it often takes considerable thought and effort to produce a simple design. Early astronomers developed all manner of complicated calculations for celestial mechanics until Copernicus simplified the model by making the Sun the central reference point instead of the Earth, which in turn allowed Newton to radically simplify the computations by inferring the laws of gravity. My favorite example of brilliant software design is the heart of the *nix operating system, much of which remains in use to this day. The quest to create a beautifully simple design, even if rarely achieved, often directly contributes to better security.

In software design, simplicity appears in many guises, but there are no easy formulations of how to discover the simplest, most elegant design. Several of the patterns discussed in Chapter 4 embrace simplicity, such as Economy of Design and Least Common Mechanism. Any time security depends on getting some complicated decision or mechanism just right, be wary: see if there is a simpler way of achieving the same ends.

When intricate functionality interacts with security mechanisms, the result often explodes with complexity. One study concluded that the 1979 failure at the Three Mile Island nuclear facility had no specific cause but was due to the immense complexity of the system, including its many redundant safety measures. Security can get in the way of what you are trying to do, and in turn, making it all secure gets trickier. The solution here is often to separate security from functionality and create a layered model, usually with security on the "outside" as a protective shell and all the functionality separately existing "inside." However, when you design with a hard shell and "soft insides," it becomes critical to enforce that separation. It's relatively easy to design a secure moat around a castle, but in software, it's easy to inadvertently open up a pathway to the inside that circumvents the outer protective layer.

# 7

## SECURITY DESIGN REVIEWS

*A good, sympathetic review is always a wonderful surprise.*
—Joyce Carol Oates

One of the best ways to bake security into software is to separately review designs with your "security hat" on. This chapter explains how to apply the security and privacy design concepts discussed in the last chapter in a *security design review (SDR)*. Think of this process as akin to when an architect designs a building and an engineer then reviews the design to ensure that it's safe and sound. Both the designer and the reviewer need to understand structural engineering and building codes, and by working together, they can achieve higher levels of quality and trust.

Ideally, the security reviewer is someone not involved in the design work, giving them distance and objectivity, and also someone familiar with the systems and context within which the software runs and how it will be used. However, these are not firm prerequisites; reviewers less familiar with the design will tend to ask a lot more questions but can also do a fine job.

Sharing these methods and encouraging more software professionals to perform SDRs themselves was one of my core goals in writing this book. You will almost certainly do a better SDR on the software systems that you work with and know well than someone with more security experience who is unfamiliar with those systems. This book provides guidance to help you with this task, and it's my hope that in doing so it will contribute in some small way to raising the bar for software security.

## SDR Logistics

Before presenting the methodology for an SDR, it's important to give a little background and discuss some basic logistics. What purpose does an SDR serve? If we're going to perform one, during what stage of the design process should this be done? Finally, I'll give a few tips on preparation and the importance of documentation in particular.

### Why Conduct an SDR?

Having done a few hundred SDRs myself, I can report that it never feels like a waste of time. SDRs take only a tiny fraction of the total design time, and will either identify important improvements to enhance security or provide strong assurance that the design properly addresses security. Simple, straightforward designs are quick to review, and for larger designs the review process provides a useful framework for identifying and validating the major hotspots. Even when you review a design that ostensibly covers all the bases for security, it's good due diligence to confirm this. And of course, when the SDR does turn up significant issues, the effort proves extremely worthwhile, because detecting these issues during implementation would be difficult and remedying them after the fact would be costly.

In addition, SDRs can yield valuable new insights, resulting in design changes unrelated to security. An SDR offers a great opportunity to involve diverse perspectives (user experience, customer support, marketing, legal, and so forth), with everyone pondering easily overlooked topics such as the potential for abuse and unintended consequences.

### When to Conduct an SDR

Plan on performing an SDR when the design (or design iteration) is complete and stable, typically following the functional review, but before the design is finalized, since there may be changes needed. I strongly recommend against trying to handle security as part of the functional review, because the mindset and areas of focus are so different. Also, it's important for everyone—not just the reviewer—to focus on security, and that's difficult to do during a combined review when there's a tendency to concentrate more on the workings of the designs.

Designs that are complicated or security-critical often benefit from an additional preliminary SDR, when the design is beginning to gel but still not fully formed, in order to get early input on major threats and overall strategy. The preliminary SDR can be less formal, previewing points of particular security interest (where you would expect to dig further) and discussing security trade-offs at a high level. Good software designers should always consider and address security and privacy issues throughout the design. To be clear, designers should *never* ignore security and rely on the SDR to fix those issues for them. They should always expect to be fully responsible for the security of their designs, with security reviewers in a support role helping to ensure that they do a thorough job. In turn, security reviewers shouldn't pontificate, but instead clearly and persuasively present their findings to designers without judgment.

### Documentation Is Essential

Effective SDRs depend on up-to-date documentation so that all parties have an accurate and consistent understanding of the design under review. Informal word-of-mouth SDRs are better than nothing, but crucial details are easily omitted or miscommunicated, and without a written record, valuable results are easily lost. Personally, I always prefer having design documents to preview ahead of a meeting, so I can start studying the design in advance and not take up meeting time with learning what we are working on.

The quality of the design documentation is, in my experience, an invaluable aid in delivering a great SDR. Of course, thorough documentation may not be available in practice, and the case study beginning on page 122 talks about handling that situation as well. Any design document vaguely specifying to "store customer data securely," for example, deserves a big red flag, unless it goes on to describe what that means and how to do that. Blanket statements without specifics almost always betray naivety and a lack of a solid understanding of security.

## The SDR Process

The following explanation of the SDR process describes how I conducted them at a large software company with a formal, mandatory review process. That said, software design is practiced in countless different ways, and you can adapt the same strategies and analysis to less formal organizations.

Starting from a clear and complete design in written form, the SDR consists of six stages:

1. *Study* the design and supporting documents to gain a basic understanding of the project.
2. *Inquire* about the design and ask clarifying questions about basic threats.
3. *Identify* the most security-critical parts of the design for closer attention.
4. *Collaborate* with the designer(s) to identify risks and discuss mitigations.
5. *Write* a summary report of findings and recommendations.
6. *Follow up* with subsequent design changes to confirm resolution before signing off.

For small designs, you can often run through most of these in one session; for larger designs, break up the work by stage, with some stages possibly requiring multiple sessions to complete. Sessions dedicated to meeting with the design team are ideal, but if necessary the reviewer can work alone and then exchange notes and questions with the design team via email or other means.

Everyone has a different style. Some reviewers like to dive in and do a "marathon." I prefer (and recommend) working incrementally over several days, affording myself an opportunity to "sleep on it," which is often where my best thinking happens.

The following walkthrough of the SDR process explains each stage, with bullet points summarizing useful techniques. When you perform an SDR you can refer to the bullets for each stage as you work through the process.

## 1. Study

Study the design and supporting documents to gain a basic understanding of the software as preparation for the review. In addition to security know-how, reviewers ideally bring domain-specific expertise. Lacking that, try to pick up what you can, and stay curious throughout the process. Trade-offs are inherent in most security decisions, so a single-minded push for more and more security is likely to overdo things, and risk ruining the design in the process. To understand how too much security can be bad, think of a house designed solely to reduce the risk of fire. Built entirely of concrete, with one thick steel door and no windows, it would be costly as well as ugly, and nobody would want to live in it.

In this preparatory stage:

- First, read the documentation to get a high-level understanding of the design.

- Next, put on your "security hat" and go through it again with a threat-aware mindset.

- Take notes, capturing your ideas and observations for future reference.

- Flag potential issues for later, but at this stage it's premature to do much security analysis.

## 2. Inquire

Ask the designer clarifying questions to understand the basic threats to the system. For simpler designs that are readily understood, or when the designer has produced rock-solid documentation, you may be able to skip this stage. Consider it an opportunity to confirm your understanding of the design and to resolve any ambiguities or open questions before proceeding further. Reviewers certainly don't need to know a design inside and out to be effective—that's the designer's job—but you do need a solid grasp of the broad outlines and how its major components interact.

This stage is your opportunity to fill in gaps before digging in. Here are some pointers:

- Ensure that the design document is clear and complete.
- If there are omissions or corrections needed, help get them fixed in the document.
- Understand the design enough to be conversant, but not necessarily at an expert level.
- Ask members of the team what they worry about most; if they have no security concerns, ask follow-up questions to learn why not.

There's no need to limit the questions you ask as a security reviewer to strictly what's in the design document. Understanding peer systems can be extremely helpful for gauging their impact on the design's security. Omitted details can be hardest to spot. For example, if the design implicitly stores data without providing any details of how this is handled, ask about the storage and its security.

## 3. Identify

Identify the security-critical parts of the design and zero in on them for close analysis. Work from basic principles to see through a security lens: think in terms of C-I-A, the Gold Standard, assets, attack surfaces, and trust boundaries. While these parts of the design deserve special attention, keep the security review focused on the whole for now, so as not to completely ignore the other parts. That said, it's fine to skip over aspects of the design with little or no relevance to security.

In this exploratory stage you should:

- Examine interfaces, storage, and communications—these will typically be central points of focus.
- Work inward from the most exposed attack surfaces toward the most valuable assets, just as determined attackers would.
- Evaluate to what degree the design addresses security explicitly.
- If needed, point out key protections and get them called out in the design as important features.

## 4. Collaborate

Collaborate with the designer, conveying findings and discussing alternatives. Ideally, the designer and reviewer meet for discussion and go through the issues one by one. This is a learning process for everyone: the designer gets a fresh perspective on the design while learning about security, and the reviewer gains insights about the design and the designer's intentions, deepening their understanding of the security challenges and the best mitigation alternatives. The joint goal is making the design better overall; security is the focus of the review, but not the only consideration. There's no need to make final decisions on changes on the spot, but it is important to reach an agreement eventually about what design changes deserve consideration.

Here are some guidelines for effective collaboration:

- As a reviewer, provide a security perspective on risks and mitigations where needed. This can be valuable even when the design is already secure, reinforcing good security practice.

- Consider sketching a scenario illustrating how a security change could pay off down the line to help convince the designer of the need for mitigations.

- Offer more than a single solution to a problem when you can, and help the designer see the strengths and weaknesses of these alternatives.

- Accept that the designer gets the last word, because they are ultimately responsible for the design.

- Document the exchange of ideas, including what will or will not go into the design.

Expanding on "the last word": in practice, this balance will depend on the organization and its culture, applicable industry standards, possible regulatory requirements, and other factors. In large or highly regimented organizations, the last word may involve sign-offs by multiple parties, including an architecture board, standards compliance officers, usability assessors, and executive stakeholders. When multiple approvals are required, designers must balance competing interests, so security reviewers should be especially conscientious of this dynamic and be as flexible as possible.

## 5. Write

Write an *assessment report* of the review findings and recommendations. The findings are the security reviewer's assessment of the security of a design. The report should focus on potential design changes to consider, and an analysis of the security of the design as it stands. Any changes the designer has already agreed to should be prominently identified as such, and subject to later verification. Consider including priority rankings for suggested changes, such as this simple three-level scheme:

- *Must* is the strongest ranking, indicating there should be no choice, and often implying urgency.

- *Ought* is intermediate: I use it to say that I, the reviewer, lean "Must" but that it's debatable.

- *Should* is the weakest ranking for optional recommended changes.

More precise rankings are difficult at the design stage, but if you want to try, Chapter 13 includes guidance on ways to systematically assign more fine-grained rankings for security bugs that can be readily adapted for this purpose.

SDRs vary enough that I have never used a standardized template for the assessment report, but instead write a narrative describing the findings. I like to work from my own rough notes taken over the course of the review, with the final form of the report evolving organically. If you can hold all the details in your head reliably, then you may want to write up the report after the review meeting.

The following tips can also be used as a framework for the write-up:

- Organize the report around specific design changes that address security risks.

- Spend most of your effort and ink on the highest-priority issues, and proportionally less on lower priorities.

- Suggest alternatives and strategies without attempting to do the designer's job for them.

- Prioritize findings and recommendations using priority rankings.

- Focus on security, but feel free to offer separate remarks for the designer's consideration as well. Be more deferential outside the scope of the SDR, don't nitpick, and avoid diluting the security message.

Separating the designer and reviewer roles is important, but in practice how this is done varies greatly depending on the responsibilities of each and their ability to collaborate. In your assessment report, avoid doing design work, while offering clear direction for needed changes so the designer knows what to do. Offer to review and comment on any significant redesign that results from the current review. As a rule of thumb, a good reviewer helps the designer see security threats and the potential consequences, as well as suggests mitigation strategies without dictating actual design changes. Reviewers who are too demanding often find that their advice is ineffective, even if it is correct, and they risk forcing designers into making changes that they do not fully understand or see the need for.

You can skimp on writing up the report if this level of rigor feels too fussy, but the chances are good that you, or someone else working on the software, will later wish that the details had been recorded for future reference. At a bare minimum, I suggest taking the time to send an email summary to the team for the record. Even a minimal report should not just say "Looks good!" but should back that up with a substantive summary. If the design covered all the security bases, reference a few of the most important design features that security depends on to underscore their importance. In the case of a design where security is a non-factor (for example, I once reviewed an informational website that collected no private information), outline the reasoning behind that conclusion.

The style, length, and level of detail in these reports varies greatly depending on the organizational culture, available time, number of stakeholders, and many other factors. When, as reviewer, you collaborate closely with the software designer, you may be able to incorporate needed provisions directly into the design document, rather than enumerating issues in need of change in a report. Even for small, informal projects, assigning separate designer and reviewer roles is worthwhile so there are multiple sets of eyes on the work, and to ensure that security is duly considered. However, even a solo design benefits from the designer going back over their own work with their security hat on for fresh perspective.

## 6. Follow Up

Follow up on agreed design changes resulting from a security review to confirm they were resolved correctly. When the collaboration has gone well, I usually just check that documentation updates happened without looking at the implementation (and that approach has never backfired in my experience). In other circumstances, and subject to your judgment, reviewers may need to be more vigilant. Sign off on the review when it's complete, including the verification of all necessary changes. Assigning the SDR in the project bug tracker is a great way to track progress reliably. Otherwise, use a more or less formal process if you prefer. Here are a few pointers for this final stage:

- For major security design changes, you might want to collaborate with the designer to ensure that changes are made correctly.

- Where opinions differ, the reviewer should include a statement of both positions and the specific recommendations that weren't followed to flag it as an open issue. ("Managing Disagreement" on page 121 talks about this topic in more detail.)

In the best case, the designer looks to the reviewer as a security resource and will continue engaging as needed over time.

## Assessing Design Security

Now that we've covered the SDR process, this section delves into the thought processes behind conducting the review. The material in this book up to this point has given you the concepts and tools you need to perform an SDR. The foundational principles, threat modeling, design techniques, patterns, mitigations, crypto tools—it all goes into the making of a secure design.

### Using the Four Questions as Guidance

The Four Questions used for threat modeling in Chapter 2 are an excellent guide to help you conduct an effective SDR. Explicit threat modeling is great if you have the time and want to invest the effort, but if you don't, using the Four Questions as touchstones is a good way to integrate a threat perspective into your review. More detailed explanations will be given in the subsections that follow, but at the highest level, here is how these questions map onto an SDR:

1. *What are we working on?*
   The reviewer should understand the high-level goals of the design as context for the review. *What's the most secure way of accomplishing the goal?*

2. *What can go wrong?*
   This is where "security hat" thinking comes in, and where to apply threat modeling. *Did the design fail to anticipate or underestimate a critical threat?*

3.  *What are we going to do about it?*
    Review what protections and mitigations you find in the design. *Can we respond in better ways to the important threats?*

4.  *Did we do a good job?*
    Assess whether the mitigations in the design suffice, if some might need more work, or if any are missing. *How secure is the design, and if lacking, how can we bring it up to snuff?*

You can use the Four Questions as a tickler while working on an SDR. If you've read the design document and noted areas of focus but don't know exactly what you are looking for yet, run through the Four Questions—especially #2 and #3—and consider how they apply to specific parts of the design. From there, your assessment will naturally shift to #4. If the answer isn't "We're doing just fine," it likely suggests a good topic of discussion, or an entry you should include in the assessment report.

## What Are We Working On?

There are a few specific ways this question keeps you on track. First, it's important to know the purpose of the design so you can confidently suggest cutting any part that incurs risk but is not actually necessary. Conversely, when you do suggest changes, you don't want to break a feature that's actually needed. Perhaps most importantly, you may be able to suggest an alternative to a risky feature that takes a new direction.

For example, in the privacy space, if you're reviewing a payroll system that collects personal information from all employees, you might identify a health question as particularly sensitive. If the data item in question is truly superfluous, then cutting it from the design is the right move. However, if it's important to the business function the design serves, instead you can propose ways to stringently protect against disclosure of this data (such as early encryption, or deletion within a short time frame).

## What Can Go Wrong?

The review should confirm that the designer has anticipated the important threats that the system faces. And it's not enough for the designer to be aware of these threats; they must have actually created a design that lives up to the task of withstanding them.

Certain threats may be acceptable and left unmitigated, and in this case, the reviewer's job is to assess that decision. But it's important to be sure that the designer is aware of the threat and chose to omit mitigation. If the design doesn't say explicitly that this is what they are doing, note this in the SDR to double-check that it's intentional. Also note the risk being accepted and explain why it's tolerable. For example, you might write: "Unencrypted data on the wire represents a snooping threat. However, we determined that the risk is acceptable because the datacenter is physically secured, and there is no potential for exposure of PII or business-confidential data."

Try to anticipate future changes that might invalidate this decision to accept the risk. Building on the example just mentioned, you might add, "If the system moves to a third-party datacenter we should revisit this physical network access risk decision."

### What Are We Going to Do About It?

Security protection mechanisms and mitigations should become apparent in the design as the reviewer studies it. Reviewers typically spend most of their time on the last two questions: identifying what makes the design secure and assessing how secure it is. One way of approaching this task is by matching the threats to the mitigations to see if all bases are covered. Pointing out issues arising from this question and confirming that the design is satisfactory are among the most important contributions of an SDR.

If the design is not doing enough to mitigate security risks, then you should itemize what's missing. To make this feedback useful, you need to explain the specific threats that are unaddressed, as well as why they are important, and perhaps provide a rough set of options for addressing each. For a number of reasons, I recommend against proposing specific remedies in an SDR. However, it's great to offer help informally, and if asked, to collaborate with the designer to consider alternatives or even elaborate on design changes. For example, your feedback might say: "The monitoring API should not be exposed publicly because it discloses our website's levels of use, which could give competitors an advantage. I recommend requiring an access key to authenticate requests to the RESTful API."

When the design does provide a mitigation for a given threat, evaluate its effectiveness and consider whether there might be better alternatives. Sometimes, designers "reinvent the wheel" by building security mechanisms from scratch: good feedback would be to suggest using a standard library instead. If the design is secure but that's achieved at a great performance cost, propose another way if you can. An example of this might be pointing out redundant security mechanisms, such as encrypting data that is sent over an encrypting HTTPS connection, and describing how to streamline the design.

### Did We Do a Good Job?

This last question goes to the bottom line: Do you consider the design secure? Competent designers should have already addressed security, so much of the value of the SDR is in assuring that they saw the whole picture and anticipated the major threats. In my experience, SDRs quickly identify issues and opportunities, or at minimum suggest interesting trade-off decisions worth considering now (because later you won't have the luxury of making changes so easily).

I recommend summarizing your overall appraisal of the whole design in one statement at the top of the report. Here are some examples of what that might look like:

- I found the design to be secure as is, and have no suggested changes.
- The design is secure, but I have a few changes to suggest that would make it even more so.
- I have concerns about the current design, and offer a set of recommendations to make it more secure.

After the summary, if there are multiple subpar areas that require fixing, break those out and explain them one by one. If you can attribute the weakness to a specific part of the design, it will be easier for the designer to pinpoint the problem, see it clearly, and make the necessary remedies.

Of course, no design is perfect, so in judging a design to be lacking, it's important to be clear about what standard you are holding it to. This is difficult to express in the abstract, so a good approach is to point out specific threats, vulnerabilities, and consequences to make your case. It may be best to couch your assessment in terms of the security of a comparable product; for example, "Our main competitor claims to be ransomware-resistant as a major selling point, but this design is particularly susceptible to such attacks due to maintaining the inventory database locally on a computer that employees also use to surf the web."

## *Where to Dig*

It's impractical to dig into every corner of a large design, so reviewers need to focus as quickly as possible on key areas that are security-critical. I encourage security reviewers to follow their instincts when deciding where to direct their efforts within the design. Begin by reading through the design and noting areas of interest according to your intuition. Next, go back to the areas of largest concern, study them more carefully, and collect questions to ask, letting potential threats and the Four Questions be your guide. Some of these leads will be more productive than others. If you do start down an unproductive path, you will usually realize this before long, so you can refocus your efforts elsewhere.

It's fine to skim parts of the design that are extraneous to security and privacy, absorbing just enough to have a basic understanding of all the moving parts. If you locked yourself out of your home, you would know to check for an open window or unlocked door: nobody would spend time going over the entire exterior inch by inch. In the same way, it's most effective to zero in on places in the design where you detect a hint of weakness, or focus closely on how the design protects the most valuable assets.

Keep an eye out for attack surfaces and give them due attention. The more readily available they are—anonymous internet exposure is the classic worst case—the more likely they are to be a potential source of attacks.

Trust boundaries guarding valuable resources, especially when reachable from an attack surface, are the major generic feature of a design that reviewers should be sure to emphasize in their analysis. Sometimes valuable assets can be better isolated from external-facing components, but often the exposure is unavoidable. These are the kinds of factors that reviewers need to search out and assess throughout the process.

## Privacy Reviews

Depending on your skill set and organizational responsibilities, you may want to handle information privacy within the scope of an SDR, or separately. Privacy feedback within an SDR should center on applicable privacy policies and how they relate to data collection, use, storage, and sharing within the scope of the design.

A good technique is to run through the privacy policy and note passages that pertain to the design, then look for ways to protect against violations. As the previous chapter describes, the technical focus is on ensuring that the design is in compliance with policy. Get sign-offs from privacy specialists and legal for issues requiring more expertise.

## Reviewing Updates

Once released, software seems to take on a life of its own, and over time, change is inevitable. This is especially true in Agile or other iterative development practices, where design change is a constant process. Design documents can easily become neglected along the way and, years later, lost or irrelevant. Yet changes to a software design potentially impact its security properties, so it's wise to perform an incremental SDR update to ensure that the design stays secure.

Design documents should be living documents that track the evolution of the architectural form of the software. Versioned documents are an important record of how the design has matured, or in some cases become convoluted. You can use these same documents as a guide to focus an incremental review on the precise set of changes (the design delta) since the previous SDR to update it. When there are changes to (or near) security-critical areas of the design, it's often wise for the reviewer to follow up to ensure that no small but important details were omitted in the design document that might have significant impact. If the incremental review does turn up anything substantial, add that to the existing assessment report so it now tells the complete story. If not, just update the report to note what design version it covers.

Underestimating the impact of a "simple change" is a common invitation to a security disaster, and re-reviewing the design is a great way to proactively assess such impacts effectively. If the design change is so minor that a review is unnecessary, it's also true that a reviewer could confirm right away that there is no security impact. For anything but a trivial design change, I would suggest that there is little to gain from skipping the SDR update, given the risk of missing this important safeguard.

# Managing Disagreement

*Whatever you do in life, surround yourself with smart people who'll argue with you.*

—John Wooden

An important lesson from my years of evangelizing security—learned the hard way, though obvious in hindsight—is that good interpersonal communication is critical to conducting successful SDRs. The analysis is technical, of course, but critiquing a design requires good communication and collaboration, so human factors are also key. Too often, security specialists, be they in-house or outsourced, get reputations (deservedly or not) of being hyper-critical interlopers who are never satisfied. That perception subtly poisons interactions, not only making the work difficult, but adversely impacting the effectiveness of everybody's efforts. We have to acknowledge this factor in order to do better.

## Communicate Tactfully

SDRs are inherently adversarial, in that they largely consist of pointing out risks and potential flaws in designs in which people are often heavily invested. Once identified, design weaknesses often look painfully obvious in hindsight, and it's easy for reviewers to slip into casting this as carelessness, or even incompetence—but it is *never* productive to communicate that way. Instead, treat the issues that do arise as teaching opportunities. Once the designer understands the problem, often they will lead the discussion into other productive areas the reviewer might have missed. Having someone point out a vulnerability in your own design is the best way there is to learn security.

An SDR spent ruthlessly tearing apart a weak design with a one-sided lecture on the importance of maximizing security over everything else is unlikely to be productive (for reasons that should be obvious if you imagine yourself on the receiving end). While this does, unfortunately, sometimes happen, I don't think it's necessarily because the reviewers are mean, but rather because in focusing on the technical changes needed, it's easy to forget about keeping the tone respectful. It's well worth bending over backwards to maintain good will and reinforce that everybody is on the same team, bringing a diversity of perspectives and working toward the common goal of striking the right balance. Sports coaches frequently walk this same fine line, pointing out weaknesses they see (that they know opponents will exploit) without asking too much, in order to help their teams do the work necessary to play their best game. As Mark Cuban says, "Nice goes much further than mean."

Getting along with people while delivering possibly unwelcome messages is, of course, desirable, but it is also much easier said than done. This is a technical software book, so I offer no self-help advice on how to win friends and influence developers. But the human factor is important enough—or more precisely, ignoring it potentially undermines the work enough—that it merits prominent mention. My fundamental guidance is simple: be aware of how you deliver messages and consider how others will receive them and likely respond. To show how this works for an SDR, I offer a true story, and a set of tips that I have come to rely on.

## Case Study: A Difficult Review

One of my most memorable SDRs is a great object lesson in the importance of soft skills. It began with a painful email exchange I initiated just to get documentation and ask a few basic questions. The exchange made it immediately clear that the team lead viewed the SDR as a complete waste of time. On top of that, because they had been unaware of this product launch requirement, it had suddenly become an unwelcome new obstacle blocking the release they were working so hard toward. The first key takeaway from this story is the importance of recognizing the other participants' perspective on the process, right or wrong, and adapting accordingly.

What documentation I eventually got I found to be sloppy, incomplete, and considerably outdated. Directly pointing this out in so many words would have been unproductive and further soured the relationship. The second key point is that to spur improvement, work around the problem, and handle the SDR effectively, it's more productive to use strategies like the following:

- Suggest fixes or additions, including the security rationale behind each suggestion.

- When feasible, offer to help review documents, suggest edits, or anything else you can do to facilitate the process (but short of doing their job for them).

- Present preliminary SDR feedback as "my perspective" rather than as demands.

- Use the "sandwich" method: begin with a positive remark, point out needed improvements, then close on a positive (such as how the changes will help).

- If your feedback is extensive, ask first how best to communicate it. (Don't surprise them with a 97-bullet-point email, or by filing tons of bugs out of the blue.)

- Explore all the leads that you notice, but limit your feedback to the most significant points. (Don't be a perfectionist.)

- A good rule of thumb is that if missing information is going to be generally useful to many readers it's worth documenting, but if it's particular to your needs you should just ask the question less formally. (If necessary, you can include the details of the issue in the assessment report.)

Instead of complaining about or judging the quality of the documentation, find creative alternative ways to learn about the software, such as using an internal prototype if available, or perusing the code and code reviews. Asking to observe a regular team meeting can be a great way to learn about the design without taking up anyone's time.

Over email, it felt like they were being rude, but when we finally met I could see that this was just a stressed-out lead developer. Instead of relying exclusively on the lead, I found another team member who was less stretched and was glad to answer my questions. To save time in preparing for the SDR meeting, I pursued only the questions that were important to resolve ahead of time, saving others for the meeting when I had a captive audience.

Preparing for an SDR meeting is a balancing act. You shouldn't go in cold with zero preparation, because the team may not appreciate having to describe everything, especially after providing you with documentation. Ahead of time, try to identify major components and dependencies you are unfamiliar with, and at least get up to speed enough to ask questions at the meeting. During preparation, a good practice is to jot down issues and questions, then to sort these into categories:

- Questions to ask in advance so you are ready to dig into security when you meet
- Questions you can find answers to yourself
- Topics best explored at the meeting
- Observations you will include in the assessment report that don't need discussion

By the time we finally held a meeting, the lead engineer was overtly unhappy that the SDR was now the major obstacle to launching the product. The first meeting was a little rocky, but we made good progress, with everyone staying focused. After a few more meetings (which gradually became easier and shorter each time), I signed off on the design. We agreed on a few changes at the first meeting, but confirming the details and meeting to finalize them was an important assurance to all. If you don't take the time to confirm that needed changes to the design get made, it's easy for a miscommunication to slip through the cracks.

It's never easy to convince busy people that you are helping them by taking up their time, and *telling* them so rarely works. However, flagging even small opportunities to improve security and *showing* how these contribute to the final product is a great way to reach a mutually satisfactory result.

By the completion of the SDR, the product team had a far better understanding of security—and by extension, of their own product. In the end, they did see the value of the review, and acknowledged that the product had been improved as a result. Better yet, for version two, the team proactively reached out to me and we sailed through the update SDR with flying colors.

## Escalating Disagreements

When the designer and reviewer fail to reach consensus, they should agree to disagree. If the issue is minor, the reviewer can simply note the point of disagreement in the assessment report and defer to the designer. In such cases, make the disagreement explicit, perhaps in a section called "Recommendations Declined," explaining the suggested design change and why you recommended it, as well as the potential consequences of not making the change. However, if there is a serious dispute about a major decision, the reviewer should escalate the issue.

In this case both the designer and the reviewer should write up their positions, starting with an attempt at identifying some common starting ground that they do agree on, and exchange drafts so everyone knows both perspectives. Their respective positions combine to form a memo explaining the risk, along with proposed outcomes and their costs. This memo supplements the assessment report and serves as the basis for a meeting, or as a guide for management to decide how to proceed. The results of the final decision, along with the escalation memo, should go into the assessment report.

Over many years of conducting security reviews, I have never had occasion to escalate an issue, but I have come close a few times. Strong disagreement almost always originates from a deep split in basic assumptions that, once identified, usually leads to resolution. Such differences often stem from implicit assumptions about the software's use, or what data it will process. In actual practice, how software gets used is extremely hard to control, and over time use cases usually evolve, so leaning to the safe side is usually the best course.

Another major cause of disconnect happens when the designer fails to see that data confidentiality or integrity matters, usually because they are missing the necessary end user perspective or not considering the full range of possible use cases. One more important factor to consider is this: Hypothetically, if we changed our minds after release, how much harder would the change be to make at that stage? Nobody wants to say "I told you so" after the fact, but putting the opposing conditions in writing is usually the best way to make the right choice.

## Practice, Practice, Practice

To solidify what you have learned in this chapter and truly make it your own, I strongly encourage readers to take the leap, find a software design, and perform an SDR for it. If there is no current software design in your sphere of interest just now, choose any available existing design and review it as an exercise. If the software you chose has no formal written design, start by creating a rough representation of the design yourself (it doesn't have to be a complete or polished document, even a block diagram will do), and review that. Generally, it's best to start with a modest-sized design so you don't get in over your head, or carve out a component from a large system and review just that part. Having read this far should have prepared you to begin. You can start by doing quick reviews for your own use if you don't feel confident enough yet to share your assessment reports.

As you acquire the critical skills of SDR, you can apply them to any software you encounter. Studying lots of designs is a great way to learn about the art of software design—both by seeing how the masters do it and by spotting mistakes that others have made—and practicing applying them in this way is an excellent exercise to grow your skills.

An especially easy way to start is to review the sample design document in Appendix A. The security provisions are highlighted, to provide a realistic example of what to look for in designs. Read the design, noting the highlighted portions, and then imagine how you would identify and supply those security-related details if they were missing. For a greater challenge, look for additional ways to make the design even more secure (by no means do I claim or expect it to be a flawless ideal!).

With each SDR, you will improve your proficiency. Even when you don't find any significant vulnerabilities, you will enhance your knowledge of the design, as well as your security skills. There certainly is no shortage of software in need of security attention, so I invite you to get started. I believe how quickly you acquire this valuable skill set will surprise you.

**NOTE**   *See Appendix D for a cheat sheet summarizing the SDR process as a handy aid doing security design reviews.*

# PART III

## IMPLEMENTATION

# 8

## SECURE PROGRAMMING

*The first principle is that you must not fool yourself, and you are the easiest person to fool.*
—Richard P. Feynman

A completed software design, created and reviewed with security in mind, is only the beginning of a product's journey: next comes the work of implementing, testing, deploying, operating, monitoring, maintaining, and, ultimately, retiring it at end of life. While the particular details of all this will vary greatly in different operating systems and languages, the broad security themes are so common as to be nearly universal.

Developers must not only faithfully implement the explicit security provisions of a good design, but in doing so they must also take care to avoid inadvertently introducing additional vulnerabilities with flawed code. A carpenter building a house based on the architect's plans is a good metaphor: sloppy construction with lousy materials leads to all kinds of problems in the finished product. If the carpenter misstrikes a nail and bends it, the problem is noticeable and easily remedied. By contrast, flawed code is easily overlooked, but may nevertheless create a vulnerability that can be exploited with dire consequences. The purpose of this chapter is not to teach you how to code—I'll assume you already know about that—but rather how code becomes vulnerable and how to make it more secure. The following chapters cover many of the commonplace implementation vulnerabilities that continue to plague software projects.

The line between design and implementation is not always clear, nor should it be. Thoughtful designers can anticipate programming issues, provide advice about areas where security will be critical, and much more. The programmers doing the implementation must flesh out the design and resolve any ambiguities in order to make functional code with precisely defined interfaces. Not only must they securely render the design—in itself a daunting task—but they must also avoid introducing additional vulnerabilities in the course of supplying the necessary code in full detail.

In an ideal world, the design should specify proactive security measures: features of the software built for the purpose of protecting the system, its assets, and its users. Conversely, security in development is about avoiding pitfalls that software is liable to—rough edges on the components and tools, if you will. Where new risks emerge during the process of implementation, mitigations specific to these are in order, because there is no reason to expect that designers could have anticipated them.

This chapter focuses on how some bugs become vulnerabilities, how they occur, and how to avoid the various pitfalls. It approaches these issues in general terms as a lead-in to the following chapters, which drill into major areas that, historically, have proven to be fraught with security problems. We'll begin by exploring the essence of the challenge of secure coding, including how attackers exploit openings and extend their influence deeper into code. We'll also talk about bugs: how vulnerabilities arise from them, how minor bugs can form vulnerability chains that potentially create bigger problems, and how code appears through the lens of entropy.

Avoiding vulnerabilities in your code requires vigilance, but that requires knowledge of how code undermines security. To make the concept of a coding vulnerability concrete, we'll walk through a simplified version of the code for a devastating real vulnerability that shows how a one-line editing slip-up broke security across the internet. Then we'll look at a few classes of common vulnerabilities as examples of bugs that are potentially exploitable with serious consequences.

Throughout Part III, most code examples will be in Python and C, widely used languages that span the range from high-level to low-level abstraction. This is real code using the particulars of the specific language, but the concepts in this book apply generally. Even if you are unfamiliar with Python or C, the code snippets should be simple enough for readers familiar with any modern programming language to follow.

## The Challenge

The term "secure programming" was the obvious choice for the title of this chapter, though it is potentially misleading. A more accurate expression of the goal (unsuitable as a chapter title) would be "avoiding coding insecurely." What I mean by that is that the challenge of secure coding largely amounts to not introducing flaws that become exploitable vulnerabilities. Programmers certainly do build protection mechanisms that proactively improve security, but these are typically explicit in the design or features of APIs. I want to focus primarily on the inadvertent pitfalls because they are nonobvious and constitute the root causes of most security failings. Think of secure coding as similar to learning where the potholes are in a road, diligently paying attention at the wheel, and navigating them consistently.

I believe that many programmers, perhaps quite rightfully, have unfavorable attitudes toward software security (and in some cases, more viscerally, about "security cops"—or worse names—who they perceive as bothering them) because they often hear the message "don't mess up" when it comes to implementation. "Don't mess up!" is unhelpful advice to a jeweler about to cut a rare diamond for the same reasons: they have every intention of doing their best, and the added stress only makes it harder to concentrate and do the job right. The well-meaning "cops" are providing necessary advice, but often they don't phrase it in the most kindly and constructive way. Having made this mistake plenty of times myself, I am endeavoring to walk that fine line here, and ask for the reader's understanding.

Caution is indeed necessary, because one slip by a programmer (as we shall see when we look at the GotoFail vulnerability later in this chapter) can easily result in disastrous consequences. The root of the problem is the great fragility and complexity of large modern software systems, which are only expected to grow in the future. Professional developers know how to test and debug code, but security is another matter, because vulnerable code usually works fine absent a diligent attack.

Software designers create idealized conceptions that, by virtue of not yet being realized, can even be perfectly secure in theory. But making software that actually works introduces new levels of complexity and requires fleshing out details beyond the design, all of which inevitably carries the risk of security problems. The good news is that perfection isn't the goal, and the coding failure modes that account for most of the common vulnerabilities are both well understood and not that difficult to get right. The trick is constant vigilance and learning how to look out for dangerous flaws in code. This chapter presents a few concepts that should help you get a good grasp of what secure versus vulnerable code looks like, along with some examples.

## Malicious Influence

When thinking about secure coding, a key consideration is understanding how attackers potentially *influence* running code. Think of a big, complicated machine purring away smoothly, and then a prankster takes a stick and starts poking the mechanism. Some parts, such as the cylinders of a gasoline engine, will be completely protected within the block, while other parts, such as a fan belt, are exposed, making it easy to jam something in, causing a failure. This is analogous to how attackers prod systems when attempting to penetrate them: they start from the attack surface and use cleverly crafted, unexpected inputs to try and foul the mechanism, then attempt to trick code inside the system into doing their bidding.

Untrusted inputs potentially influence code in two ways: directly and indirectly. Beginning wherever they can inject some untrusted input—say, the string "BOO!"—they experiment in hopes that their data will avoid rejection and propagate deeper into the system. Working down through layers of I/O and various interfaces, the string "BOO!" typically will find its way into a number of code paths, and its influence will permeate deeper into the system. Occasionally, the untrusted data and code interaction triggers a bug, or a feature that may have an unfortunate side effect. A web search for "BOO!" may involve hundreds of computers in a datacenter, each contributing a little to the search result. As a result, the string must get written to memory in thousands of places. That's a lot of influence spread, and if there is even a minuscule chance of harm, it could be dangerous.

The technical term for this kind of influence of data on code is *tainting*, and a few languages have implemented features to track it. The Perl interpreter can track tainting for the purpose of mitigating injection attacks (covered in Chapter 10). Early versions of JavaScript had taint checking for similar reasons, though it has long since been removed due to lack of use. Still, the concept of influence on code by data from untrusted sources is important to understand to prevent vulnerabilities.

There are other ways that input data can influence code indirectly without the data being stored. Suppose that, given an input of the string "BOO!", the code avoids storing any further copies of it: Does that insulate the system from its influence? It certainly does not. For example, consider this given input = "BOO!":

```
if "!" in input:
    PlanB()
else:
    PlanA()
```

The presence of the exclamation point in the input has caused the code to now pursue PlanB instead of PlanA, even though the input string itself is neither stored nor passed on for subsequent processing.

This simple example illustrates how the influence of an untrusted input can propagate deep into code, even though the data (here, "BOO!") may not itself propagate far. In a large system, you can appreciate the potential of penetration into lots of code when you consider the transitive closure (the aggregate extent of all paths), starting from the attack surface. This ability to extend through many layers is important, because it means that attackers can reach into more code than you might expect, affording them opportunities to control what the code does. We'll talk more about managing untrusted input in Chapter 10.

## Vulnerabilities Are Bugs

*If debugging is the process of removing bugs, then programming must be the process of putting them in.*

—Edsger Dijkstra

That all software has bugs is so widely accepted that it is hardly necessary to substantiate the claim at this point. Of course, exceptions to this generalization do exist: trivial code, provably correct code, and highly engineered software that runs aviation, medical, or other critical equipment. But for everything else, awareness of the ubiquity of bugs is a good starting point from which to approach secure coding, because a subset of those bugs are going to be useful to attackers. So, bugs are our focus here.

*Vulnerabilities* are a subset of software bugs useful to attackers to cause harm. It's nearly impossible to accurately separate vulnerabilities from other bugs, so it may be easiest to start by identifying bugs that clearly are not vulnerabilities—that is, totally harmless bugs. Let's consider some examples of bugs in an online shopping website. A good example of an innocuous bug might be a problem with the web page layout not working as designed: it's a bit of a mess, but all important content is fully visible and functional. While this might be important to fix for reasons of brand image or usability, it's clear that there is no security risk associated with this bug. But to emphasize how tricky vulnerability spotting can be, there could be similar bugs that mess up layout and are also harmful, such as if they obscure important information the user must see to make an accurate security decision.

At the harmful end of the spectrum, here's a nightmarish vulnerability to contemplate: the administrative interface becomes accidentally exposed, unprotected, on the internet. Now, anyone visiting the website can click a button to go into the console used by managers to change prices, see confidential business and financial data, and more. It doesn't take a genius to see that this is a complete failure of authorization and a clear security threat.

Of course, there is a continuum between those extremes, with a large murky area in the middle that requires subjective judgments about the potential of a bug to cause harm. And as we will see in the next section, the often unforeseen cumulative effects of multiple bugs make determining their potential for harm particularly challenging. In the interests of security, naturally, I would urge you to err on the safe side and lean toward remedying more bugs if there is any chance they might be vulnerabilities.

Every project I've ever worked on had a tracking database filled with tons of bugs, but no concerted effort to reduce even the known bug count (which is very different from the actual bug count) to zero. So it's safe to say that, generally, all of us program alongside a trove of known bugs, not to mention the unknown bugs. If it isn't already actively done, consider working through the known bugs and flagging possible vulnerabilities for fixing. It's important to mention, too, that it's almost always easier to just fix a bug than to investigate and prove that it's harmless. Chapter 13 offers guidance on assessing and ranking security bugs to help you prioritize vulnerabilities.

## Vulnerability Chains

The idea behind *vulnerability chains* is that seemingly harmless bugs can combine to create a serious security bug. It's bug synergy for the attackers. Think of taking a walk and coming upon a stream you would like to cross. It's far too wide to leap across, but you notice a few stones sticking up above the surface: by hopping from stone to stone, it's easy to cross without getting your shoes wet. These stones represent minor bugs, not vulnerabilities themselves, but together they form a new path right through the stream, allowing the attacker to reach deep inside the system. These stepping-stone bugs form, in combination, an exploitable vulnerability.

Here's a simple example of how such a vulnerability chain could arise in an online shopping web app. After a recent code change, the app's order form has a new field prefilled with a code indicating which warehouse will handle the shipment. Previously, business logic in the backend assigned a warehouse after the customer placed the order. Now a field that's editable by the customer determines the warehouse that will handle the order. Call this Bug #1. The developer responsible for this change suggests that nobody will notice the addition, and furthermore, even should anyone modify the warehouse designation that the system supplies by default, another warehouse won't have the requested items in stock, so it will get flagged and corrected: "No harm, no foul." Based on this analysis, but without any testing, the team schedules Bug #1 for the next release cycle. They're glad to save themselves a fire drill and schedule slip, and push the buggy code change into production.

Meanwhile, a certain Bug #2 is languishing in the bug database with a Priority-3 ranking (meaning "fix someday," which is to say, probably never), long forgotten. Years ago, a tester filed Bug #2 after discovering that if you place an order with the wrong warehouse designation, the system immediately issues a refund because that warehouse is unable to fulfill it; but then another processing stage reassigns the order to the correct warehouse, which fulfills and ships it. The tester saw this as a serious problem—the company would be giving away merchandise for free—and filed it as Priority-1. In the triage meeting, the programmers insisted that the tester was "cheating" because the backend handled the warehouse assignment (before Bug #1 was introduced) after confirming available inventory. In other words, at the time of discovery, Bug #2 was purely hypothetical and could never have happened in production. Since the interaction of various stages of business logic would be difficult to untangle, the team decided to leave it alone and make the bug Priority-3, and it was quickly forgotten.

If you followed this story of "letting sleeping bugs lie" you probably already can see that it has an unhappy ending. With the introduction of Bug #1, in combination with Bug #2, a fully fledged vulnerability chain now exists, almost certainly unbeknownst to anyone. Now that the warehouse designation field is writable by customers, the wrong warehouse case that triggers Bug #2 is easy to produce. All it takes is for one devious, or even curious, customer to try editing the warehouse field; pleasantly surprised to receive free merchandise with a full refund, they might go back for a lot more the next time, or share the secret with others.

Let's look at where the bug triage went wrong. Bug #2 (found earlier) was a serious fragility that they should have fixed in the first place. The reasoning in favor of leaving it alone hinged on the warehouse trusting other backend logic to direct it flawlessly, under the assumption (correct, at the time) that the warehouse assignment field in an order was completely isolated from any attack surface. Still, it's clearly a worrisome fragility that clearly has bad consequences, and the fact that the business logic would be difficult to fix suggests that a rewrite might be a good idea.

Bug #1, introduced later on, opened up a new attack surface, exposing the warehouse designation field to tampering. The unfortunate decision not to fix this depended on the incorrect assumption that tampering was harmless. With the benefit of hindsight, had anyone done a little testing (in a test environment, of course, never in production), they could have easily found the flaw in their reasoning and done the right thing before releasing Bug #1. And, ideally, had the tester who found Bug #2, or anyone familiar with it, been present, they might have connected the dots and slated both bugs for fixing as Priority-1.

Compared to this artificial example, recognizing when bugs form vulnerability chains is, in general, very challenging. Once you understand the concept, it's easy to see the wisdom of fixing bugs proactively whenever possible. Furthermore, even when you do suspect a vulnerability chain might exist, I should warn you that in practice it's often hard to convince others to spend time implementing a fix for what looks like a vague hypothetical, especially when fixing the bug in question entails significant work. It's likely that most large systems are full of undetected vulnerability chains, and our systems are weaker for it.

This example illustrates how two bugs can align into a causal chain, much like a tricky billiards shot with the cue ball hitting another ball, that in turn knocks the target ball into the pocket. Believe it or not, vulnerability chains can be a good deal more involved: one team in the Pwn2Own competitive hacking contest managed to chain together *six bugs* to achieve a difficult exploit.

When you understand vulnerability chains, you can better appreciate the relationship of code quality to security. Bugs introducing fragility, especially around critical assets, should be fixed aggressively. Punting a bug because "it will never happen" (like our Bug #2) is risky, and you should bear in mind that one person's opinion that it will be fine is just that, an opinion, not a proof. Such thinking is akin to the Security by Obscurity anti-pattern and at best a temporary measure rather than a good final triage decision.

## Bugs and Entropy

Having surveyed vulnerabilities and vulnerability chains, next consider that software is also liable to less precise sequences of events that can do damage. Some bugs tend to break things in unpredictable ways, which makes an analysis of their exploitability (as with a vulnerability chain) difficult. As evidence of this phenomenon, we commonly reboot our phones and computers to clear out the entropy that accumulates over time due to the multitude of bugs. (Here I'm using the word *entropy* loosely, to evoke an image of disorder and metaphorical corrosion.) Attackers can sometimes leverage these bugs and their aftereffects, so countermeasures can help improve security.

Bugs arising from unexpected interactions between threads of execution are one class prone to this kind of trouble, because they typically present in a variety of ways, seemingly at random. Memory corruption bugs are another such class, because the contents of the stack and heap are in constant flux. These sorts of bugs, which perturb the system in unpredictable ways, can almost be juicier targets for attack because they offer potentially endless possibilities. Attackers can be quite adept at exploiting such messy bugs, and automation makes it easy to retry low-yield attempts until they get lucky. On the flip side, most programmers dislike taking on these elusive bugs that are hard to pin down and frequently deemed too flaky to be of concern, and hence they tend to persist unaddressed.

Even if you cannot nail down a clear causal chain, entropy-inducing bugs can be dangerous and are well worth fixing. All bugs introduce amounts of something like entropy into systems, in the sense that they are slight departures from the correct behavior, and those small amounts of disturbance quickly add up—especially if abetted by a wily attacker. By analogy with the Second Law of Thermodynamics, entropy inevitably builds up within a closed system, raising the risk of harm due to bugs of this type becoming exploitable at some point.

## *Vigilance*

I love hiking, and the trails in my area are often muddy and slippery, with exposed roots and rocks, so slipping and falling is a constant threat. With practice and experience, slips have become rare, but what's uncanny is that in particularly treacherous spots, where I focus, I never slip. While occasionally I do still fall, rather than due to any obstacle, it's usually on an easier part of the trail, because *I just wasn't paying attention.* The point here is that with awareness, difficult challenges can be mastered; and conversely, inattention easily undermines you, even when the going is easy.

Software developers face just such a challenge: without awareness of potential security pitfalls and sustained focus, it's easy to unwittingly fall into them. Developers instinctively write code to work for the normal use case, but attackers often try the unexpected in hopes of finding a flaw that might lead to an exploit. Maintaining vigilance to anticipate the full range of possible inputs and combinations of events is critical, as described previously in terms of vulnerability chains and entropy, to delivering secure code.

The following section and chapters present a broad representative survey of the vulnerabilities that plague modern software, with "toy" code examples used to show what implementation vulnerabilities look like. As Marvin Minsky, one of the artificial intelligence legends at MIT, whom I was fortunate to meet during my time there, points out, "In science one can learn the most by studying the least." In this context, that means that simplified code examples aid explanation by making it easy to focus on the critical flaw. In practice, vulnerabilities are woven into the fabric of a great profusion of code, along with a lot of other things that are important to the task but irrelevant to the security implications, and are not so easily recognized. If you want to look at real-world code examples, browse the bug database of any open source software project—they are all sure to have security bugs.

Vigilance requires discipline at first, but with practice it becomes second nature when you know what to watch out for. Remember that if your vigilance pays off and you do manage to fend off a would-be attacker, you probably will never know it—so celebrate each small victory, as you avert hypothetical future attacks with every fix.

# Case Study: GotoFail

Some vulnerabilities are nasty bugs that don't follow any pattern, somehow slip past testing, and get released. One property of vulnerabilities that makes this more likely to happen than you might expect is that the code often works for typical usage, and only displays harmful behavior when stressed by an intentional attack. In 2014, Apple quietly released a set of critical security patches for most of its products, declining to explain the problem for "the protection of our customers." It didn't take long for the world to learn that the vulnerability was due to an apparent editing slip-up that effectively undermined a critical security protection. It's easy to understand what happened by examining a short excerpt of the actual code. Let's take a look.

## One-Line Vulnerability

To set the stage, the code in question runs during secure connection establishment. It checks that everything is working properly in order to secure subsequent communications. The security of the Secure Sockets Layer (SSL) protocol rests on checking that the server signs the negotiated key, authenticated according to the server's digital certificate. More precisely, the server signs the hash of several pieces of data that the ephemeral key derives from. Chapter 11 covers the basics of SSL, but you can follow the code behind this vulnerability without knowing any of those details. Here is the C++ code:

*vulnerable code*

```
/*
 * Copyright (c) 1999-2001,2005-2012 Apple Inc. All Rights Reserved.
 *
 * @APPLE_LICENSE_HEADER_START@
 *
 * This file contains Original Code and/or Modifications of Original Code
 * as defined in and that are subject to the Apple Public Source License
 * Version 2.0 (the 'License'). You may not use this file except in
 * compliance with the License. Please obtain a copy of the License at
 * http://www.opensource.apple.com/apsl/ and read it before using this
 * file.
 *
 * The Original Code and all software distributed under the License are
 * distributed on an 'AS IS' basis, WITHOUT WARRANTY OF ANY KIND, EITHER
 * EXPRESS OR IMPLIED, AND APPLE HEREBY DISCLAIMS ALL SUCH WARRANTIES,
 * INCLUDING WITHOUT LIMITATION, ANY WARRANTIES OF MERCHANTABILITY,
```

```
 * FITNESS FOR A PARTICULAR PURPOSE, QUIET ENJOYMENT OR NON-INFRINGEMENT.
 * Please see the License for the specific language governing rights and
 * limitations under the License.
 *
 * @APPLE_LICENSE_HEADER_END@
 */
--snip--
    if ((err = SSLHashSHA1.update(&hashCtx, &clientRandom)) != 0)
      goto fail;
    if ((err = SSLHashSHA1.update(&hashCtx, &serverRandom)) != 0)
      goto fail;
      goto fail;
    if ((err = SSLHashSHA1.update(&hashCtx, &signedParams)) != 0)
      goto fail;
--snip--

fail:
    SSLFreeBuffer(&signedHashes);
    SSLFreeBuffer(&hashCtx);
    return err;
```

The three calls to SSLHashSHA1.update feed their respective chunks of data into the hash function and check for the nonzero return error case. The details of the hash computation are beside the point for our purposes, and not shown; just know that this computation is critical to security, since its output must match an expected value in order to authenticate the communication.

At the bottom of the function, the code frees up a couple of buffers, and then returns the value of err: zero for success, or a nonzero error code.

The intended pattern in the code is clear: keep checking for nonzero return values indicating error, or sail through with zeros if everything is fine, and then return that. You probably already see the error—the duplicated goto fail line. Notwithstanding the suggestive indentation, this unconditionally shunts execution down to the fail label, skipping the rest of the hash computation and skipping the hash check altogether. Since the last assignment to err before the extra jump was a zero value, this function suddenly unconditionally approves of everything. Presumably this bug went undetected because valid secure connections still worked: the code didn't check the hash, but if it had, they all would have passed anyway.

### Beware of Footguns

GotoFail is a great argument for the wisdom of structuring code by indentation, as languages such as Python do. The C language enables a kind of *footgun* (a feature that makes it easy to shoot yourself in the foot) by instead determining a program's structure syntactically. This allows indentation that, by standard code style conventions, is potentially misleading because it implies different semantics, even though it's completely ignored by the compiler. When looking at this code:

```
if ((err = SSLHashSHA1.update(&hashCtx, &serverRandom)) != 0)
  goto fail;
  goto fail;
```

programmers might easily see the following (unless they are careful and mentally compiling the code):

```
if ((err = SSLHashSHA1.update(&hashCtx, &serverRandom)) != 0) {
    goto fail;
    goto fail;
}
```

Meanwhile, the compiler unambiguously sees:

```
if ((err = SSLHashSHA1.update(&hashCtx, &serverRandom)) != 0) {
    goto fail;
}
goto fail;
```

A simple editing error happened to be easily missed, and also dramatically changed the code, right at the heart of a critical security check. That's the epitome of a serious vulnerability.

Beware of other such footguns in languages, APIs, and other programming tools and data formats. You'll see many examples in the following chapters, but another one from C syntax that I'll mention here is writing if (x = 8) instead of if (x == 8). The former assigns 8 to x, unconditionally executing the then-clause, since that value is nonzero; the latter compares x to 8, executing the then-clause only if it's true—quite different, indeed. While some would argue against it stylistically, I like to write such C statements as if (8 == x) because if I forget to double the equal sign, it is a syntax error and the compiler will catch it.

Compiler warnings can help flag this sort of slip-up. The GCC compiler's -Wmisleading-indentation warning option is intended for just the sort of problem that caused the GotoFail vulnerability. Some warnings indicate potential trouble in subtler ways. An unused variable warning seems benign enough, but say there are two variables with similar names and you accidentally typed the wrong one in an important access test, resulting in the warning and also the use of the wrong data for a crucial test. While warnings are by no means reliable indicators of all vulnerabilities, they are easy to check and just might save the day.

### Lessons from GotoFail

There are several important lessons we can learn from GotoFail:

- Small slips in critical code can have a devastating impact on security.
- The vulnerable code still works correctly in the expected case.
- It's arguably more important for security to test that code like this rejects invalid cases than that it passes the normal legit uses.
- Code reviews are an important check against bugs introduced by oversight. It's hard to imagine how a careful reviewer looking at a code diff could miss this.

This vulnerability suggests a number of countermeasures that could have prevented it from occurring. Some of these are specific to this particular bug, but even those should suggest the sorts of precautions you could apply elsewhere to save yourself the pain of creating flawed code. Useful countermeasures include:

- Better testing, of course. At a minimum, there should have been a test case for each of those `ifs` to ensure that all necessary checks worked.

- Watch out for unreachable code (many compilers have options to flag this). In the case of GotoFail, this could have tipped the programmers off to the introduction of the vulnerability.

- Make code as explicit as possible, for example by using parentheses and curly braces liberally, even where they could be omitted.

- Use source code analysis tools such as "linters," which can improve code quality, and in the process may flag some potential vulnerabilities for preemptive fixing.

- Consider ad hoc source code filters to detect suspect patterns such as, in this case, duplicated source code lines, or any other recurrent errors.

- Measure and require full test coverage, especially for security-critical code.

These are just some of the basic techniques you can use to spot bugs that could undermine security. As you encounter new classes of bugs, consider how tools might be applied to systemically avoid repeated occurrences in the future—doing so should reduce vulnerabilities in the long term.

## Coding Vulnerabilities

*All happy families are alike; each unhappy family is unhappy in its own way.*

—Leo Tolstoy

Sadly, the famous opening line from Leo Tolstoy's novel *Anna Karenina* applies all too well to software: the prospects for new kinds of bugs are endless, and attempting to compile a complete list of all potential software vulnerabilities would be a fool's errand. Categories are useful, and we will cover many of them, but do not confuse them with a complete taxonomy covering the full range of possibilities.

This book by no means presents an exhaustive list of all potential flaws, but it does cover a representative swath of many of the most common categories. This basic survey should provide you with a good start, and with experience you will begin to intuit additional issues and learn how to safely steer clear of them.

### Atomicity

Many of the worst coding "war stories" that I have heard involve multi-threading or distributed processes sporadically interacting in bizarre ways due to an unexpected sequence of events. Vulnerabilities often stem from these same conditions, and the only saving grace is that the sensitive timing required may make the exploit too unreliable for the perpetrators—though you should not expect this to easily dissuade them from trying anyway.

Even if your code is single threaded and well behaved, it's almost always running in a machine with many other active processes, so when you interact with the filesystem, or any common resource, you are potentially dealing with race conditions involving code you know nothing about. *Atomicity* in software describes operations that are guaranteed to effectively be completed as a single step. This is an important defensive weapon in such cases in order to prevent surprises that potentially can lead to vulnerabilities.

To explain what can happen, consider a simple example of copying sensitive data to a temporary file. The deprecated Python `tempfile.mktemp` function returns the name of a temporary file guaranteed not to exist, intended for use by applications as the name of a file they create and then use. Don't use it: use the new `tempfile.NamedTemporaryFile` instead. Here's why. Between the time that `tempfile.mktemp` returns the temporary file path and the time at which your code actually opens the file, another process may have had a chance to interfere. If the other process can guess the name generated next, it can create the file first and (among many possibilities) inject malicious data into the temporary file. The clean solution that the new function provides is to use an atomic operation to create and open the temporary file, without the possibility of anything intervening in the process.

## Timing Attacks

A *timing attack* is a side-channel attack that infers information from the time it takes to do an operation, indirectly learning about some state of the system that should be private. Differences in timing can sometimes provide a hint—that is, they leak a little bit of protected information—benefiting an attacker. As a simple example, consider the task of trying to guess a secret number between 1 and 100; if it is known that the time to answer "No" is proportional to how far off the guess is, this quirk helps the guesser home in on the correct answer much more quickly.

Meltdown and Spectre are timing attacks on modern processors that operate below the software level, but the principles are directly applicable. These attacks exploit quirks of *speculative execution*, where the processor races forward to precompute results while tentatively relaxing various checks in the interest of speed. When this includes operations that are normally disallowed, the processor detects this eventually and cancels the results before they become final. This complicated speculation all works according to the processor design and is essential to achieve the incredible speeds we enjoy. However, during the speculative, rules-are-suspended execution, whenever the computation accesses memory, this has the side effect of causing it to be cached. When the speculative execution is canceled, the cache is unaffected, and that side effect represents a potential hint, which these attacks utilize to infer what happened during the speculative execution. Specifically, the attack code can deduce what happened during the canceled speculative execution by checking the state of the cache. Memory caching speeds up execution but is not directly exposed to software; however, code can tell whether or not the memory location contents were in the cache by measuring memory access time, because cached memory is way faster. This is a complicated attack on a complex processor architecture, but for our purposes the point is that when timing correlates to protected information state, it can be exploitable as a leak.

For a simpler, purely software-based example of a timing attack, suppose you want to determine whether or not your friend (or frenemy?) has an account with a particular online service, but you don't know their account name. The "forgot password" option asks users for their account name and phone number in order to send a "reminder." However, suppose that the implementation first looks up the phone number in a database, and if found, proceeds to look up the associated account name to see if it matches the input. Say that each lookup takes a few seconds, so the time delay is noticeable to the user. First, you try a few random account names (say, by mashing the keyboard) and phone numbers that likely won't match actual users, and learn that it reliably takes about three seconds to get a "No such account" response. Next, you sign up with your own phone number and try the "forgot password" feature using your number with one of the random unused account names. Now you observe that in this case it takes five seconds, or almost twice as long, to get the response.

Armed with these facts, you can try your friend's phone number with an unused account name: if it takes five seconds to get a reply, then you know that their phone number is in the database, and if it takes three seconds, then it isn't. By observing the timing alone, you can infer whether a given phone number is in the database. If membership might reveal sensitive private information, such as in a forum for patients with a certain medical condition, such timing attacks could enable a harmful disclosure.

Timing differences naturally occur due to software when there is a sequence of slow operations (think if...if...if...if...), and there is valuable information to be inferred from knowing how far down the sequence of events the execution proceeded. Precisely how much or little timing difference is required to leak information depends on many factors. In the online account checking example, it takes a few seconds to represent a clear signal, given the normal delays the web imposes on access. By contrast, when exploiting Meltdown or Spectre using code running on the same machine, sub-millisecond time differences may be measurable and also significant.

The best mitigation option is to reduce the time differential to an acceptable—that is, imperceptible—level. To prevent the presence of a phone number in the database from leaking, changing the code to use a single database lookup to handle both cases would be sufficient. When there is an inherent timing difference and the timing side channel could result in a serious disclosure, about all you can do to mitigate the risk is introduce an artificial delay to blur the timing signal.

### Serialization

*Serialization* refers to the common technique of converting data objects to a byte stream, a little like a *Star Trek* transporter does, to then "beam" them through time and space. Storing or transmitting the resulting bytes allows you to subsequently reconstitute equivalent data objects through *deserialization*. This ability to "dehydrate" objects and then "rehydrate" them is handy for object-oriented programming, but the technique is inherently a security risk if there is any possibility of tampering in between. Not only can an attacker cause critical data values to morph, but by constructing invalid byte sequences, they can even cause the deserialization code to perform harmful operations. Since deserialization is only safe when used with trusted serialized data, this is an example of the untrusted input problem.

The problem is not that these libraries are poorly built, but that they require trust to be able to perform the operations necessary to construct arbitrary objects in order to do their job. Deserialization is, in effect, an interpreter that does whatever the serialized bytes of its input tell it to do, so its use with untrusted data is never a good idea. For example, Python's deserialization operation (called "unpickling") is easily tricked into executing arbitrary code by embedding a malicious byte sequence in the data to be unpickled. Unless serialized byte data can be securely stored and transmitted without the possibility of tampering, such as with a MAC or digital signature (as discussed in Chapter 5), it's best avoided completely.

## The Usual Suspects

> *The greatest trick the devil ever pulled was convincing the world he didn't exist.*
>
> —Charles Baudelaire

The next several chapters cover many of the "usual suspects" that keep cropping up in code as vulnerabilities. In this chapter we considered GotoFail and issues with atomicity, timing attacks, and serialization. Here is a preview of the topics we'll explore next:

- Fixed-width integer vulnerabilities
- Floating-point precision vulnerabilities
- Buffer overflow and other memory management issues
- Input validation
- Character string mishandling
- Injection attacks
- Web security

Many of these issues will seem obvious, yet all continue to recur largely unabated as root causes of software vulnerabilities, with no end in sight. It's important to learn from past failings, because many of these vulnerability classes have existed for decades. Yet, it would be a mistake to take a backward-looking approach as if all possible security bugs were cataloged exhaustively. No book can forewarn of all possible pitfalls, but you can study these examples to get an idea of the deeper patterns and lessons behind them.

# 9

## LOW-LEVEL CODING FLAWS

*Low-level programming is good for the programmer's soul.*
—John Carmack

The next few chapters will survey a multitude of coding pitfalls programmers need to be aware of for security reasons, starting with the classics. This chapter covers basic flaws that are common to code that works closer to the machine level. The issues discussed here arise when data exceeds the capacity of either fixed-size numbers or allocated memory buffers. Modern languages tend to provide higher-level abstractions that insulate code from these perils, but programmers working in these safer languages will still benefit from understanding these flaws, if only to fully appreciate all that's being done for them, and why it matters.

Languages such as C and C++ that expose these low-level capabilities remain dominant in many software niches, so the potential threats they pose are by no means theoretical. Modern languages such as Python usually abstract away the hardware enough that the issues described in this chapter don't occur, but the lure of approaching the hardware level for maximum efficiency remains powerful. A few popular languages offer programmers their choice of both worlds. In addition to type-safe object libraries, the Java and C# base types include fixed-width integers, and they have "unsafe" modes that remove many of the safeguards normally provided. Python's float type, as explained in "Floating-Point Precision Vulnerabilities" on page 149, relies on hardware support and accrues its limitations, which must be coped with.

Readers who never use languages exposing low-level functionality may be tempted to skip this chapter, and can do so without losing the overall narrative of the book. However, I recommend reading through it anyway, as it's best to understand what protections the languages and libraries you use do or do not provide, and to fully appreciate all that's being done for you.

Programming closer to the hardware level, if done well, is extremely powerful, but comes at a cost of increased effort and fragility. In this chapter, we focus on the most common classes of vulnerability specific to coding with lower-level abstractions.

Since this chapter is all about bugs that arise from issues where code is near or at the hardware level, you must understand that the exact results of many of these operations will vary across platforms and languages. I've designed the examples to be as specific as possible, but implementation differences may cause varying results—and it's exactly because computations can vary unpredictably that these issues are easily overlooked and can have an impact on security. The details will vary depending on your hardware, compiler, and other factors, but the concepts introduced in this chapter do apply generally.

## Arithmetic Vulnerabilities

Different programming languages variously define their arithmetic operators either mathematically or according to the processor's corresponding instructions, which, as we shall see shortly, are not quite the same. By *low-level*, I mean features of programming languages that depend on machine instructions, which requires dealing with the hardware's quirks and limitations.

Code is full of integer arithmetic. It's used not only for computing numerical values but also for string comparison, indexed access to data structures, and more. Because the hardware instructions are so much faster and easier to use than software abstractions that handle a larger range of values, they are hard to resist, but with that convenience and speed comes the risk of *overflow*. Overflow happens when the result of a computation exceeds the capacity of a fixed-width integer, leading to unexpected results, which can create a vulnerability.

Floating-point arithmetic has more range than integer arithmetic, but its limited precision can cause unexpected results, too. Even floating-point numbers have limits (for single precision, on the order of $10^{38}$), but when the limit is exceeded, they have the nice property of resulting in a specific value that denotes infinity.

Readers interested in an in-depth treatment of the implementation of arithmetic instructions down to the hardware level can learn more from *The Secret Life of Programs* by Jonathan E. Steinhart (No Starch Press, 2019).

## Fixed-Width Integer Vulnerabilities

At my first full-time job, I wrote device drivers in assembly machine language on minicomputers. Though laughably underpowered by modern standards, minicomputers provided a great opportunity to learn how hardware works, because you could look at the circuit board and see every connection and every chip (which had a limited number of logic gates inside). I could *see* the registers connected to the arithmetic logic unit (which could perform addition, subtraction, and Boolean operations only) and memory, so I knew exactly how the computer worked. By contrast, modern processors are fabulously complicated, containing billions of logic gates, well beyond human understanding by casual observation.

Today, most programmers learn and use higher-level languages that shield them from machine language and the intricacies of CPU architecture. Fixed-width integers are the most basic building blocks of many languages, including Java and C/C++, and if any computation exceeds their limited range, you get the wrong result *silently*.

Modern processors often have either a 32- or 64-bit architecture, but we can understand how they work by discussing smaller sizes. Let's look at an example of overflow based on unsigned 16-bit integers. A 16-bit integer can represent any value from 0 to 65,535 ($2^{16} - 1$). For example, multiplying 300 by 300 should give us 90,000, but that number is beyond the range of the fixed-width integer we are using. So, due to overflow, the result we actually get is 24,464 (65,536 less than the expected result).

Some people think about overflow mathematically as *modular arithmetic*, or the remainder of division (for instance, the previous calculation gave us the remainder of dividing 90,000 by 65,536). Others think of it in terms of binary or hexadecimal truncation, or in terms of the hardware implementation—but if none of these make sense to you, just remember that the results for oversized values will not be what you expect. Since mitigations for overflow will attempt to avoid it in the first place, the precise resulting value is not usually important.

What's important here is anticipating the foibles of binary arithmetic, rather than knowing exactly what value results from a calculation—which, depending on the language and compiler, may not be well defined (that is, the language specification refuses to guarantee any particular value). Operations technically specified as "not defined" in a language may seem predictable, but you are on thin ice if the language specification doesn't offer a guarantee. The bottom line for security is that it's important to know the language specification and avoid computations that are potentially undefined. Do not get clever and experiment to find a tricky way to detect the undefined result, because with different hardware or a new version of the compiler, your code might stop working.

## A QUICK BINARY MATH REFRESHER
## USING 16-BIT ARCHITECTURE

For readers less familiar with binary arithmetic, here is a graphical breakdown of the 300 × 300 computation mentioned in the preceding text. Just as decimal numbers are written with the digits 0 through 9, binary numbers are written with the digits 0 and 1. And just as each digit further left in a decimal number represents another tenfold larger position, in binary, the digits double (1, 2, 4, 8, 16, 32, 64, and so on) as they extend to the left. Figure 9-1 shows the 16-bit binary representation of the decimal number 300, with the power-of-two binary digit positions indicated by decimal numbers 0 through 15.

15 14 13 12 11 10 9  8  7  6  5  4  3  2  1  0

**0000000100101100  =  300**

$$(2^8 + 2^5 + 2^3 + 2^2) = 300$$

Figure 9-1: An example of a binary number

The binary representation is the sum of values shown as powers of two that have a 1 in the corresponding binary digit position. That is, 300 is $2^8 + 2^5 + 2^3 + 2^2$ (256 + 32 + 8 + 4), or binary 100101100.

Now let's see how to multiply 300 times itself in binary (Figure 9-2).

```
           15 14 13 12 11 10 9 8 7 6 5 4 3 2 1 0
              0000000100101100
            × 0000000100101100
           00 00000100101100
          000 0000100101100
        00000 00100101100
     00000001 00101100
              0101111110010000
```

Figure 9-2: An example of multiplication in binary

Just as you do with decimal multiplication on paper, the multiplicand is repeatedly added and shifted to the position corresponding to a digit of the multiplier. Working from the right, we shift the first instance two digits left because the first 1 is two positions from the right, and so on, with each copy aligned on the right below one of the 1s in the multiplier. The grayed-out numbers extending on the left are beyond the capacity of a 16-bit register and therefore truncated—this is where overflow occurs. Then we just add up the parts, in binary of course, to get the result. The value 2 is 10 ($2^1$) in binary, so position 5 is the first carry (1 + 1 + 0 = 10): we put down a 0 and carry the 1. That's how multiplication of fixed-width integers works, and that's how values get silently truncated.

If you miscompute an arithmetic result your code may break in many ways, and the effects often snowball into a cascade of dysfunction, culminating in a crash or blue screen. Common examples of vulnerabilities due to integer overflow include buffer overflows (discussed in "Buffer Overflow" on page 157), incorrect comparisons of values, situations in which you give a credit instead of charging for a sale, and so on.

It's best to mitigate these issues before any computation that could go out of bounds is performed, while all numbers are still within range. The easy way to get it right is to use an integer size that is larger than the largest allowable value, preceded by checks ensuring that invalid values never sneak in. For example, to compute 300 × 300, as mentioned earlier, use 32-bit arithmetic, which is capable of handling the product of any 16-bit values. If you must convert the result back to 16-bit, protect it with a 32-bit comparison to ensure that it is in range.

Here is what multiplying two 16-bit unsigned integers into a 32-bit result looks like in C. I prefer to use an extra set of parentheses around the casts for clarity, even though operator precedence binds the casts ahead of the multiplication (I'll provide a more comprehensive example later in this chapter for a more realistic look at how these vulnerabilities slip in):

```
uint32_t simple16(uint16_t a, uint16_t b) {
  return ((uint32_t)a) * ((uint32_t)b);
}
```

The fact that fixed-width integers are subject to silent overflow is not difficult to understand, yet in practice these flaws continue to plague even experienced coders. Part of the problem is the ubiquity of integer math in programming—including its implicit usages, such as pointer arithmetic and array indexing, where the same mitigations must be applied. Another challenge is the necessary rigor of always keeping in mind not just what the reasonable range of values might be for every variable, but also what possible ranges of values the code could encounter, given the manipulations of a wily attacker.

Many times when programming, it feels like all we are doing is manipulating numbers, yet we must not lose sight of the fragility of these calculations.

### Floating-Point Precision Vulnerabilities

Floating-point numbers are, in many ways, more robust and less quirky than fixed-width integers. For our purposes, you can think of a floating-point number as a sign bit (for positive or negative numbers), a fraction of a fixed precision, and an exponent of two that the fraction is multiplied by. The popular IEEE 754 double-precision specification provides 15 decimal digits (53 binary digits) of precision, and if you exceed its extremely large bounds, you get a signed infinity—or *NaN (not a number)*—for a few operations instead of truncation to wild values, as you do with fixed-width integers.

Since 15 digits of precision is enough to tally the federal budget of the United States (currently several trillion dollars) in pennies, the risk of loss of precision is rarely a problem. Nonetheless, it does happen silently in the low-order digits, which can be surprising because the representation of floating-point numbers is binary rather than decimal. For example, since decimal fractions do not necessarily have exact representations in binary, 0.1 + 0.2 will yield 0.30000000000000004—a value that is *not* equal to 0.3. These kinds of messy results can happen because just as a fraction such as 1/7 is a repeating decimal in base 10, 1/10 repeats infinitely in base 2 (it's 0.00011001100. . . with 1100 continuing forever), so there will be error in the lowest bits. Since these errors are introduced in the low-order bits, this is called *underflow*.

Even though underflow discrepancies are tiny proportionally, they can still produce unintuitive results when values are of different magnitudes. Consider the following code written in JavaScript, a language where all numbers are floating point:

*vulnerable code*
```
var a = 10000000000000000
var b = 2
var c = 1
console.log(((a+b)-c)-a)
```

Mathematically, the result of the expression in the final line should equal b-c, since the value a is first added and then subtracted. (The console.log function is a handy way to output the value of an expression.) But in fact, the value of a is large enough that adding or subtracting much smaller values has no effect, given the limited precision available, so that when the value a is finally subtracted, the result is zero.

When calculations such as the one in this example are approximate, the error is harmless, but when you need full precision, or when values of differing orders of magnitude go into the computation, then a good coder needs to be cautious. Vulnerabilities arise when such discrepancies potentially impact a security-critical decision in the code. Underflow errors may be a problem for computations such as checksums or for double-entry accounting, where exact results are essential.

For many floating-point computations, even without dramatic underflow like in the example we just showed, small amounts of error accumulate in the lower bits when the values do not have an exact representation. It's almost always unwise to compare floating-point values for equality (or inequality), since this operation cannot tolerate even tiny differences in computed values. So, instead of (x == y), compare the values within a small range (x > y - delta && x < y + delta) for a value of delta suitable for the application. Python provides the math.isclose helper function that does a slightly more sophisticated version of this test.

When you must have high precision, consider using the super-high-precision floating-point representations (IEEE 754 defines 128- and 256-bit formats). Depending on the requirements of the computation, arbitrary-precision decimal or rational number representations may be the best choice. Libraries often provide this functionality for languages that do not include native support.

### Example: Floating-Point Underflow

Floating-point underflow is easy to underestimate, but lost precision has the potential to be devastating. Here is a simple example in Python of an online ordering system's business logic that uses floating-point values. The following code's job is to check that purchase orders are fully paid, and if so, approve shipment of the product:

*vulnerable code*

```python
from collections import namedtuple
PurchaseOrder = namedtuple('PurchaseOrder', 'id, date, items')
LineItem = namedtuple('LineItem', 'kind, detail, amount, quantity',
                       defaults=(1,))
def validorder(po):
    """Returns an error text if the purchase order (po) is invalid,
    or list of products to ship if valid [(quantity, SKU), ...].
    """
    products = []
    net = 0
    for item in po.items:
        if item.kind == 'payment':
            net += item.amount
        elif item.kind == 'product':
            products.append(item)
            net -= item.amount * item.quantity
        else:
            return "Invalid LineItem type: %s" % item.kind
    if net != 0:
        return "Payment imbalance: $%0.2f." % net
    return products
```

Purchase orders consist of line items that are either product or payment details. The total of payments, minus the total cost of products ordered, should be zero. The payments are already validated beforehand, and let me be explicit about one detail of that process: if the customer immediately cancels a charge in full, both the credit and debit appear as line items without querying the credit card processor, which incurs a fee. Let's also posit that the prices listed for items are correct.

Focusing on the floating-point math, see how for payment line items the amount is added to net, and for products the amount times quantity is subtracted (these invocations are written as Python doctests, where the >>> lines are code to run followed by the expected values returned):

```python
>>> tv = LineItem(kind='product', detail='BigTV', amount=10000.00)
>>> paid = LineItem(kind='payment', detail='CC#12345', amount=10000.00)
>>> goodPO = PurchaseOrder(id='777', date='6/16/2022', items=[tv, paid])
>>> validorder(goodPO)
[LineItem(kind='product', detail='BigTV', amount=10000.0, quantity=1)]
>>> unpaidPO = PurchaseOrder(id='888', date='6/16/2022', items=[tv])
>>> validorder(unpaidPO)
'Payment imbalance: $-10000.00.'
```

The code works as expected, approving the first transaction shown for a fully paid TV and rejecting the order that doesn't note a payment.

Now it's time to break this code and "steal" some TVs. If you already see the vulnerability, it's a great exercise to try and deceive the function yourself. Here is how I got 1,000 TVs for free, with explanation following the code:

```
>>> fake1 = LineItem(kind='payment', detail='FAKE', amount=1e30)
>>> fake2 = LineItem(kind='payment', detail='FAKE', amount=-1e30)
>>> tv = LineItem(kind='product', detail='BigTV', amount=10000.00, \
                quantity = 1000)
>>> nonpayment = [fake1, tv, fake2]
>>> fraudPO = PurchaseOrder(id='999', date='6/16/2022', items=nonpayment)
>>> validorder(fraudPO)
[LineItem(kind='product', detail='BigTV', amount=10000.0, quantity=1000)]
```

The trick here is in the fake payment of the outrageous amount 1e30, or $10^{30}$, followed by the immediate reversal of the charge. These bogus numbers get past the accounting check because they sum to zero ($10^{30} - 10^{30}$). Note that between the canceling debit and the credit is a line item that orders 1,000 TVs. Because the first number is so huge, when the cost of the TVs is subtracted, it underflows completely; then, when the credit (a negative number) is added in, the result is zero. Had the credit immediately followed the payment followed by the line item for the TVs, the result would be different and an error would be correctly flagged.

To give you a more accurate feel for underflow—and more importantly, to show how to gauge the range of safe values to make the code secure—we can drill in a little deeper. The choice of $10^{30}$ for this attack was arbitrary, and this trick works with numbers as low as about $10^{24}$, but not $10^{23}$. The cost of 1,000 TVs at $10,000 each is $10,000,000, or $10^7$. So with a fake charge of $10^{23}$, the value $10^7$ starts to change the computation a little, corresponding to about 16 digits of precision ($23 - 7$). The previously mentioned 15 digits of precision was a safe rule-of-thumb approximation (the binary precision corresponds to 15.95 decimal digits) that's useful because most of us think naturally in base 10, but since the floating-point representation is actually binary, it can differ by a few bits.

With that reasoning in mind, let's fix this vulnerability. If we want to work in floating point, then we need to constrain the range of numbers. Assuming a minimum product cost of $0.01 ($10^{-2}$) and 15 digits of precision, we can set a maximum payment amount of $$10^{13}$ ($15 - 2$), or $10 trillion. This upper limit avoids underflow, though in practice, a smaller limit corresponding to a realistic maximum order amount would be best.

Using an arbitrary-precision number type avoids underflow: in Python, that could be the native integer type, or fractions.Fraction. Higher-precision floating-point computation will prevent this particular attack but would still be susceptible to underflow with more extreme values. Since Python is dynamically typed, when the code is called with values of these types, the attack fails. But even if we had written this code with one of these arbitrary precision types and considered it safe, if the attacker managed to sneak in a float somehow, the vulnerability would reappear. That's why doing a range check—or, if the caller cannot be trusted to present the expected type, converting incoming values to safe types before computing—is important.

### Example: Integer Overflow

Fixed-width integer overflow vulnerabilities are often utterly obvious in hindsight, and this class of bugs has been well known for many years. Yet experienced coders repeatedly fall into the trap, whether because they don't believe the overflow can happen, because they misjudge it as harmless, or because they don't consider it at all. The following example shows the vulnerability in a larger computation to give you an idea of how these bugs can easily slip in. In practice, vulnerable computations tend to be more involved, and the values of variables harder to anticipate, but for explanatory purposes, this simple code will make it easy to see what's going on.

Consider this straightforward payroll computation formula: the number of hours worked times the rate of pay gives the total dollars of pay. This simple calculation will be done in fractional hours and dollars, which gives us full precision. On the flip side, with rounding, the details get a little complicated, and as will be seen, integer overflow easily happens.

Using 32-bit integers for exact precision, we compute dollar values in cents (units of $0.01), and hours in thousandths (units of 0.001 hours), so the numbers do get big. But as the highest possible 32-bit integer value, UINT32_MAX, is over 4 billion ($2^{32} - 1$), we assume we'll be safe by the following logic: company policy limits paid work to 100 hours per week (100,000 in thousandths), so at an upper limit of $400/hour (40,000 cents), that makes a maximum paycheck of 4,000,000,000 (and $40,000 is a nice week's pay).

Here is the computation of pay in C, with all variables and constants defined as uint32_t values:

```
if (millihours > max_millihours       // 100 hours max
   || hourlycents > max_hourlycents) // $400/hour rate max
  return 0;
return (millihours * hourlycents + 500) / 1000; // Round to $.01
```

The if statement, which returns an error indication for out-of-range parameters, is an essential guard for preventing overflow in the computation that follows.

The computation in the return statement deserves explanation. Since we are representing hours in thousandths, we must divide the result by 1,000 to get the actual pay, so we first add 500 (half of the divisor) for rounding. A trivial example confirms this: 10 hours (10,000) times $10.00/hour (1,000) equals 10,000,000; add 500 for rounding, giving 10,000,500; and divide by 1,000, giving 10,000 or $100.00, the correct value. Even at this point, you should consider this code fragile, to the extent that it flirts with the possibility of truncation due to fixed-width integer limitations.

So far the code works fine for all inputs, but suppose management has announced a new overtime policy. We need to modify the code to add 50 percent to the pay rate for all overtime hours (any hours worked after the first 40 hours). Further, the percentage should be a parameter, so management can easily change it later.

To add the extra pay for overtime hours, we introduce overtime_percentage. The code for this isn't shown, but its value is 150, meaning 150 percent of normal pay for overtime hours. Since the pay will increase, the $400/hour limit won't work anymore, because it won't be low enough to prevent integer overflow. But that pay rate was unrealistic as a practical limit anyhow, so let's halve it, just to be safe, and say $200/hour is the top pay rate:

*vulnerable code*

```
if (millihours > max_millihours        // 100 hours max
    || hourlycents > max_hourlycents) // $200/hour rate max
  return 0;
if (millihours > overtime_millihours) {
  overage_millihours = millihours - overtime_millihours;
  overtimepay = (overage_millihours * hourlycents * overtime_percentage
                 + 50000) / 100000;
  basepay = (overtime_millihours * hourlycents + 500) / 1000;
  return basepay + overtimepay;
}
else
  return (millihours * hourlycents + 500) / 1000;
```

Now, we check if the number of hours exceeds the overtime pay threshold (40 hours), and if not, the same calculation applies. In the case of overtime, we first compute overage_millihours as the hours (in thousandths) over 40.000. For those hours, we multiply the computed pay by the overtime_percentage (150). Since we have a percentage (two digits of decimal fraction) and thousandths of hours (three digits of decimals), we must divide by 100,000 (five zeros) after adding half of that for rounding. After computing the base pay on the first 40 hours, without the overtime adjustment, the code sums the two to calculate the total pay. For efficiency, we could combine these similar computations, but the intention here is for the code to structurally match the computation for clarity.

This code works most of the time, but not always. One example of an odd result is that 60.000 hours worked at $50.00/hour yields $2,211.51 in pay (it should be $3,500.00). The problem is with the multiplication by overtime_percentage (150), which easily overflows with a number of overtime hours at a good rate of pay. In integer arithmetic, we cannot precompute 150/100 as a fraction—as an integer that's just 1—so we have to do the multiplication first.

To fix this code, we could replace (X*150)/100 with (X*3)/2, but that ruins the parameterization of the overtime percentage and wouldn't work if the rate changed to a less amenable value. One solution that maintains the parameterization would be to break up the computation so that the multiplication and division use 64-bit arithmetic, downcasting to a 32-bit result:

```
if (millihours > max_millihours        // 100 hours max
    || hourlycents > max_hourlycents) // $200/hour rate max
  return 0;
if (millihours > overtime_millihours) {
  overage_millihours = millihours - overtime_millihours;
  product64 = overage_millihours * hourlycents;
  adjusted64 = (product64 * overtime_percentage + 50000) / 100000;
  overtimepay = ((uint32_t)adjusted64 + 500) / 1000;
  return basepay + overtimepay;
}
else
  return (millihours * hourlycents + 500) / 1000;
```

For illustrative purposes, the 64-bit variables include that designation in their names. We could also write these expressions with a lot of explicit casting, but it would get long and be less readable.

The multiplication of three values was split up to multiply two of them into a 64-bit variable before overflow can happen; once upcast, the multiplication with the percentage is 64-bit and will work correctly. The resultant code is admittedly messier, and comments to explain the reasoning would be helpful. The cleanest solution would be to upgrade all variables in sight to 64-bit at a tiny loss of efficiency. Such are the trade-offs involved in using fixed-width integers for computation.

## Safe Arithmetic

Integer overflow is more frequently problematic than floating-point underflow because it can generate dramatically different results, but we can by no means safely ignore floating-point underflow, either. Since by design compilers do arithmetic in ways that potentially diverge from mathematical correctness, developers are responsible for dealing with the consequences. Once aware of these problems, you can adopt several mitigation strategies to help avoid vulnerabilities.

Avoid using tricky code to handle potential overflow problems because any mistakes will be hard to find by testing and represent potentially exploitable vulnerabilities. Additionally, a trick might work on your machine but not be portable to other CPU architectures or different compilers. Here is a summary of how to do these computations safely:

- Be careful using type conversions that can potentially truncate or distort results, just as calculations can.

- Where possible, constrain inputs to the computation to ensure that all possible values are representable.

- Use a larger fixed-size integer to avoid possible overflow; check that the result is within bounds before converting it back to a smaller-sized integer.

- Remember that intermediate computed values may overflow, causing a problem, even if the final result is always within range.

- Use extra care when checking the correctness of arithmetic in and around security-sensitive code.

If the nuances of fixed-width integer and floating-point computations still feel arcane, watch them closely and expect surprises in what might seem like elementary calculations. Once you know they can be tricky, a little testing with some ad hoc code in your language of choice is a great way to get a feel for the limits of the basic building blocks of computer math.

Once you have identified the code at risk of these sort of bugs, make test cases that invoke calculations with extreme values for all inputs, then check the results. Well-chosen test cases can detect overflow problems, but a limited set of tests is not proof that the code is immune to overflow.

Fortunately, more modern languages, such as Python, increasingly use arbitrary-precision integers and are not generally subject to these problems. Getting arithmetic computation right begins with understanding precisely how the language you use works in complete detail. You can find an excellent reference with details for several popular languages at the memorable URL *floating-point-gui.de*, which provides in-depth explanation and best-practice coding examples.

## Memory Access Vulnerabilities

The other vulnerability class we'll discuss involves improper memory access. Direct management of memory is powerful and potentially highly efficient, but it comes with the risk of arbitrarily bad consequences if the code gets anything wrong.

Most programming languages offer fully managed memory allocation and constrain access to proper bounds, but for reasons of efficiency or flexibility, or sometimes because of the inertia of legacy, other languages (predominantly C and C++) make the job of memory management the responsibility of the programmer. When programmers take on this job—even experienced programmers—they can easily get it wrong, especially as the code gets complicated, creating serious vulnerabilities. And as with the arithmetic flaws described earlier, the great danger is when a violation of memory management protocol goes uncaught and continues to happen silently.

In this section, the focus is on the security aspects of code that directly manages and accesses memory, absent built-in safeguards. Code examples will use the classic dynamic memory functions of the original C standard library, but these lessons apply generally to the many variants that provide similar functionality.

### Memory Management

Pointers allow direct access to memory by its address, and they are perhaps the most powerful feature of the C language. But just like when wielding any power tool, it's important to use responsible safety precautions to manage the attendant risk. Software allocates memory when needed, works within its available bounds, and releases it when no longer needed. Any access outside of this agreement of space and time will have unintended consequences, and that's where vulnerabilities arise.

The C standard library provides dynamic memory allocation for large data structures, or when the size of a data structure cannot be determined at compile time. This memory is allocated from the *heap*—a large chunk of address space in the process used to provide working memory. C programs use malloc(3) to allocation memory, and when it's no longer needed, they release each allocation for reuse by calling free(3). There are many variations on these allocation and deallocation functions; we will focus on these two for simplicity, but the ideas should apply anytime code is managing memory directly.

Access after memory release can easily happen when lots of code shares a data structure that eventually gets freed, but copies of the pointer remain behind and get used in error. After the memory gets recycled, any use of those old pointers violates memory access integrity. On the flip side, forgetting to release memory after use risks exhausting the heap over time and running out of memory. The following code excerpt shows the basic correct usage of heap memory:

```
uint8_t *p;
// Don't use the pointer before allocating memory for it.
p = malloc(100);  // Allocate 100 bytes before first use.
p[0] = 1;
p[99] = 123 + p[0];
free(p);          // Release the memory after last use.
// Don't use the pointer anymore.
```

This code accesses the memory between the allocation and deallocation calls, inside the bounds of allotted memory.

In actual use, the allocation, memory access, and deallocation can be scattered around the code, making it tricky to always do this just right.

## Buffer Overflow

A *buffer overflow* (or, alternatively, *buffer overrun*) occurs when code accesses a memory location outside of the intended target buffer. It's important to be very clear about its meaning because the terminology is confusing. *Buffer* is a general term for any region in memory: data structures, character strings, arrays, objects, or variables of any type. *Access* is a catch-all term for reading or writing memory. That means a buffer overflow involves reading or writing outside of the intended memory region, even though "overflow" more naturally describes the act of writing. While the effects of reading and writing differ fundamentally, it's useful to think of them together to understand the problem.

Buffer overflows are not exclusive to heap memory, but can occur with any kind of variable, including static allocations and local variables on the stack. All of these potentially modify other data in memory in arbitrary ways. Unintended writes out of bounds could change just about anything in memory, and clever attackers will refine such an attack to try to cause maximum damage. In addition, buffer overflow bugs may read memory unexpectedly, possibly leaking information to attackers or otherwise causing the code to misbehave.

Don't underestimate the difficulty and importance of getting explicit memory allocation, access within bounds, and release of unused storage exactly right. Simple patterns of allocation, use, and release are best, including exception handling to ensure that the release is never skipped. When allocation by one component hands off the reference to other code, it's critical to define responsibility for subsequently releasing the memory to one side of the interface or the other.

Finally, be cognizant that even in a fully range-checked, garbage-collected language, you can still get in trouble. Any code that directly manipulates data structures in memory can make errors equivalent to buffer overflow issues. Consider, for example, manipulating a byte string, such as a TCP/IP packet in a Python array of bytes. Reading the contents and making modifications involves computing offsets into data and can be buggy, even if access outside the array does not occur.

## Example: Memory Allocation Vulnerabilities

Let's look at an example showing the dangers of dynamic memory allocation gone wrong. I'll make this example straightforward, but in actual applications the key pieces of code are often separated, making these flaws much harder to see.

### A Simple Data Structure

This example uses a simple C data structure representing a user account. The structure consists of a flag that's set if the user is an admin, a user ID, a username, and a collection of settings. The semantics of these fields don't matter to us, except if the isAdmin field is nonzero, as this confers unlimited authorization (making this field an attractive target for attack):

```
#define MAX_USERNAME_LEN 39
#define SETTINGS_COUNT 10
typedef struct {
  bool isAdmin;
  long userid;
  char username[MAX_USERNAME_LEN + 1];
  long setting[SETTINGS_COUNT];
} user_account;
```

Here's a function that creates these user account records:

```
user_account* create_user_account(bool isAdmin, const char* username) {
    user_account* ua;
    if (strlen(username) > MAX_USERNAME_LEN)
        return NULL;
    ua = malloc(sizeof (user_account));
    if (NULL == ua) {
        fprintf(stderr, "malloc failed to allocate memory.");
        return NULL;
    }
    ua->isAdmin = isAdmin;
    ua->userid = userid_next++;
    strcpy(ua->username, username);
    memset(&ua->setting, 0, sizeof ua->setting);
    return ua;
}
```

The first parameter specifies whether the user is an admin or not. The second parameter provides a username, which must not exceed the specified maximum length. A global counter (userid_next, declaration not shown) provides sequential unique IDs. The values of all the settings are set to zero initially, and the code returns a pointer to the new record unless an error causes it to return NULL instead. Note that the code checks the length of the username string before the allocation, so that allocation happens only when the memory will get used.

### Writing an Indexed Field

After we've created a record, the values of all the settings can be set using the following function:

*vulnerable code*
```
bool update_setting(user_account* ua,
                    const char *index, const char *value) {
    char *endptr;
    long i, v;
    i = strtol(index, &endptr, 10);
    if (*endptr)
        return false;  // Terminated other than at end of string.
    if (i >= SETTINGS_COUNT)
        return false;
    v = strtol(value, &endptr, 10);
    if (*endptr)
        return false;  // Terminated other than at end of string.
    ua->setting[i] = v;
    return true;
}
```

This function takes an index into the settings and a value as decimal number strings. After converting these to integers, it stores the value as the indexed setting in the record. For example, to assign setting 1 the value 14, we would invoke the function update_setting(ua, "1", "14").

The function strtol converts the strings to integer values. The pointer that strtol sets (endptr) tells the caller how far it parsed; if that isn't the null terminator, the string wasn't a valid integer and the code returns an error. After ensuring that the index (i) does not exceed the number of settings, it parses the value (v) in the same way and stores the setting's value in the record.

## Buffer Overflow Vulnerability

All this setup is simplicity itself, though C tends to be verbose. Now let's cut to the chase. There's a bug: no check exists for a negative index value. If an attacker can manage to get this function called as update_setting(ua, "-12", "1") they can become an admin. This is because the assignment into settings accesses 48 bytes backward into the record, since each item is of type long, which is 4 bytes. Therefore, the assignment writes the value 1 into the isAdmin field, granting excess privileges.

In this case, the fact that we allowed negative indexing within a data structure caused an unauthorized write to memory that violated a security protection mechanism. You need to watch out for many variations on this theme, including indexing errors due to missing limit checks or arithmetic errors such as overflow. Sometimes, a bad access out of one data structure can modify other data that happens to be in the wrong place.

The fix is to prevent negative index values from being accepted, which limits write accesses to the valid range of settings. The following addition to the if statement rejects negative values of i, closing the loophole:

```
if (i < 0 || i >= SETTINGS_COUNT)
```

The additional i < 0 condition will now reject any negative index value, blocking any unintended modification by this function.

## Leaking Memory

Even once we've fixed the negative index overwrite flaw, there's still a vulnerability. The documentation for malloc(3) warns, with underlining, "The memory is not initialized." This means that the memory could contain anything, and a little experimentation does show that leftover data appears in there, so recycling the uninitialized memory represents a potential leak of private data.

Our create_user_account function does write data to all fields of the structure, but it still leaks bytes that are in the data structure as recycled memory. Compilers usually align field offsets that allow efficient writing: on my 32-bit computer, field offsets are a multiple of 4 (4 bytes of 8 bits is 32), and other architectures perform similar alignments. The alignment is needed because writing a field that spans a multiple-of-4 address (for example, writing 4 bytes to address 0x1000002) requires two memory accesses. So in this example, after the single-byte Boolean isAdmin field at offset 0, the userid field follows at offset 4, leaving the three intervening bytes (offsets 1–3) unused. Figure 9-3 shows the memory layout of the data structure in graphical form.

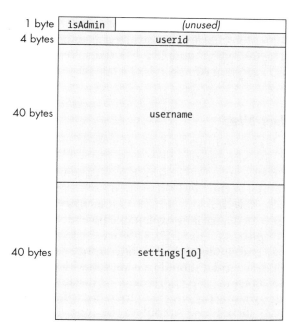

| 1 byte | isAdmin | (unused) |
| --- | --- | --- |
| 4 bytes | userid | |
| 40 bytes | username | |
| 40 bytes | settings[10] | |

*Figure 9-3: The memory layout of the user_account record*

Additionally, the use of strcpy for the username leaves another chunk of memory in its uninitialized state. This string copy function stops copying at the null terminator, so, for example, a 5-character string would only modify the first 6 bytes, leaving 34 bytes of whatever malloc happened to grab for us. The point of all this is that the newly allocated structure contains residual data which may leak unless every byte is overwritten.

Mitigating the risk of these inadvertent memory leaks isn't hard, but you must diligently overwrite all bytes of data structures that could be exposed. You shouldn't attempt to anticipate precisely how the compiler might allocate field offsets, because this could vary over time and across platforms. Instead, the easiest way to avoid these issues is to zero out buffers once allocated unless you can otherwise ensure they are fully written, or know they won't be disclosed across a trust boundary. Remember that even if your code doesn't use sensitive data itself, this memory leak path could expose other data anywhere in the process.

Generally speaking, you should avoid using strcpy to copy strings because there are so many ways to get it wrong. The strncpy function both fills unused bytes in the target with zeros and protects against overflow with strings that exceed the buffer size. However, strncpy does *not* guarantee that the resultant string will have a null terminator. This is why it's essential to allocate the buffer to be of size MAX_USERNAME_LEN + 1, ensuring that there is always room for the null terminator. Another option is to use the strlcpy function, which does ensure null termination; however, for efficiency, it does not zero-fill unused bytes. As this example shows, when you handle memory directly there are many factors you must deal with carefully.

Now that we've covered the mechanics of memory allocation and seen what vulnerabilities look like in a constructed example, let's consider a more realistic case. The following example is based on a remarkable security fiasco from several years ago that compromised a fair share of the world's major web services.

## Case Study: Heartbleed

In early April 2014, headlines warned of a worldwide disaster narrowly averted. Major operating system platforms and websites rolled out coordinated fixes, hastily arranged in secret, in an attempt to minimize their exposure as details of the newly identified security flaw became public. Heartbleed made news not only as "the first security bug with a cool logo," but because it revealed a trivially exploitable hole in the armor of any server deploying the popular OpenSSL TLS library.

What follows is an in-depth look at one of the scariest security vulnerabilities of the decade, and it should provide you with context for how serious mistakes can be. The purpose of this detailed discussion is to illustrate how bugs managing dynamically allocated memory can become devastating vulnerabilities. As such, I have simplified the code and some details of the complicated TLS communication protocol to show the crux of the vulnerability. Conceptually, this corresponds directly with what actually occurred, but with fewer moving parts and much simpler code.

Heartbleed is a flaw in the OpenSSL implementation of the TLS Heartbeat Extension, proposed in 2012 with RFC 6520. This extension provides a low-overhead method for keeping TLS connections alive, saving clients from having to re-establish a new connection after a period of inactivity. The so-called heartbeat itself is a round-trip message exchange consisting of a *heartbeat request*, with a payload of between 16 and 16,384 ($2^{14}$) bytes of arbitrary data, echoed back as a *heartbeat response* containing the same payload. Figure 9-4 shows the basic request and response messages of the protocol.

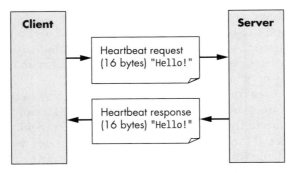

*Figure 9-4: The Heartbeat protocol (simplified)*

Having downloaded an HTTPS web page, the client may later send a heartbeat request on the connection to let the server know that it wants to maintain the connection. In an example of normal use, the client might send the 16-byte message "Hello!" (padded with zeros) comprising the request, and the server would respond by sending the same 16 bytes back. (That's how it's supposed to work, at least.) Now let's look at the Heartbleed bug.

The critical flaw occurs in malformed heartbeat requests that provide a small payload yet claim a larger payload byte count. To see exactly how this works, let's first look at the internal structure of one of the simplified heartbeat messages that the peers exchange. All of the code in this example is in C:

```
typedef struct {
  HeartbeatMessageType type;
  uint16_t payload_length;
  char bytes[0];  // Variable-length payload & padding
} hbmessage;
```

The data structure declaration hbmessage shows the three parts of one of these heartbeat messages. The first field is the message type, indicating whether it's a request or response. Next is the length in bytes of the message payload, called payload_length. The third field, called bytes, is declared as zero-length, but is intended to be used with a dynamic allocation that adds the appropriate size needed.

A malicious client might attack a target server by first establishing a TLS connection to it, and then sending a 16-byte heartbeat request with a byte count of 16,000. Here's what that looks like as a C declaration:

```
typedef struct {
  HeartbeatMessageType type = heartbeat_request;
  uint16_t payload_length = 16000;
  char bytes[16] = {"Hello!"};
} hbmessage;
```

The client sending this is lying: the message says its payload is 16,000 bytes long but the actual payload is only 16 bytes. To understand how this message tricks the server, look at the C code that processes the incoming heartbeat request message:

```
hbmessage *hb(hbmessage *request, int *message_length) {
  int response_length = request->payload_length+sizeof(hbmessage);
  hbmessage* response = malloc(response_length);
  response->type = heartbeat_response;
  response->payload_length = request->payload_length;
  memcpy(&response->bytes, &request->bytes, response->payload_length);
  *message_length = response_length;
  return response;
}
```

The hb function gets called with two parameters: the incoming heartbeat request message and a pointer named message_length, which stores the length of the response message that the function returns. The first two lines compute the byte length of the response as response_length, then a memory block of that size gets allocated as response. The next two lines fill in the first two values of the response message: the message type and its payload_length.

Next comes the fateful bug. The server needs to send back the message bytes received in the request, so it copies the data from the request into the response. Because it trusts the request message to have accurately reported its length, the function copies 16,000 bytes—but since there are only 16 bytes in the request message, the response includes thousands of bytes of internal memory contents. The last two lines store the length of the response message and then return the pointer to it.

Figure 9-5 illustrates this exchange of messages, detailing how the preceding code leaks the contents of process memory. To make the harm of the exploit concrete, I've depicted a couple of additional buffers, containing secret data, already sitting in memory in the vicinity of the request buffer. Copying 16,000 bytes from a buffer that only contained a 16-byte payload—illustrated here by the overly large dotted-line region—results in the secret data ending up in the response message, which the server sends to the client.

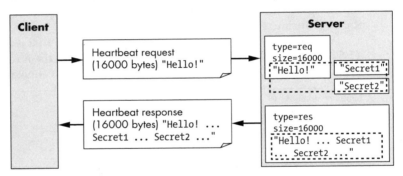

Figure 9-5: Attacking with the Heartbleed bug (simplified)

This flaw is tantamount to configuring your server to provide an anonymous API that snapshots and sends out thousands of bytes of working memory to all callers—a complete breach of memory isolation, exposed to the internet. It should come as no surprise that web servers using HTTPS security have any number of juicy secrets in working memory. According to the discoverers of the Heartbleed bug, they were able to easily steal from themselves "the secret keys used for our X.509 certificates, user names and passwords, instant messages, emails and business critical documents and communication." Since exactly what data leaked depended on the foibles of memory allocation, the ability of attackers exploiting this vulnerability to repeatedly access server memory eventually yielded all kinds of sensitive data. For a simpler view of Heartbleed, see Figure 9-6.

Figure 9-6: Heartbleed Explanation (courtesy of Randall Munroe, xkcd.com/1354)

The fix was straightforward in hindsight: anticipate "lying" heartbeat requests that ask for more payload than they provide, and, as the RFC explicitly specifies, ignore them. Thanks to Heartbleed, the world learned how dependent so many servers were on OpenSSL, and how few volunteers were laboring on the critical software that so much of the internet's infrastructure depended on. The bug is typical of why many security flaws are difficult to detect, because everything works flawlessly in the case of well-formed requests, and only malformed requests that well-intentioned code would be unlikely to ever make cause problems. Furthermore, the leaked server memory in heartbeat responses causes no direct harm to the server: only by careful analysis of the excessive data disclosure does the extent of the potential damage become evident.

As arguably one of the most severe security vulnerabilities discovered in recent years, Heartbleed should serve as a valuable example of the nature of security bugs, and how small flaws can result in a massive undermining of our systems' security. From a functional perspective, one could easily argue that this is a minor bug: it's unlikely to happen, and sending back more payload data than the request provided seems, at first glance, utterly harmless.

Heartbleed is an excellent object lesson in the fragility of low-level languages. Small errors can have massive impact. A buffer overflow potentially exposes high-value secrets if they happen to be lying around in memory at just the wrong location. The design (protocol specification) anticipated this very error by directing that heartbeat requests with incorrect byte lengths should be ignored, but without explicit testing, nobody noticed the vulnerability for over two years.

This is just one bug in one library. How many more like it are still out there now?

# 10

## UNTRUSTED INPUT

*I like engineering, but I love the creative input.*
—John Dykstra

*Untrusted inputs* are perhaps the greatest source of concern for developers writing secure code. The term itself can be confusing, and may best be understood as encompassing all inputs to a system that are not *trusted inputs*, meaning inputs from code that you can trust to provide well-formed data. Untrusted inputs are those that are out of your control and might be manipulated, and include any data entering the system that you do not fully trust. That is, they're inputs you *should not trust*, not inputs you *mistakenly trust*.

Any data coming from the outside and entering the system is best considered untrusted. The system's users may be nice, trustworthy people, but when it comes to security they are best considered untrusted, because they could do anything—including falling victim to the tricks of others. Untrusted inputs are worrisome because they represent an *attack vector*, a way to reach into the system and cause trouble. Maliciously concocted inputs that cross trust boundaries are of special concern because they can penetrate deep into the system, causing exploits in privileged code, so it's essential to have good first lines of defense. The world's greatest source of untrusted inputs has to be the internet, and since it's so rare for software to be fully disconnected, this represents a serious threat for almost all systems.

*Input validation* (or *input sanitization*) is defensive coding that imposes restrictions on inputs, forcing conformity to prescribed rules. By validating that inputs meet specific constraints and ensuring that code works properly for all valid inputs, you can successfully defend against these attacks. This chapter centers on managing untrusted inputs using input validation, and why doing so is important to security. The topic may seem mundane and it isn't technically difficult, but the need is so commonplace that doing a better job at input validation is perhaps the most impactful low-hanging fruit available to developers for reducing vulnerabilities. As such, it's covered in depth. Character string inputs present specific challenges and the security implications of Unicode are too little known, so we'll also survey the basic issues they present. Then we'll walk through some examples of injection attacks perpetrated using untrusted data with various technologies: SQL, path traversal, regular expressions, and XML external entities (XXE). Finally, I'll summarize the available mitigation techniques for this broad set of vulnerabilities.

# Input Validation

*Before you look for validation in others, try and find it in yourself.*

—Greg Behrendt

Now that you understand what untrusted inputs are, consider their potential effects within a system and how to protect against harm. Untrusted inputs routinely flow through systems, often reaching down many layers into trusted components—so just because your code is directly invoked from trusted code, there is no guarantee that those inputs can be trusted. The problem is that components might be passing through data from anywhere. The more ways an attacker can potentially manipulate the data, the more untrusted it is. Upcoming examples should make this point clear.

Input validation is a good defense, as it dials untrusted input down to a range of values that the application can safely process. The essential job of input validation is to ensure that untrusted inputs conform to design specifications so that code downstream of the validation only deals with well-formed data. Let's say you are writing a user login authentication service that receives a username and password, and issues an authentication token if the credentials are correct. By restricting usernames to between 8 and 40 characters and requiring that they consist of a well-defined subset of Unicode code points, you can make the handling of that input much simpler, because it's a known quantity. Subsequent code can use fixed-size buffers to hold a copy of the username, and it need not worry about the ramifications of obscure characters. You could likely simplify processing based on that assurance in other ways, too.

We have already seen input validation used to fix low-level vulnerabilities in the previous chapter. The paycheck integer computation code had input validation consisting of one `if` statement to guard against overly large input values:

```
if (millihours > max_millihours        // 100 hours max
    || hourlycents > max_hourlycents)   // $200/hour rate
  return 0;
```

There's no need to repeat the explanation for this, but it serves as a fine example of basic input validation. Almost any code you write will only work correctly within certain limitations: it won't work for extreme values such as massive memory sizes, or perhaps text in different languages. Whatever the limitations are, we don't want to expose code to inputs it wasn't designed for, as this risks unintended consequences that could create vulnerabilities. One easy method to mitigate this danger is to impose artificial restrictions on inputs that screen out all problematic inputs.

There are some nuances worth pointing out, however. Of course, restrictions should never reject inputs that should have been rightfully handled; for instance, in the paycheck example, we cannot reject 40-hour work weeks as invalid. If the code cannot handle all valid inputs, then we need to fix it so it can handle a broader scope of inputs. Also, an input validation strategy may need to consider the interaction of multiple inputs. In the paycheck example, the product of the pay rate and hours worked could exceed the fixed-width integer size, as we saw in Chapter 9, so validation could limit the product of these two inputs, or set limits on each separately. The former approach is more permissive but may be more difficult for callers to accommodate, so the right choice depends on the application.

Generally, you should validate untrusted inputs as soon as possible, so as to minimize the risk of unconstrained input flowing to downstream code that may not handle it properly. Once validated, subsequent code benefits from only being exposed to well-behaved data; this helps developers write secure code, because they know exactly what the range of inputs will be. Consistency is key, so a good pattern is to stage input validation in the first layer of code that handles incoming data, then hand the valid input off to business logic in deeper layers that can confidently assume that all inputs are valid.

We primarily think of input validation as a defense against untrusted inputs—specifically, what's on the attack surface—but this does not mean that all other inputs can be blithely ignored. No matter how much you trust the provider of some data, it may be possible for a mistake to result in unexpected inputs, or for an attack to somehow compromise part of the system and effectively expand the attack surface. For all of these reasons, defensive input validation is your friend. It's safest to err on the side of redundant input validation rather than risk creating a subtle vulnerability—if you don't know for certain that incoming data is reliably validated, you probably need to do it to be sure.

## Determining Validity

Input validation begins with deciding what's valid. This is not as straightforward as it sounds, because it amounts to anticipating all future valid input values and figuring out how, with good reason, to disallow the rest. This decision is usually made by the developer, who must weigh what users may want against the extra coding involved in permitting a wider range. Ideally, software requirements specify what constitutes valid input, and a good design may provide guidance.

For an integer input, the full range of 32-bit integers may appear to be an obvious choice because it's a standard data type. But thinking ahead, if the code will add these values together at some point, that'll require a bigger integer, so the 32-bit restriction becomes arbitrary. Alternatively, if you can reasonably set a lower limit for validity, then you can make sure the sum of the values will fit into 32 bits. Determining the right answer for what constitutes a valid input will require examining the application-specific context—a great example of how domain knowledge is important to security. Once the range of values deemed valid is specified, it's easy to determine the appropriate data type to use.

What usually works well is to establish an explicit limit on inputs and then leave plenty of headroom in the implementation to be certain of correctly processing all valid inputs. By headroom, I mean if you are copying a text string into a 4,096-byte buffer, use 4,000 bytes as the maximum valid length so you have a little room to spare. (In C, the additional null terminator overflowing a buffer by one byte is a classic mistake that's easy to make.) Some programmers like a good challenge, but if you're too generous (by allowing the widest possible range of input), then you are forcing the implementation to take on a bigger and harder job than is necessary, leading to greater code complexity and test burden. Even if your online shopping application can manage a cart with a billion items, attempting to process such an unrealistic transaction would be counterproductive. It would be kindest to reject the input (which may well be due to somebody's cat sitting on their keyboard).

## Validation Criteria

Most input validation checks consist of several criteria, including ensuring the input doesn't exceed a maximum size, that the data arrives in the proper format, and that it's within a range of acceptable values.

Checking the value's size is a quick test primarily intended to avoid DoS threats to your code, which would cause your application to lumber or even crash under the weight of megabytes of untrusted input. The data format may be a sequence of digits for a number, strings consisting of certain allowed characters, or a more involved format, such as XML or JSON. Typically, it's wise to check these in this order: limit size first, so you don't waste time trying to deal with excessively massive inputs, then make sure the input is well formed before parsing it, and then check that the resulting value is within the acceptable range.

Deciding on a valid range of values can be the most subjective choice, but it's important to have specific limits. How that range is defined will depend on the data type. For integers, the range will be no less than a minimum and no greater than a maximum value. For floating-point numbers, there may be limits on precision (decimal places) as well. For strings, it's a maximum length, encoding, and usually an allowable format or syntax, as determined by a regular expression or the like. I recommend specifying maximum string lengths in characters rather than bytes, if only so that non-programmers have some hope of knowing what this constraint means.

It's helpful to think about inputs as valid for a purpose, rather than in the abstract. For example, a language translation system might accept input that is first validated to conform to the supported character set and maximum length common to all supported languages. If the next processing stage analyzes the text to determine what language it is, having chosen the language you can then further restrict the text to the appropriate character set.

Or consider validating an integer input that represents the quantity of items ordered on a purchase invoice. The maximum quantity any customer might ever actually order is not easy to determine, but it's a good question to consider up front. If you have access to past data, a quick SQL query might return an interesting example worth knowing for reference. While one could argue that the maximum 32-bit integer value is the least limiting and hence best choice, in practice this rarely makes much sense. Who wouldn't consider an order of 4,294,967,295 of any product as anything but some sort of mistake? Since non-programmers are never going to remember such strange numbers derived from binary, choosing a more user-friendly limit, such as 1,000,000, makes more sense. Should anyone ever legitimately run up against such a limit, it probably is worth knowing about, and should be easy to adjust. What's more, the developer will learn about a real use case in the process that was previously unimagined.

The primary purpose of input validation is to ensure that no invalid input gets past it. The simplest way to do this is to simply reject invalid inputs, as we have been doing implicitly in the discussion so far. A more forgiving alternative is to detect any invalid input and modify it into a valid form. Let's look at these different approaches, and when to do which.

## Rejecting Invalid Input

Rejection of input that does not conform to specified rules is the simplest and arguably safest approach. Complete acceptance or rejection is cleanest and clearest, and usually easiest to get right. It's like the common-sense advice for deciding if it's safe to swim in the ocean: "When in doubt, don't go out." This can be as simple as refusing to process a web form if any field is improperly filled out, or as extreme as rejecting an entire batch of incoming data because of a single violation in some record.

Whenever people are providing the input directly, such as in the case of a web form, it's kindest to provide informative error messages, making it easy for them to correct their mistakes and resubmit. Users presumably submit invalid input either as a mistake or due to ignorance of the validation rules, neither of which is good. Calling a halt and asking the data source to provide valid input is the conservative way to do input validation, and it affords a good chance for regular providers to learn and adapt.

When input validation rejects bad input from people, best practices include:

- Explain what constitutes a valid entry as part of the user interface, saving at least those who read it from having to guess and retry. (How am I supposed to know that area codes should be hyphenated rather than parenthesized?)
- Flag multiple errors at once, so they can be corrected and resubmitted in one step.
- When people are directly providing the input, keep the rules simple and clear.
- Break up complicated forms into parts, with a separate form for each part, so people can see that they're making progress.

When inputs come from other computers, not directly from people, more rigid input validation may be wise. The best way to implement these requirements is by writing documentation precisely describing the expected input format and any other constraints. In the case of input from professionally run systems, fully rejecting an entire batch of inputs, rather than attempting to partially process the valid subset of data, may make the most sense, as it indicates something is out of spec. This allows the error to be corrected and the full dataset submitted again without needing to sort out what was or wasn't processed.

### Correcting Invalid Input

Safe and simple as it may be to insist on receiving completely valid inputs and rejecting everything else, by no means is this always the best way to go. For online merchants seeking customers at all costs, rejecting inputs during checkout could lead to more instances of the dreaded "abandoned cart," and lost sales. For interactive user input, rigid rules can be frustrating, so if the software can help the user provide valid input, it should.

If you don't want to stop the show for a minor error, then your input validation code may attempt to correct the invalid inputs, transforming them into valid values instead of rejecting them. Easy examples of this include truncating long strings to whatever the maximum length is, or removing extraneous leading or trailing spaces. Other examples of correcting invalid inputs are more complicated. Consider the common example of entering a mailing address in the exact form allowed by the postal service. This is a considerable challenge because of the precise spacing, spelling of street names, and form of abbreviation expected. Just about the only way to do this is to offer best-guess matches of similar addresses in the official format for the respondent to choose from.

The best cure for tricky validation requirements is to design inputs to be as simple as possible. For example, many of us have struggled when providing phone numbers that require area codes in parentheses, or dashes in certain positions. Instead, let phone numbers be strings of digits and avoid syntax rules in the first place.

While adjustments may save time, any correction introduces the possibility that the correction will modify the input in an unintended fashion (from the user's standpoint). Take the example of a telephone number form field where the input is expected to be 10 digits long. It should be safe to strip out common characters such as hyphens and accept the input if the result produces 10 valid digits, but if the input has too many digits, the user might have intended to provide an international number, or they might have made a typo. Either way, it probably isn't safe to truncate it.

Proper input validation requires careful judgment, but it makes software systems much more reliable, and hence more secure. It reduces the problem space, eliminates needless tricky edge cases, improves testability, and results in the entire system being better defined and stable.

# Character String Vulnerabilities

*If you are a programmer working in 2006 and you don't know the basics of characters, character sets, encodings, and Unicode, and I catch you, I'm going to punish you by making you peel onions for six months in a submarine.*

—Joel Spolsky

Nearly all software components process character strings, at least as command line parameters or when displaying output in legible form. Certain applications process character strings extensively; these include word processors, compilers, web servers and browsers, and many more. String processing is ubiquitous, so it's important to be aware of the common security pitfalls involved. What follows is a sampling of the many issues to be aware of to avoid inadvertently creating vulnerabilities.

## Length Issues

Length is the first challenge because character strings are potentially of unbounded length. Extremely long strings invite buffer overflow when copied into fixed-length storage areas. Even if handled correctly, massive strings can result in performance problems if they consume excessive cycles or memory, potentially threatening availability. So, the first line of defense is to limit the length of incoming untrusted strings to reasonable sizes. At the risk of stating the obvious, don't confuse character count with byte length when allocating buffers.

## Unicode Issues

Modern software usually relies on Unicode, a rich character set that spans the world's written languages, but the cost of this richness is a lot of hidden complexity that can be fertile ground for exploits. There are numerous character encodings to represent the world's text as bytes, but most often software uses Unicode as a kind of *lingua franca*. The Unicode standard (version 13.0) is just over 1,000 pages long, specifying over 140,000 characters, canonicalization algorithms, legacy character code standard compatibility, and bidirectional language support; it covers nearly all the world's written languages, encoding more than one million code points.

Unicode text has several different encodings that you need to be aware of. UTF-8 is the most common, but there are also UTF-7, UTF-16, and UTF-32 encodings. Accurately translating between bytes and characters is important for security, lest the contents of the text inadvertently morph in the process. *Collation* (sorted order) depends on the encoding and the language, which can create unintended results if you aren't aware of it. Some operations may work differently in the context of a different locale, such as when run on a computer configured for another country or language, so it's important to test for correctness in all these cases. When there is no need to support different locales, consider specifying the locale explicitly rather than inheriting an arbitrary one from the system configuration.

Because Unicode has many surprising features, the bottom line for security is to use a trustworthy library to handle character strings, rather than attempting to work on the bytes directly. You could say that in this regard, Unicode is analogous to cryptography in that it's best to leave the heavy lifting to experts. If you don't know what you are doing, some quirk of an obscure character or language you've never heard of might introduce a vulnerability. This section details some of the major issues that are well worth being aware of, but a comprehensive deep dive into the intricacies of Unicode would deserve a whole book. Detailed guidance about security considerations for developers who need to understand the finer points is available from the Unicode Consortium. *UTR#36: Unicode Security Considerations* is a good starting point.

### Encodings and Glyphs

Unicode encodes characters, not *glyphs* (rendered visual forms of characters). This simple dictum has many repercussions, but perhaps the easiest way to explain it is that the capital letter I (U+0049) and the Roman numeral one (U+2160) are separate characters that may appear as identical glyphs (called *homomorphs*). Web URLs support international languages, and the use of look-alike characters is a well-known trick that attackers use to fool users. Famously, someone got a legitimate server certificate using a Cyrillic character (U+0420) that looks just like the P in PayPal, creating a perfect phishing setup.

Unicode includes combining characters that allow different representations for the same character. The Latin letter Ç (U+00C7) also has a two-character representation, consisting of a capital C (U+0043) followed by the "Combining Cedilla" character (U+0327). Both the one- and two-character forms display as the same glyph, and there is no semantic difference, so code should generally treat them as equivalent forms. The typical coding strategy would be to first normalize input strings to a canonical form, but unfortunately, Unicode has several kinds of normalization, so getting the details right requires further study.

### Case Change

Converting strings to upper- or lowercase is a common way of canonicalizing text so that code treats test, TEST, tEsT, and so forth as identical. Yet it turns out that there are characters beyond the English alphabet that have surprising properties under case transformations.

For example, the following strings are different yet nearly identical to casual observers: 'This ıs a test.' and 'This is a test.' (Note the missing dot over the second lowercase i in the first sentence.) Converted to uppercase, they both turn into the identical 'THIS IS A TEST.' since the lowercase dotless ı (U+0131) and the familiar lowercase i (U+0069) both become uppercase I (U+0049). To see how this leads to a vulnerability, consider checking an input string for the presence of <script>: the code might convert to lowercase, scan for that substring, then convert to uppercase for output. The string <scrıpt> would slip through but appear as <SCRIPT> in the output, which could allow script injection on a web page—the very thing the code was trying to prevent.

# Injection Vulnerabilities

*If you ever injected truth into politics you would have no politics.*

—Will Rogers

Unsolicited credit card offers comprise a major chunk of the countless tons of junk mail that clog up the postal system, but one clever recipient managed to turn the tables on the bank. Instead of tossing out a promotional offer to sign up for a card with terms he did not like, Dmitry Agarkov scanned the attached contract and carefully modified the text to specify terms extremely favorable to him, including 0 percent interest, unlimited credit, and a generous payment that he would receive should the bank cancel the card. He signed the modified contract and returned it to the bank, and soon received his new credit card. Dmitry enjoyed the generous terms of his uniquely advantageous contract for a while, but things got ugly when the bank finally caught on. After a protracted legal battle that included a favorable judgment upholding the validity of the modified contract, he eventually settled out of court.

This is a real-world example of an *injection attack*: contracts are not the same as code, but they do compel the signatories to perform prescribed actions in much the same way as a program behaves. By altering the terms of the contract, Dmitry was able to force the bank to act against its will, almost as if he had modified the software that manages credit card accounts in his favor. Software is also susceptible to this sort of attack: untrusted inputs can fool it into doing unexpected things, and this is actually a fairly common vulnerability.

There is a common software technique that works by constructing a string or data structure that encodes an operation to be performed, and then executing that to accomplish the specified task. (This is analogous to the bank writing a contract that defines how its credit card service operates, expecting the terms to be accepted unchanged.) When data from an untrusted source is involved, it may be able to influence what happens upon execution. If the attacker can change the intended effect of the operation, that influence may cross a trust boundary and get executed by software at a higher privilege. This is the idea of injection attacks in the abstract.

Before explaining the specifics of some common injection attacks, let's consider a simple example of how the influence of untrusted data can be deceptive. According to an apocryphal story, just this kind of confusion was exploited successfully by an intramural softball team that craftily chose the name "No Game Scheduled." Several times opposing teams saw this name on the schedule, assumed it meant that there was no game that day, and lost by forfeit as no-shows. This is an example of an injection attack because the team name is an input to the scheduling system, but "No Game Scheduled" was misinterpreted as being a message from the scheduling system.

The same injection attack principles apply to many different technologies (that is, forms of constructed strings that represent an operation), including but not limited to:

- SQL statements
- Filepath names
- Regular expressions (as a DoS threat)
- XML data (specifically, XXE declarations)
- Shell commands
- Interpreting strings as code (for example, JavaScript's eval function)
- HTML and HTTP headers (covered in Chapter 11)

The following sections explain the first four kinds of injection attacks in detail. Shell command and code injection work similarly to SQL injection, where sloppy string construction is exploitable by untrusted inputs. We'll cover web injection attacks in the next chapter.

## SQL Injection

The classic xkcd comic #327 (Figure 10-1) portrays an audacious SQL injection attack, wherein parents give their child an unlikely and unpronounceable name that includes special characters. When entered into the local school district's database, this name compromises the school's records.

Figure 10-1: Exploits of a Mom (courtesy of Randall Munroe, xkcd.com/327)

To understand how this works, assume that the school registration system uses a SQL database and adds student records with a SQL statement of the form shown here:

```
INSERT INTO Students (name) VALUES ('Robert');
```

In this simplified example, that statement adds the name "Robert" to the database. (In practice, more columns than just name would appear in the two sets of parenthesized lists; those are omitted here for simplicity.)

Now imagine a student with the ludicrous name of Robert'); DROP TABLE students;--. Consider the resultant SQL command, with the parts corresponding to the student's name highlighted:

```
INSERT INTO Students (name) VALUES ('Robert'); DROP TABLE Students;--');
```

According to SQL command syntax rules, this string actually contains two statements:

```
INSERT INTO Students (name) VALUES ('Robert');
DROP TABLE Students; --');
```

The first of these two SQL commands inserts a "Robert" record as intended. However, since the student's name contains SQL syntax, it also injects a second, unintended command, DROP TABLE, that deletes the entire table. The double dashes denote a comment, so the SQL engine ignores the following text. This trick allows the exploit to work by consuming the trailing syntax (single quote and close parenthesis) in order to avoid a syntax error that would prevent execution.

Now let's look at the code a little more closely to see what a SQL injection vulnerability looks like and how to prevent it. The hypothetical school registration system code works by forming SQL commands as text strings, such as in the first basic example we covered, and then executing them. The input data provides names and other information to fill out student records. In theory, we can even suppose that staff verified this input against official records to ensure their accuracy (assuming, with a large grain of salt, that legal names can include ASCII special characters).

The programmer's fatal mistake was in writing a string concatenation statement such as the following without considering that an unusual name could "break out" of the single quotes:

*vulnerable code*

```
sql_stmt = "INSERT INTO Students (name) VALUES ('" + student_name + "');";
```

Mitigating injection attacks is not hard but requires vigilance, lest you get sloppy and write code like this. Mixing untrusted inputs and command strings is the root cause of the vulnerability, because those inputs can break out of the quotes with unintended harmful consequences.

Determining what strings constitute a valid name is an important requirements issue, but let's just focus on the apostrophe character used in this SQL statement as a single quote. Since there are names (such as O'Brien) that contain the apostrophe, which is key to cracking open the SQL command syntax, the application cannot forbid this character as part of input validation. This name could be correctly written as the quoted string 'O''Brien', but there could be many other special characters requiring special treatment to effectively eliminate the vulnerability in a complete solution.

As a further defense, you should configure the SQL database such that the software registering students does not have the administrative privileges to delete any tables, which it does not need to do its job. (This is an example of the "Least Privilege" pattern from Chapter 4.)

Rather than "reinventing the wheel" with custom SQL sanitization code, the best practice is to use a library intended to construct SQL commands to handle these problems. If a trustworthy library isn't available, create test cases to ensure that attempted injection attacks are either rejected or safely processed, and that everything works for students with names like O'Brien.

Here are a few simple Python code snippets showing the wrong and then the right way to do this. First is the wrong way, using a mock-up of the Bobby Tables attack:

*vulnerable code*

```
import sqlite3
con = sqlite3.connect('school.db')
student_name = "Robert'); DROP TABLE Students;--"
# The WRONG way to query the database follows:
sql_stmt = "INSERT INTO Students (name) VALUES ('" + student_name + "');"
con.executescript(sql_stmt)
```

After creating a connection (con) to the SQL database, the code assigns the student's name to the variable student_name. Next, the code constructs the SQL INSERT statement by plugging the string student_name into the VALUES list and assigning that to sql_stmt. Finally, that string is executed as a SQL script.

The right way to handle this is to let the library insert parameters involving untrusted data, as shown in the following code snippet:

*fixed code*

```
import sqlite3
con = sqlite3.connect('school.db')
student_name = "Robert'); DROP TABLE Students;--"
# The RIGHT way to query the database follows:
con.execute("INSERT INTO Students (name) VALUES (?)", (student_name,))
```

In this implementation, the ? placeholder is filled in from the following tuple parameter consisting of the `student_name` string. Note that there are no quotes required within the `INSERT` statement string—that's all handled for you. This syntax avoids the injection and safely enters Bobby's strange name into the database.

There is a detail in this example that deserves clarification. Making the original exploit work requires the `executescript` library function, because `execute` only accepts a single statement, which serves as a kind of a defense against this particular attack. However, it would be a mistake to think that all injection attacks involve additional commands, and that this limitation confers much protection. For example, suppose there's another student with a different unpronounceable name at the school, `Robert', 'A+');--`. He and plain old Robert are both failing—but when his grades are recorded in another SQL table, his mark gets elevated to an A+. How so?

When plain old Robert's grades are submitted using the vulnerable code, the command enters the intended grade of an F as follows:

```
INSERT INTO Grades (name, grade) VALUES ('Robert', 'F');
```

But with the name `Robert', 'A+');--` that command becomes:

```
INSERT INTO Grades (name, grade) VALUES ('Robert', 'A+');--', 'F');
```

One final remark is in order about xkcd's "Little Bobby Tables" example that attentive readers may have noticed. Setting aside the absurdity of the premise, it is a remarkable coincidence that Bobby's parents were able to foresee the arbitrarily chosen specific name of the database table (`Students`). This is best explained by artistic license.

## Path Traversal

Filepath traversals are a common vulnerability closely related to injection attacks. Instead of escaping from quotation marks, as we saw in the previous section's examples, this attack escapes into parent directories to gain unexpected access to other parts of the filesystem. For example, to serve a collection of images, an implementation might collect image files in a directory named /server/data/image_store and then process requests for an image named X by fetching image data from the path formed from the (untrusted) input name X: /server/data/image_store/X.

The obvious attack would be requesting the name ../../secret/key, which would return the file /server/secret/key that should have been private. Recall that . (dot) is a special name for the current directory and .. (dot-dot) is the parent directory that allows traversal toward the filesystem root, as shown by this sequence of equivalent pathnames:

- /server/data/image_store/../../secret/key
- /server/data/../secret/key
- /server/secret/key

The best way to secure against this kind of attack is to limit the character set allowed in the input (X in our example). Often, input validation ensuring that the input is an alphanumeric string suffices to completely close the door. This works well because it excludes the troublesome file separator and parent directory forms needed to escape from the intended part of the filesystem.

However, sometimes that approach is too limiting. When it's necessary to handle arbitrary filenames this simple method is too restrictive, so you have more work to do (and it can get complicated because filesystems are complicated). Furthermore, if your code will run across different platforms, you need to be aware of possible filesystem differences (for example, the *nix path separator is a slash, but on Microsoft Windows it's a backslash).

Here is a simple example of a function that inspects input strings before using them as subpaths for accessing files in the directory that this Python code resides in (denoted by __file__). The idea is to provide access only to files in a certain directory or its subdirectories—but absolutely *not* to arbitrary files elsewhere. In the version shown here, the guard function safe_path checks the input for a leading slash (which goes to the filesystem root) or parent directory dot-dot and rejects inputs that contain these. To get this right you should work with paths using standard libraries, such as Python's os.path suite of functionality, rather than ad hoc string manipulation. But this alone isn't sufficient to ensure against breaking out of the intended directory:

*vulnerable code*
```python
def safe_path(path):
    """Checks that argument path is a safe file path. If not, returns None.
    If safe, returns the normalized absolute file path.
    """
    if path.startswith('/') or path.startswith('..'):
        return None
    base_dir = os.path.dirname(os.path.abspath(__file__))
    filepath = os.path.normpath(os.path.join(base_dir, path))
    return filepath
```

The remaining hole in this protection is that the path can name a valid directory, and then go up to the parent directory, and so on to break out. For example, since the current directory this sample code runs in is five levels below the root, the path ./../../../../../etc/passwd (with five dot-dots) resolves to the /etc/passwd file.

We could improve the string-based tests for invalid paths by rejecting any path containing dot-dot, but such an approach can be risky, since it's hard to be certain that we've anticipated all possible tricks and completely blocked them. Instead, there's a straightforward solution that relies on the os.path library, rather than constructing path strings with your own code:

```
def safe_path(path):
    """Checks that argument path is a safe file path. If not, returns None.
    If safe, returns the normalized absolute file path.
    """
    base_dir = os.path.dirname(os.path.abspath(__file__))
    filepath = os.path.normpath(os.path.join(base_dir, path))
    if base_dir != os.path.commonpath([base_dir, filepath]):
        return None
    return filepath
```

This protection you can take to the bank, and here's why. The base directory is a reliable path because there is no involvement of untrusted input: it's fully derived from values completely under the programmer's control. After joining with the input path string, that path gets normalized, which resolves any dot-dot parent references to produce an absolute path (filepath). Now we can check that the longest common subpath of these is the intended directory to which we want to restrict access.

## Regular Expressions

Efficient, flexible, and easy to use, a *regex* (regular expression) offers a remarkably wide range of functionality and is perhaps the most versatile tool we have for parsing text strings. They're generally faster (both to code and execute) than ad hoc code, and more reliable. Regex libraries compile state tables that an interpreter (a finite state machine or similar automaton) executes to match against a string.

Even if your regex is correctly constructed it can cause security issues, as some regular expressions are prone to excessive execution times, and if attackers can trigger these they can cause a serious DoS. Specifically, execution time can balloon if the regex incurs *backtracking*—that is, when it scans forward a long way, then needs to go back and rescan over and over to find a match. The security danger generally results from allowing untrusted inputs to specify the regex; or, if the code already contains a backtracking regex, from an untrusted input that supplies a long worst-case string that maximizes the computational effort.

A backtracking regex can look innocuous, as an example will demonstrate. The following Python code takes more than three seconds to run on my modest Raspberry Pi Model 4B. Your processor is likely much faster, but since each D added to the 24 in the example doubles the running time, it isn't hard to lock up any processor with a slightly longer string:

```
import re
print(re.match(r'(D+)+$', 'DDDDDDDDDDDDDDDDDDDDDDDD!'))
```

The danger of excessive runtime exists with any kind of parsing of untrusted inputs, in cases where backtracking or other nonlinear computations can blow up. In the next section you'll see an XML entity example along these lines, and there are many more.

The best way to mitigate these issues depends on the specific computation, but there are several general approaches to countering these attacks. Avoid letting untrusted inputs influence computations that have the potential to blow up. In the case of regular expressions, don't let untrusted inputs define the regex, avoid backtracking if possible, and limit the length of the string that the regex matches against. Figure out what the worst-case computation could be, and then test it to ensure that it's not excessively slow.

### Dangers of XML

XML is one of the most popular ways to represent structured data, as it is powerful as well as human-readable. However, you should be aware that the power of XML can also be weaponized. There are two major ways that untrusted XML can cause harm using XML entities.

*XML entity declarations* are a relatively obscure feature, and unfortunately, attackers have been creative in finding ways of abusing these. In the example that follows, a named entity big1 is defined as a four-character string. Another named entity, big2, is defined as eight instances of big1 (a total of 32 characters), and big3 is eight more of those, and so on. By the time you get up to big7, you're dealing with a megabyte of data, and it's easy to go on up from there. This example concocts an 8-megabyte chunk of XML. As you can see, you would need to add only a few lines to go into the gigabytes:

```
<!DOCTYPE dtd[
  <!ENTITY big1 "big!">
  <!ENTITY big2 "&big1;&big1;&big1;&big1;&big1;&big1;&big1;&big1;">
  <!ENTITY big3 "&big2;&big2;&big2;&big2;&big2;&big2;&big2;&big2;">
  <!ENTITY big4 "&big3;&big3;&big3;&big3;&big3;&big3;&big3;&big3;">
  <!ENTITY big5 "&big4;&big4;&big4;&big4;&big4;&big4;&big4;&big4;">
  <!ENTITY big6 "&big5;&big5;&big5;&big5;&big5;&big5;&big5;&big5;">
  <!ENTITY big7 "&big6;&big6;&big6;&big6;&big6;&big6;&big6;&big6;">
]>
<mega>&big7;&big7;&big7;&big7;&big7;&big7;&big7;&big7;</mega>
```

More tricks are possible with external entity declarations. Consider the following:

```
<!ENTITY snoop SYSTEM "file:///etc/passwd>" >
```

This does exactly what you would think: reads the password file and makes its contents available wherever &snoop; appears in the XML henceforth. If the attacker can present this as XML and then see the result of the entity expansion, they can disclose the contents of any file they can name.

Your first line of defense against these sorts of problems will be keeping untrusted inputs out of any XML that your code processes. Some modern libraries check for just this kind of attack, but you should check to be sure if you need to rely on it. If you don't need XML external entities, then protect against this sort of attack by excluding them from inputs, or by disabling the processing of such declarations.

## Mitigating Injection Attacks

Just as various kinds of injection attacks rely on the common trick of using untrusted inputs to influence statements or commands that execute in the context of the application, mitigations for these issues also have common threads, though the details do vary. Input validation is always a good first line of defense, but depending on what allowable inputs may consist of, that alone is not necessarily enough.

Avoid attempting to insert untrusted data into constructed strings for execution, for instance as commands. Modern libraries for SQL and other functionality susceptible to injection attacks should provide helper functions that allow you to pass in data separately from the command. These functions handle quoting, escaping, or whatever it takes to safely perform the intended operation for all inputs. I recommend checking for a specific note about security in the library's documentation, as there do exist slipshod implementations that just slap strings together and will be liable to injection attacks under the facade of the API. When in doubt, a security test case (see Chapter 12) is a good way to sanity-check this.

If you cannot, or will not, use a secure library—although, again, I caution against the slippery slope of "what could possibly go wrong?" thinking—first consider finding an alternative way to avoid the risk of injection. Instead of constructing a *nix ls command to enumerate the contents of a directory, use a system call. The reasoning behind this is clear: all that readdir(3) can possibly do is return directory entry information; by contrast, invoking a shell command could potentially do just about anything.

Using the filesystem as a homemade datastore may be the quickest solution in some cases, but I can hardly recommend it as a secure approach. If you insist on doing it the risky way, don't underestimate the work required to anticipate and then block all potential attacks in order to fully secure it. Input validation is your friend here; if you can constrain the string to a safe character set (for example, names consisting only of ASCII alphanumerics), then you may be all right. As an additional layer of defense, study the syntax of the command or statement you are forming and be sure to apply all the necessary quoting or escaping to ensure nothing goes wrong. It's worth reading the applicable specifications carefully, as there may be obscure forms you are unaware of.

The good news is that the dangerous operations where injections become a risk are often easy to scan for in source code. Check that SQL commands are safely constructed using parameters, rather than as ad hoc strings. For shell command injections, watch for uses of exec(3) and its variants, and be sure to properly quote command arguments (Python provides shlex.quote for exactly this purpose). In JavaScript, review uses of eval and either safely restrict them or consider not using it when untrusted inputs could possibly influence the constructed expression.

This chapter covered a number of injection attacks and related common vulnerabilities, but injection is a very flexible method that can appear in many guises. In the following chapter we will see it again (twice), in the context of web vulnerabilities.

# 11

## WEB SECURITY

*When the words appeared, everyone said they were a miracle.*
*But nobody pointed out that the web itself is a miracle.*
—E. B. White (from *Charlotte's Web*)

The enormous success of the World Wide Web is in no small part due to the remarkable fact (today, completely taken for granted) that countless millions of people use it routinely without having the slightest understanding of how it works. This singular achievement for such a complex amalgam of technology is at once a blessing and a curse. Undoubtedly, the web's ease of use has sustained widespread growth. On the flip side, securing a global network of independent digital services, used by countless millions of oblivious humans at the endpoints, is indeed an extremely difficult task. Security is perhaps the hardest part of this big hard problem.

One complicating factor that makes security especially challenging is that the early web was rather naively designed, without much consideration to security. As a result, the modern web is the product of a long evolution of standards, muddled by the competitive "browser wars" and backward compatibility restrictions. In short, the web is the most extreme instance of after-the-fact, "bolt-on security" in history—though what we have, well over a quarter of a century after its invention, is getting respectable.

Yet while the modern web can be made secure, its tangled history means that it's also quite fragile and filled with many "security and privacy infelicities," as the authors of RFC 6265, a spec for web cookies, so colorfully put it. Software professionals need to understand all of this so as not to run afoul of these issues when building for the web. Tiny missteps easily create vulnerabilities. Given the "Wild West" nature of the internet, bad actors have the freedom to easily probe how websites work, as well as anonymously muck around looking for openings to attack.

This chapter focuses on the fundamentals of how the web security model evolved, and the right and wrong ways to use it. Vulnerabilities arise from the details, and there are so many things a secure website must get exactly right. We'll cover all of the basics of web security, beginning with a plea to build on top of a secure framework that handles the intricacies for you. From there, we will see how secure communication (HTTPS), proper use of the HTTP protocol (including cookies), and the Same Origin Policy combine to keep websites safe. Finally, we'll cover two of the major vulnerabilities specific to the web (XSS and CSRF) and discuss a number of other mitigations that, when combined, go a long way toward securing a modern web server. Nonetheless, this chapter is by no means a complete compendium of web security, the specifics of which are voluminous and evolve rapidly.

The goal here is to convey a broad-brush sense of the major common pitfalls so you will recognize and know how to deal with them. Web applications are also subject to the many other vulnerabilities covered elsewhere in this book: the focus in this chapter should not be interpreted to suggest that these are the only potential security concerns.

**NOTE** *The following discussion assumes that you are minimally familiar with the basics of the web: the client/server model; the basics of HTTP and HTML, including cookies; a little CSS; JavaScript at the "101" level; and the Document Object Model. Readers less familiar with the web should still be able to follow along for the most part, perhaps with a little supplemental reading to fill in any gaps.*

## Build on a Framework

> *Use design as a framework to bring order out of chaos.*
>
> —Nita Leland

Thanks to modern web development tools, building a website has become nearly as easy as using one. My top recommendations for building a secure website are to rely on a high-quality framework, never override the safeguards it provides, and let competent experts handle all the messy details.

A reliance on a solid framework should insulate you from the kinds of vulnerabilities covered in the following sections, but it's still valuable to understand exactly what frameworks do and don't do so you can use them effectively. It's also critical that you choose a secure framework from the start, because your code will heavily depend on it, making it painful to switch later if it lets you down. How do you know if a web framework is really secure? It boils down to trust—both in the good intentions and the expertise of its makers.

Web frameworks rise and fall in popularity and buzz almost as fast as Parisian fashion, and your choice will depend on many factors, so I won't attempt to make recommendations. However, I can suggest general guidelines to consider for your own evaluation:

- Choose a framework produced by a trustworthy organization or team that actively develops and maintains it in order to keep up with constantly changing web technologies and practices.

- Look for an explicit security declaration in the documentation. If you don't find one, I would disqualify the framework.

- Research past performance: the framework doesn't need a perfect record, but slow responses or ongoing patterns of problems are red flags.

- Build a small prototype and check the resulting HTML for proper escaping and quoting (using inputs like the ones in this chapter's examples).

- Build a simple test bed to experiment with basic XSS and CSRF attacks, as explained later in this chapter.

## The Web Security Model

*I'm kind of glad the web is sort of totally anarchic. That's fine with me.*

—Roger Ebert

The web is a client/server technology, and understanding its security model requires considering both of those perspectives at once. Doing so gets interesting quickly, since the security interests of the two parties are often in contention, especially given the threat of potential attackers intruding via the internet.

Consider the typical online shopping website. The security principles at play here apply, more or less, to all kinds of web activity. In order to do business, the merchant and customers must trust each other to a certain degree, and in the vast majority of cases that does actually happen. Nonetheless, there are inevitably a few bad actors out there, so websites cannot fully trust every client, and vice versa. The following points highlight some of the nuances of the tentative mutual trust between the merchant and customer.

Here are some the merchant's basic requirements:

- Other websites should be unable to interfere with my customer interactions.

- I want to minimize my competitors' ability to scrape my product and inventory details while helpfully informing legit customers.

- Customers shouldn't be able to manipulate prices or order products not in stock.

Here are some of the customer's:

- I require assurance that the website I'm accessing is authentic.
- I demand confidence that online payments are secure.
- I expect the merchant to keep my shopping activities private.

Clearly, both parties must remain vigilant for the web to work well. That said, the customer expects many things from the merchant. Solving the hard problem of educating confused or gullible customers is out of scope here, if that's even possible. Instead, in web security, we focus on securing a website from the merchant's perspective. The web only works if servers do a good job of providing that security, making it possible for the honest end user to even have a chance at a secure web experience. Merchants must not only decide how much they can trust customers, but also intuit how much customers will likely trust them.

Another odd aspect of the web's security model is the role of the client browser. Designing web services proves challenging because they need to interact with browsers that they have absolutely no control over. A malevolent client could easily use a modified browser capable of anything. Alternatively, a careless client could well be running an ancient browser full of security holes. Even if a web server attempts to limit the types of browsers clients use to certain versions, remember that the browser could easily misidentify itself to get around such restrictions. The saving grace is that honest clients want to use secure browsers and update them regularly, because it protects their own interests. Most importantly, so long as the server remains secure, one malicious client cannot interfere with the service that other clients receive.

Web servers overtrusting potentially untrustworthy client browsers is at the root of many web security vulnerabilities. I stress this point, at the risk of repetition, because it is so easily and often forgotten (as I will explain throughout the chapter).

## The HTTP Protocol

*Anyone who considers protocol unimportant has never dealt with a cat.*

—Robert A. Heinlein

The HTTP protocol itself is at the heart of the web, so before we dig into web security, it's worth briefly reviewing how it works. This hyper-simplified explanation serves as a conceptual framework for the rest of the security discussion, and we'll focus on the parts where security enters the picture. For many, web browsing has become so commonplace in daily life that it's worth stepping back and thinking through all the steps of the process— many of which we hardly notice, as modern processors and networks routinely provide blazing-fast responses.

Web browsing always begins with a uniform resource locator (URL). The following example shows its parts:

```
http://www.example.com/page.html?query=value#fragment
```

The *scheme* precedes the colon, and specifies the protocol (here, http) the browser must use to request the desired resource. IP-based protocols begin with // followed by the *hostname*, which for web pages is the domain name of the web server (in this case, www.example.com). The rest is all optional: the / followed by the *path*, the ? followed by the *query*, and the # followed by the *fragment*. The path specifies which web page the browser is requesting. The query allows the web page content to be parameterized. For example, when searching for something on the web, the URL path for results might be /search?q=something. The fragment names a secondary resource within the page, often an anchor as the destination of a link. In summary, the URL specifies how and where to request the content, the specific page on the site, query parameters to customize the page, and a way to name a particular part of the page.

Your web browser has a lot of work to do in order to display the web page when you give it a URL. First, it queries the Domain Name System (DNS) for the IP address of the hostname in order to know where to send the request. The request contains the URL path and other parameters encoded as *request headers* (including any cookies, the user's preferred language, and so on) sent to the web server host. The server sends back a response containing a status code and *response headers* (which may set cookies, and many other things), followed by the content body that consists of the HTML for the web page. For all embedded resources, such as scripts, images, and so forth, this same request/response process repeats until the content is fully loaded and displayed.

Now let's look at what web servers must do correctly in order to remain secure. One important detail not yet mentioned is that the request specifies the *HTTP verb*. For our purposes here, we will focus on just the two most common verbs. *GET* requests content from the server. By contrast, clients use the *POST* verb to send form submissions or file uploads. GET requests are explicitly not state-changing, whereas POST requests intend to change the state of the server. Respecting this semantic distinction is important, as will be seen when we cover CSRF attacks. For now, keep in mind that even though the client specifies the request verb to use, the server is the one that decides what to do with it. Additionally, by offering hyperlinks and forms on its pages, the server in effect guides the client to make subsequent GET or POST requests.

Sticklers will point out that one certainly can run a server that changes state in response to GET verb requests and, perversely, refuses to change state for form POST submissions. But if you strictly follow the standard rules, it is vastly easier to make your server secure. Think of it this way: yes, it is possible to climb over fences marked "Keep Out!" at a cliff and walk along the edge of the precipice without falling, but doing so needlessly puts your security in jeopardy.

A related security no-no is embedding sensitive data in a URL; instead, use form POST requests to send the data to the server. Otherwise, the REFERER header may disclose the URL of the web page that led to the request, exposing the data. For example, clicking a link on a web page with the URL https://example.com?param=SECRET navigates to the link destination using a GET request with a REFERER header containing the URL which includes SECRET, thereby leaking the secret data. In addition, logs or diagnostic messages risk disclosing the data contained in URLs. While servers can use the Referrer-Policy header to block this, they must depend on the client honoring it—hardly a perfect solution. (The REFERER header is indeed misspelled in the spec, so we're stuck with that, but the policy name is correctly spelled.)

One easy mistake to make is including usernames in URLs. Even an opaque identifier, such as the hash of a username, leaks information, in that it potentially allows an eavesdropper to match two separately observed URLs and infer that they refer to the same user.

## Digital Certificates and HTTPS

*If what is communicated is false, it can hardly be called communication.*

—Benjamin Mays

The first challenge for secure web browsing is reliably communicating with the correct server. To do this, you must know the correct URL and query a DNS service that provides the right IP address. If the network routes and transmits the request correctly, it should reach the intended server. That's a lot of factors to get right, and a large attack surface: bad actors could interfere with the DNS lookup, the routing, or the data on the wire at any point along the route. Should the request be diverted to a malicious server, the user might never realize it; it isn't hard to put up a look-alike website that would easily fool just about anyone.

The HTTPS protocol (also called *HTTP over TLS/SSL*) is tailor-made to mitigate these threats. HTTPS secures the web using many of the techniques covered in Chapter 5. It provides a secure end-to-end tamper-proof encrypted channel, as well as assurance to the client that the intended server is really at the other end of that channel. Think of the secure channel as a tamper-evident pipeline for data that confirms the server's identity. An eavesdropping attacker could possibly see encrypted data, but without the secret key, it's indistinguishable from random bits. An attacker may be able to tamper with the data on an unprotected network, but if HTTPS is used, any tampering will always be detected. Attackers may be able to prevent communication, for example by physically cutting a cable, but you are assured that bogus data will never get through.

Nobody ever disputed the need for HTTPS to secure financial transactions on the web, but major sites delayed going fully HTTPS for far too long. (For example, Facebook only did so in 2013.) When first implemented, the protocol had subtle flaws, and the necessary computations were too heavyweight for the hardware at the time to justify widespread adoption. The good news is that, over time, developers fixed the bugs and optimized the protocol. Thanks to protocol optimizations, more efficient crypto algorithms, and faster processors, HTTPS is fast, robust, and rapidly approaching ubiquity today. It's widely used to protect private data communications, but even for a website only serving public information, HTTPS is important to ensure authenticity and strong integrity. In other words, it provides assurance that the client is communicating with the bona fide server named in the request URL, and that data transmitted between them has not been snooped on or tampered with. Today, it's difficult to think of any good reason *not* to configure a website to use HTTPS exclusively. That said, there are still plenty of non-secure HTTP websites out there. If you use them, keep in mind that the nice security properties of HTTPS do not apply, and take appropriate precautions.

Understanding precisely what HTTPS does (and does not do) to secure the client/server interaction is critical in order to grasp its value, how it helps, and what it can and cannot change. In addition to assuring server authenticity and the confidentiality and integrity of web requests and response content, the secure channel protects the URL path (in the first line of the request headers—for example, GET /path/page.html?query=secret#fragment), preventing anyone who's snooping from seeing what page of the website the client requested. (HTTPS can optionally also authenticate the client to the server.) However, the HTTPS traffic itself is still observable over the network, and because the IP addresses of the endpoints are unprotected, eavesdroppers can often deduce the identity of the server.

Table 11-1 compares of the security attributes of HTTP and HTTPS, in terms of the capabilities of an attacker lurking between the two endpoints of a client/server communication.

**Table 11-1:** HTTP vs. HTTPS Security Attributes

| Can an attacker. . . | HTTP | HTTPS |
| --- | --- | --- |
| See web traffic between client/server endpoints? | Yes | Yes |
| Identify the IP addresses of both client and server? | Yes | Yes |
| Deduce the web server's identity? | Yes | Sometimes (see note below) |
| See what page within the site is requested? | Yes | No (in encrypted headers) |
| See the web page content and the body of POSTs? | Yes | No (encrypted) |
| See the headers (including cookies) and URL (including the query portion)? | Yes | No |
| Tamper with the URL, headers, or content? | Yes | No |

**NOTE** *The reverse DNS lookup of a web server's IP address reveals its domain name. When multiple web servers share an IP address, the SNI (Server Name Indication) is visible, but the ESNI (Encrypted SNI) is protected.*

As HTTPS and the technology environment matured, the last obstacle to broad adoption was the overhead of getting server certificates. Whereas larger companies could afford the fees that trusted certificate authorities charged and had staff to manage the renewal process, the owners of smaller websites balked at the extra cost and administrative overhead. By 2015, HTTPS was mature and most internet-connected hardware operated fast enough to handle it, and with awareness of the importance of web privacy growing quickly, the internet community was approaching a consensus that it needed to secure the majority of web traffic. The lack of free and simple server certificate availability proved the biggest remaining obstacle.

Thanks to strong promotion by the wonderful Electronic Frontier Foundation and sponsorship from a wide range of industry companies, Let's Encrypt, a product of the nonprofit Internet Security Research Group, offers the world a free, automated, and open certificate authority. It provides Domain Validation (DV) certificates, free of charge, to any website owner. Here's a simplified explanation of how Let's Encrypt works. Keep in mind that the following process is automated in practice:

1.  Identify yourself to Let's Encrypt by generating a key pair and sending the public key.
2.  Query Let's Encrypt, asking what you need to do to prove that you control the domain.
3.  Let's Encrypt issues a challenge, such as provisioning a specified DNS record for the domain.
4.  You satisfy the challenge by creating the requested DNS record and ask Let's Encrypt to verify what you did.
5.  Once verified, the private key belonging to the generated key pair is authorized for the domain by Let's Encrypt.
6.  Now you can request a new certificate by sending Let's Encrypt a request signed by the authorized private key.

Let's Encrypt issues 90-day DV certificates and provides a "certbot" to handle automatic renewals. With automatically renewable certificates available as a free service, secure web serving today has widely become a turnkey solution at no additional cost. HTTPS comprised more than 85 percent of web traffic in 2020, more than double the 40 percent level of 2016, when Let's Encrypt launched.

A DV certificate is usually all you need to prove the identity of your website. DV certificates simply assert the authenticated web server's domain name, and nothing more. That is, the example.com certificate is only ever issued to the owner of the example.com web server. By contrast, certificates offering higher levels of trust, such as Organization Validation (OV) and Extended Validation (EV) certificates, authenticate not only the identity of the website but also, to some extent, the owner's identity and reputation. However, with the proliferation of free DV certificates, it's increasingly unclear if the other kinds will remain viable. Few users care about such distinctions of trust, and the technical as well as legal nuances of OV and EV certificates are subtle. Their precise benefits are challenging to grasp unless (and even if) you are a lawyer.

Once you've set up your web server to use the HTTPS protocol with a certificate, you must make sure it *always* uses HTTPS. To ensure this, you must reject *downgrade attacks*, which attempt to force the communication to occur with weak encryption or without encryption. These attacks work in two ways. In the simplest case, the attacker tries changing an HTTPS request to HTTP (which can be snooped and tampered with), and a poorly configured web server might be tricked into complying. The other method exploits the HTTPS protocol options that let the two parties negotiate *cipher suites* for the encrypted channel. For example, the server may be able to "speak" one set of crypto "dialects," and the client might "speak" a different set, so up front, they need to agree on one that's in both their repertoires. This process opens the door to an attacker, who could trick both parties into selecting an insecure choice that compromises security.

The best defense is to ensure your HTTPS configuration only operates with secure modern cryptographic algorithms. Judging exactly which cipher suites are secure is highly technical and best left to cryptographers. You must also strike a balance to avoid excluding, or degrading the experience of, older and less powerful clients. If you don't have access to reliable expert advice, you can look at what major trustworthy websites do and follow that. Simply assuming that the default configuration will be secure forever is a recipe for failure.

Mitigate such attacks by always redirecting HTTP to HTTPS, as well as restricting web cookies to HTTPS only. Include the `Strict-Transport-Security` directive in your response HTTP headers so the browser knows that the website always uses HTTPS. For an HTTPS web page to be fully secure, it must be pure HTTPS. This means all content on the server should use HTTPS, as should all scripts, images, fonts, CSS, and other referenced resources. Failing to take all the necessary precautions weakens the security protection.

### The Same Origin Policy

> *Doubt is the origin of wisdom.*
>
> —Rene Descartes

Browsers isolate resources—typically windows or tabs—from different websites so they can't interfere with each other. Known as the *Same Origin Policy (SOP)*, the rule allows interaction between resources only if their host domain names and port numbers match. The Same Origin Policy dates back to the early days of the web and became necessary with the advent of JavaScript. Web script interacts with web pages via the *Document Object Model (DOM)*, a structured tree of objects that correspond to browser windows and their contents. It didn't take a security expert to see that if any web page could use script to `window.open` any other site, and programmatically do anything it wanted with the content, countless problems would ensue. The first restrictions that were implemented—including fixes for a number of tricky ways people found of getting around them over the years—evolved into today's Same Origin Policy.

The Same Origin Policy applies to script and cookies (with a few extra twists), which both can potentially leak data between independent websites. However, web pages can include images and other content, such as web ads, from other websites. This is safely allowed, since these cannot access the content of the window they appear in.

Although the Same Origin Policy prevents script in pages from other websites from *reaching in*, web pages can always choose to *reach out* to different websites if they wish, pulling their content into the window. It's quite common for a web page to include content from other websites, to display images, to load scripts or CSS, and so forth. Including any content from other websites is an important trust decision; however, because it makes the web page vulnerable to malicious content that may originate there.

## Web Cookies

*When the going gets tough, the tough make cookies.*

—Erma Bombeck

*Cookies* are small data strings that the server asks the client to store on its behalf and then provide back to it with subsequent requests. This clever innovation allows developers to easily customize web pages for a particular client. The server response may set named cookies to some value. Then, until the cookies expire, the client browser sends the cookies applicable to a given page in subsequent requests. Since the client retains its own cookies, the server doesn't necessarily need to identify the client to bind cookie values to it, so the mechanism is potentially privacy-preserving.

Here's a simple analogy: if I run a store and want to count how many times each customer visits, an easy way would be for me to give each customer a slip of paper with "1" on it and ask them to bring it back the next time they come. Then, each time a customer returns, I take their paper, add one to the number on it, and give it back. So long as customers comply, I won't have to do any bookkeeping or even remember their names to keep accurate tallies.

We use cookies for all manner of things on the web, tracking users being among the most controversial. Cookies often establish secure sessions so the server can reliably tell all of its clients apart. Generating a unique *session cookie* for each new client allows the server to identify the client from the cookie appearing in a request.

While any client could tamper with its own cookies and pretend to be a different session, if the session cookie is properly designed, the client shouldn't be able to forge a valid session cookie. Additionally, clients could send copies of their cookies to another party, but in doing so they would only harm their own privacy. That behavior doesn't threaten innocent users and is tantamount to sharing one's password.

Consider a hypothetical online shopping website that stores the current contents of a customer's shopping cart in cookies as a list of items and the total cost. There is nothing to stop a clever and unethical shopper from modifying the local cookie store. For instance, they could change the price of a valuable load of merchandise to a paltry sum. This does not mean that cookies are useless; cookies could be used to remember the customer's preferences, favorite items, or other details, and tampering with these wouldn't hurt the merchant. It just means that you should always use client storage on a "trust but verify" basis. Go ahead and store item costs and the cart total as cookies if that's useful, but before accepting the transaction, be certain to validate the cost of each item on the server side, and reject any data that's been tampered with. This example makes the problem plain as day. However, other forms of the same trust mistake are more subtle, and attackers frequently exploit this sort of vulnerability.

Now let's look at this same example from the client's perspective. When two people use an online shopping website and browse to the same /mycart URL, they each see different shopping carts because they have distinct sessions. Usually, unique cookies establish independent anonymous sessions, or, for logged-in users, identify specific accounts.

Servers set session cookies with a time of expiration, but since they cannot always rely on the client to respect that wish, they must also enforce limits on the validity of session cookies that need renewing. (From the user's perspective, this expiration looks like being asked to log in again after a period of inactivity.)

Cookies are subject to the Same Origin Policy, with explicit provisions for sharing between subdomains. This means that cookies set by example.com are visible to the subdomains cat.example.com and dog.example.com, but cookies set on those respective subdomains are isolated from each other. Also, though subdomains can see cookies set by parent domains, they cannot modify them. By analogy, state governments rely on national-level credentials such as passports, but may not issue them. Within a domain, cookies may be further scoped by path as well (but this is not a strong security mechanism). Table 11-2 illustrates these rules in detail. In addition, cookies may specify a Domain attribute for explicit control.

**Table 11-2:** Cookie Sharing Under Same Origin Policy (SOP) with Subdomains

| Can the web pages served by the hosts below. . . | . . .see the cookies set for these hosts? | | | |
| --- | --- | --- | --- | --- |
| | *example.com* | *dog.example.com* | *cat.example.com* | *example.org* |
| *example.com* | Yes (same domain) | No (subdomain) | No (subdomain) | No (SOP) |
| *dog.example.com* | Yes (parent domain) | Yes (same domain) | No (sibling domain) | No (SOP) |
| *cat.example.com* | Yes (parent domain) | No (sibling domain) | Yes (same domain) | No (SOP) |
| *example.org* | No (SOP) | No (SOP) | No (SOP) | Yes (same domain) |

Script nominally has access to cookies via the DOM, but this convenience would give malicious script that manages to run in a web page an opening to steal the cookies, so it's best to block script access by specifying the httponly cookie attribute. HTTPS websites should also apply the secure attribute to direct the client to only send cookies over secure channels. Unfortunately, due to legacy constraints too involved to cover here, integrity and availability issues remain even when you use both of these attributes (see RFC 6265 for the gory details). I mention this not only as a caveat, but also as a great example of a repeated pattern in web security; the tension between backward compatibility and modern secure usage results in compromise solutions that illustrate why, if security isn't baked in from the start, it often proves to be elusive.

HTML5 has added numerous extensions to the security model. A prime example is Cross-Origin Resource Sharing (CORS), which allows selective loosening of Same Origin Policy restrictions to enable data access by other trusted websites. Browsers additionally provide the Web Storage API, a more modern client-side storage capability for web apps that's also subject to the Same Origin Policy. These newer features are much better designed from a security standpoint, but still are not a complete substitute for cookies.

# Common Web Vulnerabilities

*Websites should look good from the inside and out.*

—Paul Cookson

Now that we've surveyed the major security highlights of website construction and use, it's time to talk about specific vulnerabilities that commonly arise. Web servers are liable to all kinds of security vulnerabilities, including many of those covered elsewhere in this book, but in this chapter we'll focus on security issues specific to the web. The preceding sections explained the web security model, including a lot of potential ways to avoid weakening security and useful features that help better secure your web presence. Even assuming you did all of that right, this section covers still more ways web servers can get it wrong and be vulnerable.

The first category of web vulnerability, and likely the most common, is cross-site scripting (XSS). The other vulnerability we'll cover here is probably my favorite due to its subtlety: cross-site request forgery (CSRF).

## Cross-Site Scripting

*I don't let myself "surf" on the Web, or I would probably drown.*

—Aubrey Plaza

The isolation that the Same Origin Policy provides is fundamental to building secure websites, but this protection breaks easily if we don't take necessary precautions. *Cross-site scripting (XSS)* is a web-specific injection attack where malicious input alters the behavior of a website, typically resulting in running unauthorized script.

Let's consider a simple example to see how this works and why it's essential to protect against. The attack usually begins with the innocent user already logged in to a trusted website. The user then opens another window or tab and goes surfing, or perhaps unwisely clicks a link in an email, browsing to an attacking site. The attacker typically aims to commandeer the user's authenticated state with the target site. They can do so even without a tab open to the victim site, so long as the cookies are present (which is why it's good practice to log out of your banking website when you're done). Let's look at what an XSS vulnerability in a victim site looks like, exactly how to exploit it, and finally, how to fix it.

Suppose that for some reason a certain page of the victim website (www.example.com) wants to render a line of text in several different colors. Instead of building separate pages, all identical except for the color of that line, the developer chooses to specify the desired color in the URL query parameter. For example, the URL for the version of the web page with a line of green text would be:

```
https://www.example.com/page?color=green
```

The server then inserts the highlighted query parameter into the following HTML fragment:

```
<h1 style="color:green">This is colorful text.</h1>
```

This works fine if used properly, which is exactly why these flaws are easily overlooked. Seeing the root of the problem requires looking at the server-side Python code responsible for handling this task (as well as some devious thinking):

*vulnerable code*
```
query_params = urllib.parse.parse_qs(self.parts.query)
color = query_params.get('color', ['black'])[0]
h = '<h1 style="color:%s">This is colorful text.</h1>' % color
```

The first line parses the URL query string (the part after the question mark). The next line extracts the color parameter, or defaults to black if it's unspecified. The last line constructs the HTML fragment that displays text with the corresponding font color, using inline styling for the heading level 1 tag (<h1>). The variable h then forms part of the HTML response that comprises the web page.

You can find the XSS vulnerability in that last line. There, the programmer has created a path from the contents of the URL (which, on the internet, anyone can send to the server) that leads directly into the HTML content served to the client. This is the familiar pattern of injection attacks from Chapter 10, and constitutes an unprotected trust boundary crossing, because the parameter input string is now inside the web page HTML contents. This condition alone is enough to raise red flags, but to see the full dimensions of this XSS vulnerability, let's try exploiting it.

An attack requires a little imagination. Refer back to the <h1> HTML tag and consider other possible substitutions for the highlighted color name. Think outside the box, or in this case, outside the double quoted string style="color:green". Or can you break out of the <h1> tag entirely? Here's a URL that illustrates what I mean by "break out":

```
https://www.example.com/page?color=orange"><SCRIPT>alert("Gotcha!")</SCRIPT><span%20id="dummy
```

All of that highlighted stuff gets dutifully inserted into the <h1> HTML tag as before, producing a vastly different result.

In the actual HTML, this code would appear as a single line, but for legibility I've indented it here to show how it's parsed:

```
<h1 style="color:orange">
  <SCRIPT>alert("Gotcha!")</SCRIPT>
  <span id="dummy">This is colorful text.
</h1>
```

The new `<h1>` tag is syntactic, specifying an orange color. However, note that the attacker's URL parameter value supplied the closing angle bracket. This wasn't done just to be nice: the attacker needed to close the `<h1>` tag in order to make a well-formed `<SCRIPT>` tag and inject it into the HTML, ensuring that the script would run. In this case, the script opens an alert dialog—a harmless but unmistakable proof of the exploit. After the closing `</SCRIPT>` tag, the rest of the injection is just filler to obscure that tampering occurred. The new `<span>` tag has an `id` attribute merely so the following double quote and closing angle bracket will appear as part of the `<span>` tag. Browsers routinely supply closing `</span>` tags if missing, so the exploited page is well-formed HTML, making the modifications invisible to the user (unless they inspect the HTML source).

To actually attack victims remotely, the attacker has more work to do in order to get people to browse to the malicious URL. Attacks like this generally only work when the user is already authenticated to the target website—that is, when valid login session cookies exist. Otherwise, the attacker might as well type the URL into their own browser. What they're after is your website session, which shows your bank balance or your private documents. A serious attacker-defined script would immediately load additional script, and then proceed to exfiltrate data, or make unauthorized transactions in the user's context.

XSS vulnerabilities aren't hard for attackers to discover, since they can easily view a web page's content to see the inner workings of the HTML. (To be precise, they can't see code on the server, but by trying URLs and observing the resulting web pages, it isn't hard to make useful inferences about how it works.) Once they notice an injection from the URL into a web page, they can then perform a quick test, like the example shown here, to check if the server is vulnerable to XSS. Moreover, once they have confirmed that HTML metacharacters, such as angle brackets and quotes, flow through from the URL query parameter (or perhaps another attack surface) into the resultant web page, they can view the page's source code and tweak their attempts until they hit the jackpot.

There are several kinds of XSS attacks. This chapter's example is a *reflected XSS* attack, because it is initiated via an HTTP request and expressed in the immediate server response. A related form, the *stored XSS* attack, involves two requests. First, the attacker somehow manages to store malicious data, either on the server or in client-side storage. Once that's set up, a following request tricks the web server into injecting the stored data into a subsequent request, completing the attack. Stored XSS attacks can work across different clients.

For example, on a blog, if the attacker can post a comment that causes XSS in the rendering of comments, then subsequent users viewing the web page will get the malicious script.

A third attack form, called *DOM-based XSS*, uses the HTML DOM as the source of the malicious injection, but otherwise works much the same. Categories aside, the bottom line is that all of these vulnerabilities derive from injecting untrusted data that the web server allows to flow into the web page, introducing malicious script or other harmful content.

A secure web framework should have XSS protection built in, in which case you should be safe so long as you stay within the framework. As with any injection vulnerability, the defense involves either avoiding any chance for untrusted input to flow into a web page and potentially break out, or performing input validation to ensure that inputs will be handled safely. In the colored text example, the former technique could be implemented by simply serving named web pages (/green-page and /blue-page, for example) without the tricky query parameter. Alternatively, with a color parameter in the URL, you could constrain the query parameter value to be in an allowlist.

## Cross-Site Request Forgery

*One cannot separate the spider web's form from the way in which it originated.*

—Neri Oxman

*Cross-site request forgery* (*CSRF*, or sometimes *XSRF*) is an attack on a fundamental limitation in the Same Origin Policy. The vulnerability that these attacks exploit is conceptually simple but extremely subtle, so exactly where the problem lies, and how to fix it, can be hard to see at first. Web frameworks should provide CSRF protection, but a strong understanding of the underlying issue is still valuable so you can confirm that it works and be sure not to interfere with the mechanism.

Websites certainly can and often do include content, such as images from different websites, obtained via HTTP GET. The Same Origin Policy allows these requests while isolating the content, so the image data doesn't leak between different websites from different domains. For example, site X can include on its page an image from site Y; the user sees the embedded image as part of the page, but site X itself cannot "see" the image, because the browser blocks script access to image data via the DOM.

But the Same Origin Policy works the same for POST as it does for GET, and POST requests can modify a site's state. Here's exactly what happens: the browser allows site X to submit a form to site Y, and includes the Y cookies, too. The browser ensures that the response from site Y is completely isolated from site X. The threat is that a POST can modify data on the Y server, which X shouldn't be able to do, and *by design*, any website can POST to any other. Since browsers facilitate these unauthorized requests, web developers must explicitly defend against these attempts to modify data on the server.

A simple attack scenario will illustrate what CSRF vulnerabilities look like, how to exploit them, and in turn, how to defend against attack. Consider a social website Y, with many users who each have accounts. Site

Y is running a poll, and each user gets one vote. The site drops a unique cookie for each authenticated user on the voting page, and then only accepts one vote per user.

A comment posted on the voting page says, "Check this out before you vote!" and links to a page on another website, X, that offers advice on how to vote. Many users click the link and read the page. With the Same Origin Policy protecting you, what could go wrong?

If you don't see the problem yet, here's a big hint: think about what might be going on in the site X window. Suppose site X is run by some dastardly and guileful cheaters trying to steal votes. Whenever a user browses to X, script on that page submits the site owner's preferred vote to the social website in that user's browser context (using their cookies from Y).

Since site X is allowed to submit forms using each user's Y cookies, that's enough to steal votes. The attackers just want to effect the state change on the server; they don't need to see the response page confirming the user's vote, which is all the Same Origin Policy blocks.

To prevent CSRF, ensure that valid state-changing requests are unguessable. In other words, treat each valid POST request as a special snowflake that only works once in the context of its intended use. An easy way to do this is by including a secret token as a hidden field in all forms, then checking that each request includes the secret corresponding to the given web session. There is a lot of nuanced detail packed into the creation and checking of a secret token for CSRF protection, so the details are worth digging into. A decent web framework should handle this for you, but let's take a look at the details.

Here's an example of the voting form with an anti-CSRF secret token highlighted:

```
<form action="/ballot" method="post">
  <label for="name">Voting for</label>
  <input type="text" id="name" name="name" value=""/>
  <input type="hidden" name="csrf_token"
         value="mGEyoi1wE6NBWCyhBN9IZdEmaJLQtrYxioJ23XuXR4o="/>
  <input type="submit" value="Vote"/>
</form>
```

The hidden csrf_token field doesn't appear on the screen, but is included in the POST request. The field's value is a base-64 encoding of a SHA-256 hash of the contents of the session cookie, but any per-client secret works. Here's the Python code creating the anti-CSRF token for the session:

```
def csrf_token(self):
    digest = hashlib.sha256(self.session_id.encode('utf-8')).digest()
    return base64.b64encode(digest).decode('utf-8')
```

The code derives the token from the session cookie (the string value self.session_id), so it's unique to each client. Since the Same Origin Policy prevents site X from knowing the victim's site Y cookies, it's impossible for

Y's creators to concoct an authentic form that satisfies these conditions to POST and steal the vote.

The validation code on the Y server simply computes the expected token value and checks that the corresponding field in the incoming form matches it. The following code prevents CSRF attempts by returning an error message if the token doesn't match, before actually processing the form:

```
token = fields.get('csrf_token')
if token != self.csrf_token():
    return 'Invalid request: Cross-site request forgery detected.'
```

There are many ways to mitigate CSRF attacks, but deriving the token from the session cookie is a nice solution because all the necessary information to do the check arrives in the POST request. Another possible mitigation is to use a *nonce*—an unguessable token for one-time use—but to fend off CSRF attacks, you still have to tie it to the intended client session. This solution involves generating the random nonce for the form's CSRF token, storing the token in a table indexed by session, and then validating the form by looking up the nonce for the session and checking that it matches.

Modern browsers support the SameSite attribute on cookies to mitigate CSRF attacks. SameSite=Strict blocks sending cookies for any third-party requests (to other domains) on a page, which would stop CSRF but can break some useful behavior when navigating to another site that expects its cookies. There are other settings available, but support may be inconsistent across browser brands and older versions. Since this is a client-side CSRF defense it may be risky for the server to completely depend on it, so it should be considered at additional mitigation rather than the sole defense.

## More Vulnerabilities and Mitigations

*The only way you can know where the line is, is if you cross it.*

—Dave Chappelle

To recap: to be secure you should build websites in pure HTTPS, using a quality framework. Don't override protection features provided by the framework unless you really know what you are doing, which means understanding how vulnerabilities such as XSS and CSRF arise. Modern websites often incorporate external scripts, images, styling, and the like, and you should only depend on resources from sources that you can trust since you are letting them inject content into your web page.

Naturally, that isn't the end of the story, as there are still plenty of ways to get in trouble when exposing a server to the web. Websites present a large attack surface to the public internet, and those untrusted inputs can easily trigger all manner of vulnerabilities in server code, such as SQL injection (web servers frequently use databases for storage) and all the rest.

There are a number of other web-specific pitfalls worth mentioning. Here are some of the more common additional issues to watch out for (though this list is hardly exhaustive):

- Don't let attackers inject untrusted inputs into HTTP headers (similar to XSS).

- Specify accurate MIME content types to ensure that browsers process responses correctly.

- Open redirects can be problematic: don't allow redirects to arbitrary URLs.

- Only embed websites you can trust with <IFRAME>. (Many browsers support the X-Frame-Options header mitigation.)

- When working with untrusted XML data, beware of XML external entity (XXE) attacks.

- The CSS :visited selector potentially discloses whether a given URL is in the browser history.

In addition, websites should use a great new feature, the HTTP Content-Security-Policy response header, to reduce exposure to XSS. It works by specifying authorized sources for script or images (and many other such features), allowing the browser to block attempts to inject inline script or other malicious content from other domains. There are a lot of browsers out there, and browser compatibility for this feature is still inconsistent, so using this header isn't sufficient to consider the vulnerability completely fixed. Think of this as an additional line of defense, but since it is client-side and out of your control, don't consider it a free pass granting perfect immunity to XSS.

Links to untrusted third-party websites can be risky because the browser may send a REFERER header, as mentioned earlier in this chapter, and provide a window.opener object in the DOM to the target page. The rel="noreferrer" and rel="noopener" attributes, respectively, should be used to block these unless they are useful and the target can be trusted.

Adding new security features after the fact may be daunting for large existing websites, but there is a relatively easy way of moving in the right direction. In a test environment, add restrictive security policies in all web pages, and then test the website and track down what gets blocked issue by issue. If you prohibit script loading from a site that you know is safe and you intended to use, then by incrementally loosening the script policy, you'll quickly arrive at the correct policy exceptions. With automated in-browser testing just to make sure the entire site gets tested, you should be able to make great strides for security with a modest investment of effort.

There are a number of HTTP response headers that help you specify what the browser should or should not allow, including the Content-Security-Policy, Referrer-Policy, Strict-Transport-Security, X-Content-Type-Options, and X-Frame-Options headers. The specifications are still evolving, and support may vary from browser to browser, so this is a tricky, changing landscape.

Ideally, make your website secure on the server side, and then use these security features as a second layer of defense, bearing in mind that reliance *only* on client side mechanisms would be risky.

It's amazing how secure the web actually is, considering all the ways that things can go wrong, what it evolved from, and the volume of critical data it carries. Perhaps, in hindsight, it's best that security technologies have matured slowly over time as the web has seen widespread global adoption. Had the early innovators attempted to design a completely secure system back in the day, the task would have been extremely daunting, and had they failed, the entire endeavor might never have come to anything.

# 12

## SECURITY TESTING

*Testing leads to failure, and failure leads to understanding.*
—Burt Rutan

This chapter introduces security testing as an essential part of developing reliable, secure code. Testing proactively to detect security vulnerabilities is both well understood and not difficult to do, but it's vastly underutilized in practice and so represents a major opportunity to raise security assurance.

This chapter opens with a quick overview of the uses of security testing, followed by a walkthrough of how security testing could have saved the world from a major vulnerability. Next, we look at the basics of writing security test cases to detect and catch vulnerabilities or their precursors. Fuzz testing is a powerful supplementary technique that can help you ferret out deeper problems. We'll also cover security regression tests, created in response to existing vulnerabilities to ensure that the same mistakes are never made twice. The chapter concludes with a discussion of how testing helps to prevent denial-of-service (DoS) and related attacks, followed by a summary of security testing best practices (which covers a wide range of ideas for security testing, but is by no means comprehensive).

## What Is Security Testing?

To begin, it's important to define what I mean by *security testing*. Most testing consists of exercising code to check that functionality works as intended. Security testing simply flips this around, ensuring that operations that should *not* be allowed aren't (an example with code will shortly make this distinction clear).

Security testing is indispensable because it ensures that mitigations are working. Given that coders reasonably focus on getting the intended functionality to work with normal use, attacks that do the unexpected can be difficult to fully anticipate. The material covered in the preceding chapters should immediately suggest numerous security testing possibilities. Here are some basic kinds of security test cases corresponding to the major classes of vulnerabilities covered previously:

**Integer overflows**
Establish permitted ranges of values and ensure that detection and rejection of out-of-range values work.

**Memory management problems**
Test that the code handles extremely large data values correctly, and rejects them when they're too big.

**Untrusted inputs**
Test various invalid inputs to ensure they are either rejected or converted to a valid form that is safely processed.

**Web security**
Ensure that HTTP downgrade attacks, invalid authentication and CSRF tokens, and XSS attacks fail (see the previous chapter for details on these).

**Exception handling flaws**
Force the code through its various exception handling paths (using dependency injection for rare ones) to check that it recovers reasonably.

What all of these tests have in common is that they are off the beaten path of normal usage, which is why they are easily forgotten. And since all these areas are ripe for attack, thorough testing makes a big difference. Security testing makes code more secure by anticipating such cases and confirming that the necessary protection mechanisms always work. In addition, for security-critical code, I recommend thorough code coverage to ensure the highest possible quality, since bugs in those areas tend to be devastating.

Security testing is likely the best way you can start making real improvements to application security, and it isn't difficult to do. There are no public statistics for how much or how little security testing is done in the software industry, but the preponderance of recurrent vulnerabilities strongly suggests that it's an enormous missed opportunity.

## Security Testing the GotoFail Vulnerability

*What a testing of character adversity is.*

—Harry Emerson Fosdick

Recall the GotoFail vulnerability we examined in Chapter 8, which caused secure connection checks to be bypassed. Extending the simplified example presented there, let's look at how security testing would have easily detected problems like that.

The GotoFail vulnerability was caused by a single line of code accidentally being doubled up, as shown by the highlighted line in the following code snippet. Since that line was a goto statement, it short-circuited a series of important checks and caused the verification function to unconditionally produce a passing return code. Earlier we looked only at the critical lines of code (in my simplified version), but to security test it, we need to examine the entire function:

*vulnerable code*

```
/*
 * Copyright (c) 1999-2001,2005-2012 Apple Inc. All Rights Reserved.
 *
 * @APPLE_LICENSE_HEADER_START@
 *
 * This file contains Original Code and/or Modifications of Original Code
 * as defined in and that are subject to the Apple Public Source License
 * Version 2.0 (the 'License'). You may not use this file except in
 * compliance with the License. Please obtain a copy of the License at
 * http://www.opensource.apple.com/apsl/ and read it before using this
 * file.
 *
 * The Original Code and all software distributed under the License are
 * distributed on an 'AS IS' basis, WITHOUT WARRANTY OF ANY KIND, EITHER
 * EXPRESS OR IMPLIED, AND APPLE HEREBY DISCLAIMS ALL SUCH WARRANTIES,
 * INCLUDING WITHOUT LIMITATION, ANY WARRANTIES OF MERCHANTABILITY,
 * FITNESS FOR A PARTICULAR PURPOSE, QUIET ENJOYMENT OR NON-INFRINGEMENT.
 * Please see the License for the specific language governing rights and
 * limitations under the License.
 *
 * @APPLE_LICENSE_HEADER_END@
 */
```

```
int VerifyServerKeyExchange(ExchangeParams params,
                            uint8_t *expected_hash, size_t expected_hash_len)
{
  int err;
  HashCtx ctx = 0;
  uint8_t *hash = 0;
  size_t hash_len;
  if ((err = ReadyHash(&ctx)) != 0)
    goto fail;
❶ if ((err = SSLHashSHA1.update(ctx, params.clientRandom, PARAM_LEN)) != 0)
    goto fail;
❷ if ((err = SSLHashSHA1.update(ctx, params.serverRandom, PARAM_LEN)) != 0)
    goto fail;
    goto fail;
❸ if ((err = SSLHashSHA1.update(ctx, params.signedParams, PARAM_LEN)) != 0)
    goto fail;
  if ((err = SSLHashSHA1.final(ctx, &hash, &hash_len)) != 0)
    goto fail;
  if (hash_len != expected_hash_len) {
    err = -106;
    goto fail;
  }
❹ if ((err = memcmp(hash, expected_hash, hash_len)) != 0) {
    err = -100;  // Error code for mismatch
  }
  SSLFreeBuffer(hash);

fail:
  if (ctx)
    SSLFreeBuffer(ctx);
  }
  return err;
}
```

**NOTE** *This code is based on the original* sslKeyExchange.c *with the bug. Code not directly involved with the critical vulnerability is simplified and some names are changed for brevity. For example, the actual function name is* SSLVerifySignedServerKeyExchange.

The VerifyServerKeyExchange function takes a params argument consisting of three fields, computes the message digest hash over its contents, and compares the result to the expected_hash value that authenticates the data. A zero return value indicates that the hashes match, which is required for a valid request. A nonzero return value means there was a problem: the hash *values* did not match (-100), the hash *lengths* did not match (-106), or some nonzero error code was returned from the hash computation library due to an unspecified error. Security depends on this: any tampering with the hash value or the data causes the hashes to mismatch, signaling that something is amiss.

Let's first walk through the correct version of the code, before the duplicated goto statement was introduced. After setting up a HashCtx ctx context variable, it hashes the three data fields of params in turn (at ❶, ❷, and ❸). If any error occurs, it jumps to the fail label to return the error code in the variable err. Otherwise, it continues, copying the hash result into a buffer and comparing that (at ❹) to the expected hash value. The comparison function memcmp returns 0 for equal, or if the hashes are different, the code assigns an error code of -100 to err and falls through to return that result.

## Functional Testing

Before considering security testing, let's start with a functional test for the VerifyServerKeyExchange function. Functional testing checks that the code performs as expected, and this simple example is by no means complete. This example uses the MinUnit test framework for C. To follow along, all you need to know is that mu_assert(*condition, message*) checks that the expression *condition* is true; if not, the assertion fails, printing the *message* provided:

```
mu_assert(0 == VerifyServerKeyExchange(test0, expected_hash, SIG_LEN),
    "Expected correct hash check to succeed.");
```

This calls the function with known-good parameters, so we expect a return value of 0 to pass the test. In the function itself, the three fields will be hashed (at ❶, ❷, and ❸). The hashes compare equal at ❹. Not shown are the test values for the three fields of data (in the ExchangeParams struct named test0) with the precomputed correct hash (expected_hash) that the server would sign.

## Functional Testing with the Vulnerability

Now let's introduce the GotoFail vulnerability (that highlighted line of code) and see what impact it has. When we rerun the functional test with the extra goto, the test still passes. The code works fine up to the duplicated goto, but then jumps over the hashing of the third data field (at ❸) and the comparison of hashes (at ❹). The function will continue to verify correct inputs, but now it will also verify some bad inputs that it should reject. However, we don't know that yet. This is precisely why security testing is so important—and why it's so easily overlooked.

More thorough functional testing might well include additional test cases, such as to check for verification failure (a nonzero return value). However, functional testing often stops short of thoroughly covering all the cases where we need the verify function to reject inputs in the name of security. This is where security testing comes in, as we shall see next.

## Security Test Cases

Now let's write some security test cases. Since there are three chunks of data to hash, that suggests writing three corresponding tests; each of these will change the data values in some way, resulting in a hash that won't match the expected value. The target verify function should reject these inputs because the changed values potentially represent data tampering, which the hash comparison is supposed to prevent. The actual values (test1, test2, test3) are copies of the correct test0 with slight variations in one of the three data fields; the values themselves are unimportant and not shown. Here are the three test cases:

```
mu_assert(-100 == VerifyServerKeyExchange(test1, expected_hash, SIG_LEN),
    "Expected to fail hash check: wrong client random.");
mu_assert(-100 == VerifyServerKeyExchange(test2, expected_hash, SIG_LEN),
    "Expected to fail hash check: wrong server random.");
mu_assert(-100 == VerifyServerKeyExchange(test3, expected_hash, SIG_LEN),
    "Expected to fail hash check: wrong signed parameters.");
```

All three of these will fail due to the bug. The verify function works fine up to the troublesome goto, but then unconditionally jumps to the label fail, leaving its hashing job incomplete and never comparing hash values ❹. Since we wrote these tests to expect verification failure as correct, a return value of 0 causes the tests to fail. Now we have a testing safety net that would have caught this vulnerability before release, avoiding the resulting fiasco.

In the spirit of completeness, another security test case suggests itself. What if all three values are correct, as in the test0 case, but with a different signed hash (wrong_hash)? Here's the test case for this:

```
mu_assert(-100 == VerifyServerKeyExchange(test0, wrong_hash, SIG_LEN),
    "Expected check against the wrong hash value to fail.");
```

This test fails as well with the errant goto, as we would expect. While for this particular vulnerability just one of these tests would have caught it, the purpose of security testing is to cover as broad a range of potential vulnerabilities as possible.

### The Limits of Security Tests

Security testing aims to detect the potential major points of failure in code, but it will never cover all of the countless ways for code to go wrong. It's possible to introduce a vulnerability that the tests we just wrote won't detect, but it's unlikely to happen inadvertently. Unless test coverage is extremely thorough, the possibility of crafting a bug that slips through the tests remains; however, the major threat here is inadvertent bugs, so a modest set of security test cases can be quite effective.

Determining how thorough the security test cases need to be requires judgment, but the rules of thumb are clear:

- Security testing is more important for code that is crucial to security.
- The most important security tests often check for actions such as denying access, rejecting input, or failing (rather than success).
- Security test cases should ensure that each of the key steps (in our example, the three hashes and the comparison of hashes) works correctly.

Having closely examined a real security vulnerability with a simple (if unexpected) cause, and how to security test for such eventualities, let's consider the general case and see how we could have anticipated this sort of problem and proactively averted it.

# Writing Security Test Cases

*A good test case is one that has a high probability of detecting an as yet undiscovered error.*

—Glenford Myers

A security test case confirms that a specific security failure does not occur. These tests are motivated by the second of the Four Questions: What can go wrong? This differs from *penetration testing*, where honest people ethically pound on software to find vulnerabilities so they can be fixed before bad actors find them, in that it does not attempt to scope out all possible exploits. Security testing also differs from penetration testing by providing protection against future vulnerabilities being introduced.

A security test case checks that protective mechanisms work correctly, which often involves the rejection or neutralization of invalid inputs and disallowed operations. While nobody would have anticipated the GotoFail bug specifically, it's easy to see that all of the if statements in the VerifyServerKeyExchange function are critical to security. In the general case, code like this calls for test coverage on each condition that enforces a security check. With that level of testing in place, when the extraneous goto creates a vulnerability, one of those test cases will fail and call the problem to your attention.

You should create security test cases when you write other unit tests, not as a reaction to finding vulnerabilities. Secure systems protect valuable resources by blocking improper actions, rejecting malicious inputs, denying access, and so forth. Create security test cases wherever such security mechanisms exist to ensure that unauthorized operations indeed fail.

General examples of commonplace security test cases include testing that login attempts with the wrong password fail, that unauthorized attempts to access kernel resources from user space fail, and that digital certificates that are invalid or malformed in various ways are always rejected. Reading the code is a great way to get ideas for good security test cases.

## Testing Input Validation

Let's consider security test cases for input validation. As a simple example, we'll test input validation code that requires a string that is at least 10 characters and at most 20 characters long, consisting only of alphanumeric ASCII characters.

You could create helper functions to perform this sort of standardized input validation, ensuring that it happens uniformly and without fail, then combine input validation with matching test cases to confirm that the validation checks work and that the code performs properly, right up to the allowable limits. In fact, since off-by-one errors are legion in programming, it's good practice to check both right at and just beyond the limits. The following unit tests cover the input validation test cases for this example:

- Check that a valid input of length 10 works, but an input of length 9 or less fails.
- Check that a valid input of length 20 works, but an input of length 21 or more fails.
- Check that inputs with one or more invalid characters always fail.

Of course, the functional tests should have already checked that sample inputs that satisfy all constraints work properly.

For another similar example, suppose the code under test stores a byte array parameter in a fixed-length buffer of $N$ bytes. Security test cases should ensure that the code works as expected with inputs of sizes up to and including $N$, but that an input of size $N+1$ gets safely rejected.

### Testing for XSS Vulnerabilities

Now let's look at a more challenging security test case and some of the different test strategies that are available. Recall the XSS vulnerability from Chapter 11, where an untrusted input injects itself into HTML generated on the web server and breaks out into the page, such as by introducing script that runs to launch an attack. The root cause of this vulnerability is improper escaping, so that is where our security tests will focus.

Say the code under test is the following Python function, which composes a fragment of HTML based on strings that describe its contents:

*vulnerable code*
```python
def html_tag(name, attrs):
    """Build and return an HTML fragment with attribute values.
    >>> html_tag('meta', {'name': 'test', 'content': 'example'})
    '<meta name="test" content="example">'
    """
    result = '<%s' % name
    for attr in attrs:
        result += ' %s="%s"' % (attr, html.escape(attrs[attr]))
    return result + ">"
```

The doctest (marked with the >>> prefix) example in the comments (delimited by """) illustrates how to use this function to generate HTML text for a <meta> tag. The first line builds the first section of the text string result: the angle bracket (<) that opens every HTML tag, followed by the tag name. Then the loop iterates through the attributes (attrs), appending a space and its declaration (of the form X="Y") for each attribute.

The code applies the html.escape function to each attribute string value correctly, but we still should test it. (For our purposes, we'll assume that attribute values are the only potential source of untrusted input that needs escaping. While in practice this is usually sufficient, anything is possible, so more escaping or input validation might be necessary in some applications.)

Let's write the test cases with Python's unittest library:

```python
class ExampleTestCases(unittest.TestCase):
    def test_basic(self):
        self.assertEqual(html_tag('meta', {'name': 'test', 'content': '123'}),
                         '<meta name="test" content="123">')

    def test_special_char(self):
        self.assertEqual(html_tag('meta', {'name': 'test', 'content': 'x"'}),
                         '<meta name="test" content="x&quot;">')

if __name__ == '__main__':
    unittest.main()
```

The first test case is a basic functional test that shows how these unit tests work. When run from the command line, the module invokes the unit test framework main in the last line. This automatically calls each method of all subclasses of unittest.TestCase, which contain the unit tests. The assertEqual method compares its arguments, which should be equal, or else the test fails.

Now let's look at the security test case, named test_special_char. Since we know XSS can exploit the code by breaking out of the double quotes that the untrusted input goes into, we test the escaping with a string containing a double quote. Correct HTML escaping should convert this to the HTML entity &quot;, as shown in the expected string of the assertEqual statement. If we remove the html.escape function in the target method, this test will indeed fail, as we want it to.

So far, so good. But note that in order to write the test we had to know in advance what kinds of inputs might be problematic (double quote characters). Since the HTML specification is fairly involved, how do we know there aren't more important test cases needed? We could try a bunch of other special characters, a number of which the escape function would convert to various HTML entity values (for example, converting the greater-than sign to &gt;). However, adjusting our test cases to cover all the possibilities like this would involve a lot of effort.

Since we are working with HTML, we can use libraries that know all about the specification in detail to do the heavy lifting for us. The following test case checks the result of forming HTML tags as we did earlier for the same two test values, the normal case and the one with a string containing a double quote character, assigned to the variable content in turn:

```python
def test_parsed_html(self):
    for content in ['x', 'x"']:
        result = html_tag('meta', {'name': 'test', 'content': content})
        soup = BeautifulSoup(result, 'html.parser')
        node = soup.find('meta')
        self.assertEqual(node.get('name'), 'test')
        self.assertEqual(node.get('content'), content)
```

Inside the loop is the common code that tests both cases, beginning with a call to the target function to construct a string HTML <meta> tag.

Instead of checking for an explicit expected value, we invoke the BeautifulSoup parser, which produces a tree of objects that logically represent the parsed HTML structure (colorfully referred to as a *soup* of objects). The variable soup is the root of the HTML node structure, and we can use it to navigate and examine its contents through an object model.

The find method finds the first <meta> tag in the soup, which we assign to the variable node. The node object sports a get method that looks up the values of attributes by name. The code tests that both the name and content attributes of the <meta> tag have the expected values. The big advantage of using the parser is that it takes care of spaces or line breaks in the HTML text, handles escaping and unescaping, converts entity expressions, and does everything else that HTML parsing entails.

Because we used the parser library, this security test case works on the parsed objects, shielded from the idiosyncrasies of HTML. If the XSS injects a malicious input that manages to break out of the double quotes, the parsed HTML won't have the same value in the node object for the <meta> tag. So, even if you had no clue that double quote characters were problematic for some XSS attacks, you could easily try a range of special characters and rely on the parser to figure out which were working properly (or not). The next topic takes this idea of trying a number of test case variations and automates it at scale.

## Fuzz Testing

*Fuzz testing* is a technique that automatically generates test cases in an effort to bombard the target code with test inputs. This helps you determine if particular inputs might cause the code to fail or crash the process. Here's an analogy that might help: a dishwasher cleans by spraying water at many different angles from a rotating arm. Without knowledge of how dishware happens to be loaded or at what angle shooting water will be effective, it sprays at random and still manages to get everything clean. In contrast to how security test cases written with specific intentions, the scattershot method of fuzz testing can be quite effective at finding a wider range of bugs, some of which will be vulnerabilities.

For security test cases, the typical approach is to "fuzz" untrusted inputs (that is, try lots of different values) and look for anomalous results or crashes. To actually identify a security vulnerability, you will need to investigate the leads that the results of fuzz testing produce.

You could convert test_parsed_html from the previous section into a fuzz test by checking many more characters.

```
def test_fuzzy_html(self):
    for fuzz in string.punctuation:
        content = 'q' + fuzz
        result = html_tag('meta', {'name': 'test', 'content': content})
        soup = BeautifulSoup(result, 'html.parser')
        node = soup.find('meta')
        self.assertEqual(node.get('name'), 'test')
        self.assertEqual(node.get('content'), content)
```

Rather than trying a chosen list of test cases, this code loops over all ASCII punctuation characters, which are defined by a constant in the standard string library. On each iteration, the variable fuzz takes the value of a punctuation character and prepends this with the letter q to construct the two-character content value. The rest of the code is identical to the original example, only here it runs many more test cases.

This example is simplistic to the point of stretching the definition of fuzz testing a bit, but it illustrates the power of brute-force testing 32 cases programmatically instead of carefully choosing and writing a collection of test cases by hand. A more elaborate version of this code might construct many more cases using longer strings composed of the troublesome HTML quoting and escaping characters.

There are many libraries that offer various fuzzing capabilities, from random fuzzing to the generation of variations based on the knowledge of specific formats such as HTML, XML, and JSON. If you have a particular testing strategy in mind, you can certainly write your own test cases and try them. The idea is that test cases are cheap, and generating lots of them is an easy way of getting good test coverage.

## Security Regression Tests

*What regresses, never progresses.*

—Umar ibn al-Khattâb

Once identified and fixed, security vulnerabilities are the last bugs we want to come back and bite us again. Yet this does happen, more often than it should, and when it does it's a clear indication of insufficient security testing. When responding to a newly discovered security vulnerability, an important best practice is to create a *security regression test* that detects the underlying bug or bugs. This serves as a handy *repro* (a test case that reproduces the bug or bugs) as well as confirms that the fix actually eliminates the vulnerability.

That's the idea, anyway, but this practice seems to be less than diligently followed, even by the largest and most sophisticated software makers. For example, when Apple released iOS 12.4 in 2019, it reintroduced a bug identical to one already found and fixed in iOS 12.3, immediately re-enabling a vulnerability after that door should have been firmly closed. Had the original fix included a security regression test case, this should never have happened.

It's notable that in some cases security regressions can be far worse than new vulnerabilities. That iOS regression was particularly painful because the bug was already familiar to the security research community, so they quickly adapted the existing jailbreak tool built for iOS 12.3 to work on iOS 12.4 (a *jailbreak* is an escalation of privilege circumventing restrictions imposed by the maker limiting what the user can do on their device).

I recommend writing the test case first, before tackling the actual fix. In an emergency, you might prioritize the fix if it's clear-cut, but unless you're working solo, having someone develop the regression test in parallel is a good practice. In the process of developing an effective regression test, you may learn more about the issue and even get clues about related potential vulnerabilities.

A good security regression test should try more than a single specific test case that's identical to a known attack; it should be more general. For example, for the SQL injection attack described in Chapter 10, it wouldn't be sufficient to just test that the one known "Bobby Tables" attack now fails. Also try an excessively long name, which might suggest that input validation needs to length-check name input strings, too. Try variants on the attack, such as using a double quote instead of single quote, or a backslash (the SQL string escape character) at the end of the name. Also try similar attacks in other columns of the same table, or other tables. Just as you wouldn't fix the SQL injection bug by narrowly rejecting only names beginning with `Robert');`, even though it would stop that specific attack, you shouldn't write regression tests that way either.

In addition to addressing the newly discovered vulnerability, it's common that the investigation will suggest similar vulnerabilities elsewhere in the system that might also be exploitable. Use your superior knowledge of system internals and familiarity with the source code to stay ahead of potential adversaries. If possible, probe for the presence of similar bugs immediately, so you can fix them as part of the update that closes the original vulnerability. This can be important, since you can bet that attackers will also be thinking along these lines, and releasing a fix will be a big clue about new ways they might target your system. If there is no time to explore all the leads, file away the details for investigation later, when time permits.

As an example, let's consider how to write a security regression test for the Heartbleed vulnerability from Chapter 9. Recall that the exploit worked by sending a packet containing a payload of arbitrary bytes with a much larger byte count; the server response honored the byte count and sent back additional memory contents, often causing a serious internal data leak.

The correct behavior is to ignore such invalid requests. Some good security regression test cases include:

- Test that known exploit requests no longer receive a response.
- Test with request byte counts greater than 16,384 (the maximum).
- Test requests with payloads of 0 bytes and the maximum byte size.
- Investigate whether other types of packets in the TLS protocol could have similar issues, and if so test those as well.

## Availability Testing

*Worry about being unavailable; worry about being absent or fraudulent.*

—Anne Lamott

DoS attacks represent a unique potential threat because the load limits that systems should be able to sustain are difficult to characterize. In particular, the term *load* packs a lot of meaning in that statement, including:

processing power, memory consumption, operating system resources, network bandwidth, disk space, and other potential bottlenecks (recall the entropy pool of a CSPRNG from Chapter 5). Operations staff typically monitor these factors in response to production use, but there are a few cases where security testing can avert attacks that intentionally exploit performance vulnerabilities.

Security testing should include test cases for identifying code that may be subject to nonlinear performance degradation. We saw some examples of this kind of vulnerability in Chapter 10, when we considered backtracking regex and XML entity expansion blow-ups. Since these can adversely impact performance exponentially, they are particularly potent vulnerabilities. Of course, these are just two instances of a larger phenomenon, and the same issue can occur in all kinds of code.

The next sections explain two basic strategies to test for this kind of problem: measuring the performance of specific functionality and monitoring overall performance against various loads.

## Resource Consumption

For functionality that you know may be susceptible to an availability attack, add security test cases that measure and determine a sensible limit on the input to protect blow-ups from occurring. Then test further to ensure that input validation prevents larger inputs from overloading the system.

For example, in the case of a backtracking regex, you could test with strings of length $N$ and $N+1$ to estimate the geometric rate at which the computation time grows. Use that factor to extrapolate the time required for the longest valid input, and then check that it's under the maximum threshold to pass the test.

For the sake of argument, let's say that $N = 20$ takes 1 second and $N = 21$ takes 2 seconds, so the additional character doubles the runtime. If the maximum input length is 30 characters, you can estimate this will take 1,024 ($2^{10}$) seconds to process and decide if this is feasible or not. By extrapolating the processing time mathematically instead of actually executing the $N = 30$ case, you can avoid an extremely slow-running test case. However, bear in mind that actual performance times may depend on other factors, so more than two measurements may be necessary to validate a suitable model.

In addition to this kind of targeted testing, measure performance metrics for the overall system and set generous upper limits so that if an iteration causes a significant degradation, the test will flag it for inspection. Often, these measurements can be easily added to existing larger tests, including smoke tests, load tests, and compatibility tests.

One easy technique to guard against a code change causing dramatic increases in memory consumption is to run tests under artificially resource-constrained conditions. *Memory* here refers to stack and heap space, swap space, disk file and database, and so forth. Unit tests should run with little available memory; if the test suite ever hits the limit, that's worth investigating. Larger integration tests will need resources comparable to those available in production, and when run with minimal headroom they can serve as a "canary in the coal mine." For example, if you can test the system successfully with 80 percent of the memory available in production, that provides some assurance of 20 percent headroom (excess capacity).

### Threshold Testing

One important but easily overlooked protection of system availability is to establish warning signs before fundamental limits are reached. A classic example of exceeding such a limit happened to a well-known software company not long ago, when the 32-bit counter that assigned unique IDs to the objects that the system managed wrapped from 2,147,483,647 to 0, resulting in the IDs of low-numbered objects being duplicated. It took hours to remedy the problem—a disaster that could easily have been averted by monitoring for the counter approaching its limit and issuing a warning when it reached, say, `0.99*INT_MAX`. Surely, in the early days of the product, it was difficult to imagine the counter ever reaching its maximum, but as the company grew and the prospect became a potential issue, nobody considered the possibility.

Warnings for such thresholds are often considered the responsibility of operational monitoring rather than security tests, but these are so often missed, and so easy to fix, that covering these eventualities under both categories is often worthwhile. Be sure to also watch out for other limits where the system will hit a brick wall, not just counters.

Storage capacity is another area where you'll want significant advance warning, allowing you to respond smoothly. Rather than setting arbitrary thresholds, such as 99 percent of the limit, a more useful calculation looks at a *time series* (a set of measurements over time) and extrapolates the time it will take to reach the limit.

Don't forget to stay ahead of time limits, too. The expiration dates of digital certificates are easily ignored until suddenly they fail to validate. Systems that rely on the certificates of partners that supply data feeds should monitor those and provide a heads-up in order to avoid an outage that, to your customers, will look like your problem.

The "Y2K bug" is now a distant memory of a non-event (possibly due to the extraordinary efforts made at the time to avoid the chaos that might have ensued in computer systems that stored years as two-digit values when the year changed from 1999 to 2000). However, we now have the "Y2k38 bug" to look forward to on January 19, 2038, when 2,147,483,647 seconds will have passed since 00:00:00 UTC on January 1, 1970 (the Unix epoch, as referenced in Figure 12-1). In less than two decades we will reach a point where the number of seconds elapsed since the epoch overflows the range of a 32-bit number, and this is almost certain to manifest all manner of nasty bugs. If it's too soon to instrument your codebase for this, when is the right time?

Figure 12-1: Bug (courtesy of
Randall Munroe, xkcd.com/376)

### Distributed Denial-of-Service Attacks

Denial-of-service (DoS) attacks are single actions that adversely impact availability; distributed denial-of-service (DDoS) attacks accomplish this through the cumulative effect of a number of concerted actions. For internet-connected systems, the open architecture of the internet creates an additional risk of DDoS attacks, such as from a coordinated botnet. Brute-force overloading from distributed anonymous sources generally ends up as a contest of scale of computing power. Mitigating these attacks typically requires reliance on DDoS protection vendors that have networking expertise backed by massive datacenter capacity.

I point this out as separate from the other categories of availability threats because this isn't something you can easily mitigate on your own should your server be unfortunate enough to become a target of a serious DDoS attack.

## Best Practices for Security Testing

Writing solid security test cases is an important way to improve the security of any codebase. While security test cases can't guarantee perfect security, they confirm that your protections and mitigations are working, and are thus a significant step in the right direction. A robust suite of security test cases, combined with security regression tests, dramatically lowers the chances of a major security lapse.

### Test-Driven Development

Security test cases are especially important when you're writing critical code and thinking through its security implications. I strongly endorse *test-driven development (TDD)*, where you write test cases concurrently with new code—rigorous practitioners of this method actually make the tests first, only authoring new code in order to fix the initially failing tests. TDD with security test cases included from the start ensures that security is built into the code, rather than as an afterthought, but whatever methodology you use for testing, security test cases need to be part of your test suite.

If others write the tests, developers should provide guidance that describes the security test cases needed, because they can be harder to intuit without a solid understanding of the security demands on the code.

### Leveraging Integration Testing

*Integration testing* puts systems through their paces to ensure that all the components, already unit-tested individually, work together as they should. These are important tests for quality assurance purposes—but once you've invested the effort, it's easy to extend them for a little security testing, too.

In 2018, a major social media platform advised its customers to change their passwords due to a self-inflicted breach of security: a bug had caused account passwords to spew into an internal log in plaintext. By leveraging integration tests, they could easily have detected and fixed the code that introduced this vulnerability before it was released to production. Integration tests for this service should have included logging in with a fake user account, say, USER1, with some password, such as /123!abc$XYZ (even fake accounts should have secure passwords). After the test completed, a security test would scan the outputs for that distinctive password string and raise an error if it found any matches. This testing approach applies not just to log files, but to anywhere a potential leak could occur: in other residual files, publicly accessible web pages, client caches, and so forth. Tests like this can be as simple as a grep(1) command.

Passwords are a convenient example for explanatory purposes, but this technique applies to any private data. Test systems require a bunch of synthetic data to stand in for actual user data in production, and all of that private content could potentially leak in just the same way. A more comprehensive leak test would scan all system outputs not explicitly protected as confidential for any traces of test input data that are private.

### Security Testing Catch-Up

If you are working on a codebase bereft of security test cases, assuming that security is a priority, there is some important work that needs doing. If there is a design that considers security that has been threat modeled and reviewed, use it as a map of what code deserves attention first. It's usually wise to divide the job into pieces with incremental milestones, do an achievable first iteration or two, and then assess the remaining need as you work through the tasks.

Target the protection mechanisms and functional areas in order of importance, letting the code guide you in determining what needs testing. Review existing test cases, as some may already do some security testing or be close enough to easily adapt for security. If someone is new to the project and needs to learn the code, have them write some of the security test cases; this is a great way to educate them and will produce lasting value.

# 13

## SECURE DEVELOPMENT BEST PRACTICES

*They say that nobody is perfect. Then they tell you practice makes perfect. I wish they'd make up their minds.*
—Winston Churchill

So far in Part III, we have surveyed a collection of security vulnerabilities that arise in the development phase. In this chapter, we'll focus on how aspects of the development process itself relate to security and can go wrong. We'll begin by discussing code quality: the value of good code hygiene, thorough error and exception handling, documenting security properties, and the role of code reviews in promoting security. Second, we'll look at dealing with dependencies: specifically, how they introduce vulnerabilities into systems. The third area we'll cover is bug triage—a critical skill for balancing security against other exigencies. Finally, secure development depends on maintaining a secure working environment, so I provide some basic tips on what you need to do to avoid being compromised.

For practical reasons, the guidance that follows is generic. Readers should be able to apply it to their own development practices. Many other effective techniques are specific to programming languages, operating systems, and other particulars of a given system. For this reason, it's important that you recognize the big patterns in the following discussion, but also be alert to additional security-related issues and opportunities that arise in your own work.

# Code Quality

*Quality is always in style.*

—Robert Genn

The earlier chapters in Part III explained many of the ways that vulnerabilities slip into code, but here I want to focus on the relationship of bugs in general to security. If you can raise the quality of your code, you'll make it more secure in the long run, whether you recognize this or not. All vulnerabilities are bugs, so fewer bugs means fewer vulnerabilities and vulnerability chains. But of course, diminishing returns kick in long before you eliminate all bugs, so it's best to take a balanced approach.

The following discussion covers some of the key areas to focus on in the name of security.

## Code Hygiene

Programmers usually have a good sense of the quality of the code they're working with, but for various reasons, they often choose to accept known flaws instead of making needed improvements. Code smells, spaghetti code, and postponed "TODO" comments that mark further work needed all tend to be fertile ground for vulnerabilities. At least in areas where security is of special concern, identifying and smoothing out these rough edges can be one of the best ways to avoid vulnerabilities without needing to do any security analysis in order to see how bugs may be exploitable.

In addition to your native sense of the condition of the code, use tools to flag these issues. Compile your code with full warnings and then fix the code to resolve significant issues. Some of these automated warnings, such as misleading indentation or unused code for which there is no execution path, would have identified the GotoFail vulnerability we talked about in Chapter 8, and security tested in Chapter 12. Lint and other static code analysis tools offer even richer scrutiny of the code, providing tips that sometimes reveal bugs and vulnerabilities.

Code analysis doesn't always identify security bugs as such, so you'll have to cast a broader net. Use these tools frequently during development to lower the overall number of potential bugs. This way, if a tool's output changes significantly you'll have a better chance of noticing it, because the new content won't get lost in a torrent of older messages.

Fix all warnings if it's easy to do so, or when you see that an issue could be serious. For example, unreachable code suggests that although somebody wrote the code for a reason, it's now out of the picture, and that can't be right. On the other hand, warnings about variable naming conventions, while being good suggestions, probably won't relate to any security vulnerability.

Finding time to do this kind of cleanup is always challenging. Take an incremental approach; even an hour or two a week will make a big difference over time, and the process is a good way to become familiar with a big codebase. If all the warnings are too much to deal with, start with the most promising ones (for example, GCC's -Wmisleading-indentation), then fix what gets flagged.

## Exception and Error Handling

The 1996 Ariane 5 Flight 501 Failure Report painfully details the consequences of poor exception handling. While the calamitous bug was purely self-inflicted, involving no malicious actor, it stands as an example of how an attacker might exploit the resulting behavior to compromise a system.

Soon after the Ariane 5 spacecraft's launch, a floating point to integer conversion in a calculation caused an exception. An exception-handling mechanism triggered, but as the conversion error was unanticipated, the exception handler code had no contingency for the situation. The code shut down the engine, resulting in catastrophic failure after 36.7 seconds of flight.

Defending against such problems begins with recognizing the risks of slapdash exception handling and then thinking through the right response for even the most unlikely exceptions. Generally speaking, it's best to handle exceptions as close to the source as possible, where there is the most context for it and the shortest window of time for further complications to arise.

That said, large systems may need a top-level handler to field any unhandled exceptions that bubble up. One good way to do this is to identify a unit of action and fail that in its entirety. For example, a web server might catch exceptions during an HTTP request and return a generic 500 (server error) response. Typically, web applications should handle state-changing requests as transactions so that any error always results in no state change. This avoids partial changes that may leave the system in a fragile state.

Much of the reasoning that connects sloppy exception handling to potential vulnerabilities also applies to error handling in general. Like exceptions, error cases may occur infrequently, so it's easy for developers to forget them, leaving them incomplete or untested. A common trick attackers use to discover exploits is to try causing some kind of error and then observe what the code does in hopes of discovering weaknesses. Therefore, the best defense is to implement solid error handling from the start. This is a classic example of one way that security vulnerabilities are different from other bugs: in normal use, some error might be exceedingly rare, but in the context of a concerted attack, invoking an error might be an explicit goal.

Solid testing is important in order to get error and exception handling right. Ensure that there is test coverage on all code paths, especially the less common ones. Monitor logs of exceptions in production and track down their causes to make sure that exception recovery works correctly. Aggressively investigate and fix intermittent exceptions, because if a smart attacker learns how to trigger one, they may be able to fine-tune it into a malicious exploit from there.

## Documenting Security

When you're writing code with important security consequences, how much do you need to explain your decisions in comments, so others (or your own forgetful self, months or years later) don't accidentally break it?

For critical code, or wherever the security implications deserve explanation, commenting is important, as it allows anyone who is contemplating changing the code to understand the stakes. When you write comments about security, explain the security implications and be specific: simply writing `// Beware: security consequences` isn't an explanation. Be clear and stick to the point: include too much verbiage and people will either tune it out or give up. Recalling the Heartbleed bug we discussed in Chapter 9, and security tested in Chapter 12, a good comment would explain that rejecting invalid requests with byte counts exceeding the actual data provided is crucial because it could result in disclosing private data beyond the extent of the buffer. If the security analysis becomes too complex to explain in the comments, write up the details in a separate document, then provide a reference to that document.

This does not mean that you should attempt to flag all code that security depends on. Instead, aim to warn readers about the less-than-obvious issues that might be easily overlooked in the future. Ultimately, comments cannot fully substitute for knowledgeable coders who are constantly vigilant of security implications, which is why this stuff is not easy.

Writing a good security test case (as discussed in Chapter 12) is an ideal way to back up the documentation with a mechanism to prevent others from unwittingly breaking security with future changes. As a working mock-up of what an attack looks like, such a test not only guards against accidental adverse changes, but also serves to show exactly how the code might go wrong.

## Security Code Reviews

The professional software development process includes peer code reviews as standard practice, and I want to make the case for explicitly including security in those reviews. Usually this is best done as one step within the code review workflow, along with the checklist of potential issues that reviewers should be on the lookout for, including code correctness, readability, style, and so forth.

I recommend that the same code reviewer add an explicit step to consider security, typically after a first pass reading the code, going through it again with their "security hat" on. If the reviewer doesn't feel up to covering security, they should delegate that part to someone capable. Of course, you can skip this step for code changes that are clearly without security implications.

Reviewing code changes for security differs from an SDR (the topic of Chapter 7) in that you are looking at a narrow subset of the system without the big-picture view you get when reviewing a whole design. Be sure you consider how the code handles a range of untrusted inputs, check that any input validation is robust, and avoid potential Confused Deputy problems. Naturally, code that is crucial to security should get extra attention, and usually merits a higher threshold of quality. The opportunity to focus an extra pair of eyes on the security of the code has great potential for improving the system as a whole.

Code reviews are also an excellent opportunity to ensure that the security test cases that have been created (as described in Chapter 12) are sufficient. As a reviewer, if you hypothesize that certain inputs might be problematic, write a security test case and see what happens, rather than guessing. Should your exploratory test case reveal a vulnerability, raise the issue and also contribute the test case to ensure it gets fixed.

# Dependencies

*Dependence leads to subservience.*

—Thomas Jefferson

Modern systems tend to build on large stacks of external components. These dependencies are problematic in more ways than one. Many platforms, such as npm, automatically pull in numerous dependencies that are difficult to track. And using old versions of external code with known vulnerabilities is one of the biggest ongoing threats the industry has yet to systematically eliminate. In addition, there is risk of picking up malicious components in your software supply chain. This can happen in several ways; for example, packages created with similar names to well-known ones may get selected by mistake, and you can get malware indirectly via other components through their dependencies.

Adding components to a system can potentially harm security even if those components are intended to strengthen it. You must trust not only the component's source, but everything the source trusts as well. In addition to the inevitable risks of extra code that adds bugs and overall complexity, components can expand the attack surface in unexpected new ways. Binary distributions are virtually opaque, but even with source code and documentation, it's often infeasible to carefully review and understand everything you get inside the package, so it often boils down to blind trust. Antivirus software can detect and block malware, but it also uses pervasive hooks that go deep into the system, needs superuser access, and potentially increases the attack surface, such as when it phones home to get the latest database of malware and report findings. The ill-advised choice of a vulnerable component can end up degrading security, even if your intention was to add an extra layer of defense.

## *Choosing Secure Components*

For the system as a whole to be secure, each of its components must be secure. In addition, the interfaces between them must be secure. Here are some basic factors to consider when choosing secure components:

- What is the security track record of the component in question, and of its maker?

- Is the component's interface proprietary, or are there compatible alternatives? (More choices may provide more secure alternatives.)

- When (not if) security vulnerabilities are found in the component, are you confident its developers will respond quickly and release a fix?
- What are the operational costs (in other words, effort, downtime, and expenses) of keeping the component up to date?

It's important to select components with a security perspective in mind. A component used to process private data should provide guarantees against information disclosure. If, as a side effect of processing data, it will be logging the content or storing it in unsecured storage, that constitutes a potential leak. Don't repurpose software written to handle, say, ocean temperatures, which have no privacy concerns at all, for use with sensitive medical data. Also avoid prototype components, or anything other than high-quality production releases.

## Securing Interfaces

A well-documented interface should explicitly specify its security and privacy properties, but in practice this often doesn't happen. In the interest of efficiency, it's easy for programmers to omit input validation, especially when they assume that validation will have already been handled. On the other hand, making every interface perform redundant input validation is indeed wasteful. When unsure, test to find out how the interface behaves if you can, and if still in doubt, add a layer of input validation in front of the interface for good measure.

Avoid using deprecated APIs, because they often mask potential security issues. API makers commonly deprecate, rather than entirely remove, APIs that include insecure features. This discourages others from using the vulnerable code while maintaining backward compatibility for existing API consumers. Of course, deprecation happens for other reasons as well, but as an API consumer, it's important to investigate whether the reason for the deprecation has security implications. Remember that attackers may be tracking API deprecations as well, and may be readying an attack.

Beyond these basic examples, take extra care whenever an interface exposes its internals, because these often get used in unintended ways that can easily create vulnerabilities. Consider "The Most Dangerous Code in the World" (Georgiev et al., 2012), a great case study of a widely used SSL library that researchers found was repeatedly used unsafely, completely undermining the security properties it was meant to provide. The authors found that "the root cause of most of these vulnerabilities is the terrible design of the APIs to the underlying SSL libraries."

Also be wary of APIs with complicated configuration options, particularly if security depends on them. When designing your own APIs, honor the Secure by Default pattern, document how to securely configure your system, and where appropriate provide a helper method that ensures proper configuration. When you must expose potentially insecure functionality, do everything possible to ensure that nobody can plausibly use it without knowing exactly what they are doing.

## Don't Reinvent Security Wheels

Use a standard, high-quality library for your basic security functionality when possible. Every time someone attempts to mitigate, say, an XSS attack in query parameters from scratch, they risk missing an obscure form of attack, even if they know HTML syntax inside out.

If a good solution isn't available, consider creating a library for use throughout your codebase to address a particular potential flaw, and be sure to test it thoroughly. In some cases, automated tools can help find specific flaws in code that often become vulnerabilities. For example, scan C code for the older "unsafe" string functions (such as strcpy) and replace them with the newer "safe" versions (strlcpy) of the same functionality.

If you are writing a library or framework, look carefully for security foibles so they get handled properly, once and for all. Then follow through and explicitly document what protections are and aren't provided. It isn't helpful to just advertise: "Use this library and your security worries will all be solved." If I am relying on your code, how do I know what exactly is or is not being handled? For example, a web framework should describe how it uses cookies to manage sessions, prevents XSS, provides nonces for CSRF, uses HTTPS exclusively, and so forth.

While it may feel like putting all your eggs in one basket, solving a potential security problem once with a library or framework is usually best. The consistent use of such a layer provides a natural bottleneck, addressing all instances of the potential problem. When you find a new vulnerability later, you can make a single change to the common code, which is easy to fix and test and should catch all usages.

Security-aware libraries must sometimes provide raw access to underlying features that cannot be fully protected. For example, an HTML framework template might let applications inject arbitrary HTML. When this is necessary, thoroughly document wherever the usual protections cease to apply, and explain the responsibilities of the API users. Ideally, name the API in a way that provides an unmistakable hint about the risk, such as unsafe_raw_html.

The bottom line is that security vulnerabilities can be subtle, possible attacks are many, and it only takes one to succeed—so it's wise to avoid tackling such challenges on your own. For the same reasons, once someone has successfully solved a problem, it's smart to reuse that as a general solution. Human error is the attacker's friend, so using solutions that make it easy to do things the secure way is best.

## Contending with Legacy Security

Digital technology evolves quickly, but security tools tend to lag behind for a number of reasons. This represents an important ongoing challenge. Like the proverbial frog in hot water, legacy security methods often remain in use for far too long unless someone takes a hard look at them, explicitly points out the risk, and proposes a more secure solution and a transition plan.

To be clear, I'm not saying that existing security methods are necessarily weak, just that almost everything has a "best before" date. Plus, we need to periodically re-evaluate existing systems in the context of the evolving threat landscape. Password-based authentication may need shoring up with a second factor if it becomes susceptible to phishing attacks. Crypto implementations are based on modern hardware cost and capability assessments, and as Moore's law tells us, this is a moving target; as quantum computing matures, high-security systems are already moving on to post-quantum algorithms thought to be resistant to the new technology.

Weak security often persists well past its expiration date for a few reasons. First, inertia is a powerful force. Since systems typically evolve by increments, nobody questions the way authentication or authorization is currently done. Second, enterprise security architecture typically requires all subsystems to be compatible, so any changes will mean modifying every component to interoperate in a new way. That often feels like a huge job and thus raises powerful resistance.

Also, older subcomponents can be problematic, as legacy hardware or software may not support more modern security technologies. In addition, there is the easy counterargument that the current security has worked so far, so there's no need to fix what isn't broken. On top of all this, whoever designed the legacy security may no longer be around, and nobody else may fully understand it. Or, if the original designer is around, they may be defensive of their work.

No simple answer can address all of these concerns, but threat modeling may identify specific issues with weak legacy security that should make the risk it represents evident.

Once you've identified the need to phase out the legacy code, you need to plan the change. Integrating a new component with a compatible interface into the codebase makes the job easier, but sometimes this isn't possible. In some cases, a good approach is to implement better security incrementally: parts of the system can convert to the new implementation piecewise, until you can remove legacy code when it is no longer needed.

## Vulnerability Triage

*The term "triage" normally means deciding who gets attention first.*

—Bill Dedman

Most security issues, once identified, are straightforward to fix, and your team will easily reach consensus on how to do so. Occasionally, however, differences of opinion about security issues do happen, particularly in the middle ground where the exploitability of a bug is unclear or the fix is difficult. Unless there are significant constraints that compel expediency, it's generally wise to fix any bug if there is any chance that it might be vulnerable to exploit. Bear in mind how vulnerability chains can arise when several minor bugs combine to create major vulnerabilities, as we saw in Chapter 8. And always remember that just because you can't see how to exploit a bug, that by no means proves that a determined attacker won't.

## DREAD Assessments

In the rare case that your team does not quickly reach consensus on fixing a bug, make a structured assessment of the risk it represents. The *DREAD model*, originally conceived by Jason Taylor and evangelized by both of us at Microsoft, is a simple tool for evaluating the risk of a specific threat. DREAD enumerates five aspects of the risk that a vulnerability exposes:

**Damage potential**
    If exploited, how harmful could it be?

**Reproducibility**
    Will attacks succeed every time, some of the time, or only rarely?

**Exploitability**
    How hard, in terms of technical difficulty, effort, and cost, is the vulnerability to exploit? How long is the attack path?

**Affected users**
    Will all, some, or only a few users be impacted? Can specific targets be easily attacked, or are the victims arbitrary?

**Discoverability**
    How likely is it that attackers will find the vulnerability?

In my experience, it works best to think of DREAD ratings in terms of five independent dimensions. Personally, I do not recommend assigning a numerical score to each, because severity is not very linear. My preferred method is to use T-shirt sizes (S, M, L, XL) to represent subjective magnitudes, as the following example illustrates. If you do use numerical scores, I would specifically discourage adding up the five scores to get a total to use for ranking one threat against another, as this is essentially comparing apples to oranges. Unless several of the factors have fairly low DREAD scores, consider the threat a significant one likely worth mitigating.

If the issue requires a triage meeting to resolve, use DREAD to present your case. Discuss the individual factors as needed to get a clear view of the consequences of the vulnerability. Often, when one component scores low, the debate will focus on what that means to the overall impact.

Let's see how DREAD works in practice. Pretend we've just discovered the Heartbleed bug and want to make a DREAD rating for it. Recall that this vulnerability lets anonymous attackers send malicious Heartbeat requests and receive back large chunks of the web server's memory.

Here is a quick DREAD scoring of the information leakage threat:

**Damage potential: XL**
    Internal memory of the server potentially discloses secret keys.

**Reproducibility: M**
    Leaked memory contents will vary due to many factors and will be innocuous in some cases, but unpredictable.

**Exploitability: L**

An anonymous attacker needs only send a simple request packet; extracting useful secrets takes a little expertise and then some luck.

**Affected users: XL**

The server and all users are at risk.

**Discoverability: L**

It depends on whether the idea occurs to an attacker (obvious once publicly announced); it's easily tried and confirmed.

This DREAD rating is subjective because in our scenario, there has not been time to investigate the vulnerability much beyond a quick confirmation of the bug. Suppose that we have seen a server key disclosed (hence, Damage potential is XL), but that in repeated tests the memory contents varied greatly, suggesting the M Reproducibility rating. Discoverability is particularly tricky: How do you measure the likelihood of someone thinking to even try this? I would argue that if you've thought of this, then it's best to assume others will too before long.

Discussions of DREAD scores are a great way to tease out the nuances of these judgments. When you get into a discussion, listen carefully and give due consideration to other opinions. Heartbleed is among the worst vulnerabilities in history, yet we didn't rate all of its DREAD factors at the maximum, serving as a good demonstration of why ratings must be carefully interpreted. Since this flaw occurred in code running on millions of web servers and undermined the security of HTTPS, you could say that the Damage potential and Affected users scores were actually off the charts (say, XXXXXXXL), more than making up for the few moderate ratings. The value of DREAD ratings is in revealing the relative importance of different aspects of a vulnerability, providing a clear view of the risk it represents.

## Crafting Working Exploits

Constructing a working proof-of-concept attack is the strongest way to make the case to fix a vulnerability. For some bugs the attack is obvious, and when it's easy to code up the exploit, that seals the deal. However, in my opinion this is rarely necessary, for a couple of reasons. For starters, crafting a demonstration exploit usually involves a lot of work. Actual working exploits often require a lot of refinement after you've identified the underlying vulnerability. More importantly, even if you are an experienced penetration tester, just because you fail to create a functional exploit, that is by no means proof that the vulnerability is not exploitable.

This is a controversial topic, but my take is that for all these reasons it's difficult to justify the effort of creating a working exploit for the purpose of addressing a security vulnerability. That said, by all means write a regression test (as discussed in Chapter 12) that will trigger the bug directly, even if it isn't a full-fledged working attack.

## Making Triage Decisions

When using DREAD, or doing any vulnerability assessment for that matter, bear in mind that it's far easier to underestimate, rather than overestimate, actual threats. Noticing a potential vulnerability and taking no action can be a tragic mistake, and one that's obviously best avoided. I've lost a few of those battles and can assure you that there is no satisfaction in saying "I told you so" after the fact. Failing to fix significant flaws is a Russian roulette game not worth playing: "just fix it" is a great standing policy.

Here are some general rules of thumb for making better security triage decisions:

- Bugs in privileged code, or code that accesses valuable assets, should be fixed and then carefully tested to guard against the introduction of new bugs.

- Bugs that are well isolated from any attack surface and seem harmless are usually safe to defer.

- Carefully confirm claims that a bug is harmless: it may be easier to fix the bug than to accurately assess its full potential impact.

- Aggressively fix bugs that could be part of vulnerability chains (discussed in Chapter 8).

- Finally, when it's a toss-up, I always advise fixing the issue: better safe than sorry.

When more research is needed, assign someone to investigate the issue and report back with a proposal; don't waste time debating hypotheticals. In discussions, focus on understanding other perspectives rather than trying to change minds. Trust your intuition. With practice, when you know what to focus on, this will quickly become easier.

# Maintaining a Secure Development Environment

*The secret of landscapes isn't creation. . . .It's maintenance.*

—Michael Dolan

Good hygiene is a useful analogy: to produce a safe food product, manufacturers need fresh ingredients from trustworthy suppliers, a sanitary working environment, sterilized tools, and so forth. Similarly, good security practices must be observed throughout the entire development process for the resulting product to be secure.

Malicious code can slip into the product due to even a one-time lapse during development, a fact which should give you pause. The last thing that developers want is for their software to become a vector for malware.

## Separating Development from Production

Strictly separate your development and production environments, if you aren't doing this already. The core idea is to provide a "wall" between the two, typically consisting of separate subnetworks, or at least mutually exclusive access permission regimes. That is, when developing software, the programmer should not have access to production data. Nor should production machines and operations staff have access to the development environment and source code (write access). In smaller shops, where one person handles both production and development, you can switch between user accounts. The inconvenience of switching is more than compensated for by saving the product from even a single mistake. Plus, it provides peace of mind.

## Securing Development Tools

Carefully vet development tools and library code before installing and using them. Some minor utility downloaded from "somewhere," even for a one-time use, could bring more trouble than it's worth. Consider setting up a safely isolated sandbox for experiments or odd jobs not part of the core development process. This is easily done with a virtual machine.

All computers involved in development must be secure if the result is to be secure. So must all source code repositories and other services, as these are all potential openings for vulnerabilities to creep into the final product. In fact, it goes deeper: all operating systems, compilers, and libraries involved in the process of development must also be secure. It's a daunting challenge, and it may sound almost impossible, but fortunately perfection is not the goal. You must recognize these risks first, then find opportunities to make incremental improvements.

The best way to mitigate these risks is by threat modeling the development environment and processes. Analyze the attack surface for a range of threats, treating the source code as your primary asset. Basic mitigations for typical development work include:

- Securely configure and regularly update development computers.
- Restrict personal use of computers used for development.
- Systematically review new components and dependencies.
- Securely administer computers used for the build and release processes.
- Securely manage secrets (such as code signing keys).
- Secure login credential management with strong authentication.
- Regularly audit source change commits for anomalous activity.
- Keep secure backup copies of source code and the build environment.

## Releasing the Product

Use a formal release process to bridge development and production. This can happen through a shared repository that only development staff can modify, and that operations staff can only read. This Separation of Duty ensures that the responsibilities of the respective parties are not only clear but enforced, essentially rendering impossible solo "cowboy" efforts to make quick code changes and then push the new version into production, where security flaws are easily introduced, without going through approved channels.

**NOTE** *See Appendix D for a cheat sheet summarizing the DREAD model for risk assessment as a handy aid doing bug triage.*

# AFTERWORD

Having watched computing evolve over the last 50 years, I have learned that attempting to predict the future is folly. However, to conclude this book I would like to offer my thoughts about future directions in security that I think would be valuable, unlikely as some of them may be. The following are by no means predictions, but rather possibilities that would constitute significant progress.

The nascent internet received a wake-up call in 1988 when the Morris worm first demonstrated the potential power of online malware and how it can spread by exploiting existing vulnerabilities. More than 30 years later, though we have made astounding progress on many fronts, I wonder if we have fully understood these risks and prioritized our mitigation efforts sufficiently. Reports of attacks and private data disclosures are still commonplace, and no end is in sight. Sometimes, it seems that the attackers are having a field day while the defenders are frantically treading water. And it's important to bear in mind that many incidents are kept secret, or may even persist undetected, so the reality is almost certainly worse than we know. In large part, we've learned to live with vulnerable software.

What's remarkable is that, despite our imperfect systems continuing to be compromised, everything somehow manages to keep going. Perhaps this is why security problems persist: the status quo is good enough. But even though I understand the cool logic of returns on investment, deep down I just don't accept that. I believe that when, as an industry, we accept the current state of affairs as the best we can do, we block real progress. Justifying additional work in the interest of security is always difficult because we rarely learn about failed attacks, or even what particular lines of defense were effective.

This concluding chapter sketches out promising future directions to raise the level of our collective software security game. The first section recapitulates the core themes of the book, summarizing how you can apply the methods in this book to good effect. The remainder of this chapter envisions further innovations and future best practices, and is more speculative. A discussion of mobile device data protection provides an example of how much more needs to be done to actually deliver effective security in the "last mile." I hope the conceptual and practical ideas in this book spark your interest in this vital and evolving field, and serve as a springboard for your own efforts in making software secure.

## Call to Action

> *The great aim of education is not knowledge but action.*
>
> —Herbert Spencer

This book is built around promoting two simple ideas that I believe will result in better software security: involving everyone building the software in promoting its security, and integrating a security perspective and strategy from the requirements and design stage. I entreat readers of this book to help lead the charge.

In addition, a continuing focus on the quality of the software we create will contribute to better security, because fewer bugs mean fewer exploitable bugs. High-quality software requires work: competent designs, careful coding, comprehensive testing, and complete documentation, all kept up to date as the software evolves. Developers, as well as end users, must continue to push for higher standards of quality and polish to ensure this focus is maintained.

### Security Is Everyone's Job

Security analysis is best done by people who deeply understand the software. This book lays out the conceptual basis for good security practice, empowering any software professional to understand the security facets of design, learn about secure coding, and more. Instead of asking experts to find and fix vulnerabilities because security has been largely neglected, let's all pitch in to ensure at least a modest baseline is met for all the software we produce. We can then rely on experts for the more arcane and technical security work, where their skills are best applied. Here's the rationale:

- However well expert consultants know security, as outsiders, they cannot fully understand the software and its requirements in context, including how it must operate within the culture of an enterprise and its end users.

- Security works best when it's integral to the entire software lifecycle, but it isn't practical to engage security consultants for the long haul.

- Skilled software security professionals are in high demand, difficult to find, and hard to schedule on short notice. Hiring them is expensive.

Security thinking is not difficult, but it is abstract and may feel unfamiliar at first. Most vulnerabilities tend to be obvious in hindsight; nonetheless, we seem to make the same mistakes over and over. The trick, of course, is seeing the potential problem before it manifests. This book presents any number of methods to help you learn how to do just that. The good news is that nobody is perfect at this, so starting out with even a small contribution is better than nothing. Over time, you will get better at it.

Broader security participation is best understood as a team effort, where every individual does the part that they do best. The idea is not that each individual can handle the entire job alone, but rather that the combined input of team members with a diverse set of skills synergistically produces the best result. Whatever your part is in producing, maintaining, or supporting a software product, focus on that as your primary contribution. But it's also valuable to consider the security of related components, and double-check the work of your teammates to ensure they haven't overlooked something. Even if your role is a small one, you just might spot a vital flaw, just as a soccer goalie occasionally scores a goal.

It's important to be clear that outside expertise is valuable for performing tasks such as gap analysis or penetration testing, for balancing organizational capacity, and as "fresh eyes" with deep experience. However, specialist consultants should supplement solid in-house security understanding and well-grounded practice, rather than being called in to carry the security burden alone. And even if specialists do contribute to the overall security stance, they go off to other engagements at the end of the day. As such, it's always best to have as many people as possible on the team responsible for the software be thinking about security regularly.

## Baking in Security

Bridges, roads, buildings, factories, ships, dams, harbors, and rockets are all designed and meticulously reviewed to ensure quality and safety, and only then built. In any other engineering field, it's acknowledged that refining a design on paper is better than retrofitting security measures after the fact. Yet most software is built first and then secured later.

A central premise of this book, which the author has seen proven in industry time and again, is that earlier security diligence saves time and reaps significant rewards, improving the quality of the result. When designs thoroughly consider security, implementers have a much easier job of delivering a secure solution. Structuring components to facilitate security makes it easy to anticipate potential issues.

The worst-case scenario, and most compelling reason for front-loading security into the design phase ("moving left," in popular industry jargon), is to avoid by-design security flaws. Designed-in security flaws—whether in componentization, API structure, protocol design, or any other aspect of architecture—are potentially devastating, because they are nearly impossible to fix after the fact without breaking compatibility. Catching and fixing these problems early is the best way to avoid painful and time-consuming reactive redesigns.

Good security design decisions have greater benefits that often go unrecognized. The essence of good design is minimalism without compromising necessary functionality. Applied to security, this means the design minimizes the area of the attack surface and critical component interactions, which in turn means there are fewer opportunities for implementers to make mistakes.

Security-focused design reviews are important because functional reviews of software designs take a different perspective and ask questions that don't consider security. "Does it fulfill all the necessary requirements? Will it be easy to operate and maintain? Is there a better way?" In fact, an insecure design can easily pass all these tests with flying colors while being vulnerable to devastating attacks. Supplementing design review with a security assessment vets the security of the design by understanding the threats it faces and considering how it might fail or be abused.

The implementation side of software security consists of learning about, and vigilantly avoiding, the many potential ways of inadvertently creating vulnerabilities, or at least mitigating those common pitfalls. Secure designs minimize the opportunities for the implementation to introduce vulnerabilities, but it can never magically make software bulletproof. Developers must be diligent not to undermine security by stepping into any number of potential traps.

Security is a process that runs through the entire lifecycle of a software system, from conception to its inevitable retirement. Digital systems are complex and fragile, and as software "eats the world," we become increasingly dependent on it. We are imperfect humans using imperfect components to build good-enough systems for imperfect people. But just because perfection is unattainable does not mean we cannot progress. Instead, it means that every bug fixed, every design improved, and every security test case added help in ways big and small to make systems more trustworthy.

# Future Security

*The future depends on what you do today.*

—Mahatma Gandhi

This book is built around the methods of improving security that I have practiced and seen work consistently, but there is much more to do beyond this. The following subsections sketch a few ideas that I think are promising. Although these notions require additional development, I believe they may lead to significant further advances.

Artificial intelligence or other advanced technologies offer much promise, but my intuition is that a lot of the work needed is of the "chop wood, carry water" variety. One way we can all contribute is by working to ensure the quality of the software we produce, because it is from bugs that vulnerabilities arise. Second, as our systems grow in power and scope, complexity necessarily grows, but we must manage it so as not to be overwhelmed. Third, in researching this book, I was disappointed (but not surprised) by the dearth of solid data about the state of the world's software and how secure it is: surely, more transparency will enable a clearer view to better guide us forward. Fourth, authenticity, trust, and responsibility are the bedrock of how the software community works together safely, yet modern mechanisms that implement these are largely ad hoc and unreliable—advances in these areas could be game changers.

## Improving Software Quality

"The programmers get paid to put the bugs in, and they get paid to take the bugs out." This was one of the most memorable observations I heard as a Microsoft program manager 25 years ago, and this attitude about the inevitability of bugs still prevails, with little danger of changing any time soon. But bugs are the building blocks of vulnerabilities, so it's important to be aware of the full cost of buggy software.

One way to improve security is to augment the traditional bug triage by also considering whether each bug could possibly be part of an attack chain, and prioritizing fixing those where this seems more likely and the stakes are high. Even if just a fraction of these bug fixes closes an actual vulnerability, I would argue that these efforts are entirely worthwhile.

## Managing Complexity

*An evolving system increases its complexity unless work is done to reduce it.*

—Meir Lehman

As software systems grow larger, managing the resultant complexity becomes more challenging, and these systems risk becoming more fragile. The most reliable systems succeed by compartmentalizing complexity within components that present simple interfaces, loosely coupled in fault-tolerant configurations. Large web services achieve high resiliency by distributing requests over a number of machines that perform specific functions to synthesize the whole response. Designed with built-in redundancy, in the event of a failure or timeout, the system can retry using a different machine if necessary.

Compartmentalizing the respective security models of the many components of a large information system is a basic requirement for success. Subtle interactions between the assembled components may influence security, making the task of securing the system massively harder as interdependencies compound. In addition to excellent testing, well-documented security requirements and dependencies are important first lines of defense when dealing with a complex system.

## From Minimizing to Maximizing Transparency

Perhaps the bleakest assessment of the state of software security derives from this (variously attributed) aphorism: "If you can't measure it, you can't improve it." Lamentably, there is a dearth of measurements of the quality of the world's software, in particular regarding security. Public knowledge of security vulnerabilities is limited to a subset of cases: software that is open source, public releases of proprietary software (usually requiring reverse engineering of binaries), or instances when a researcher finds flaws and goes public with a detailed analysis. Few enterprises would even consider making public the full details of their software security track record. As an industry, we learn little from security incidents because full details are rarely disclosed—which is in no small part due to fear. While this fear is not unfounded, it needs to be balanced against the potential value to the greater community of more informative disclosure.

Even when we accept the barriers that exist to a full public disclosure of all security vulnerabilities, there is much room for improvement. The security update disclosures for major operating systems typically lack useful detail at the expense of their users, who would likely find additional information useful in responding to and assessing risk. In the author's opinion, major software companies often obscure the information they do provide to the point of doublespeak. Here are a few examples from a recent operating system security update:

- "A logic issue was addressed with improved restrictions." (This applies to almost any security bug.)
- "A buffer overflow issue was addressed with improved memory handling." (How is it possible to fix a buffer overflow any other way?)
- "A validation issue was addressed with improved input sanitization." (Again, this can be said of any input validation vulnerability.)

This lack of detail has become reflexive with too many products; it harms customers, and the software security community would benefit from more informative disclosure. Software publishers can almost always provide additional information without compromising future security. Realistically, adversaries are going to analyze changes in the updates and glean basic details, so useless release notes only deprive honest customers of important details. Responsible software providers of the future would do better to begin with full disclosure, then redact it as necessary so as to not weaken security. Better yet, after the risk of exploit is past, it should be safe to disclose additional details held in abeyance that would be valuable to our understanding of the security of major commercial software products, if only in the rearview mirror.

Providing detailed reporting of vulnerabilities may be embarrassing, because in hindsight the problem is usually blatantly obvious, but I maintain that honestly confronting these lapses is healthy and productive. The learning potential from a full disclosure is significant enough that if we are serious about security for the long term, we need greater transparency. As a customer, I would be much more impressed with a software vendor whose security fix release notes included:

- Dates that the bug was reported, triaged, fixed, tested, and released, with an explanation of any untoward delays.

- A description of when and how the vulnerability was created (for example, a careless edit, ignorance of the security implications, miscommunication, or a malicious attack).

- Information about whether the commit that contained the flawed code was reviewed. If so, how was it missed; if not, why not?

- An account of whether there was an effort to look for similar flaws of the same kind. If so, what was found?

- Details of any precautions taken to prevent regression or similar flaws in the future.

Shifting the industry toward a culture of sharing more forthcoming disclosures of vulnerabilities, their causes, and their mitigations enables us all to learn from these incidents. Without much detail or context, these disclosures are just going through the motions and benefit no one.

A great example of best practice is the National Transportation Safety Board, which publishes detailed reports that the aviation industry as well as pilots can follow to learn from accidents. For many reasons software cannot simply follow that process, but it serves as a model to aspire to. Ideally, leading software makers should see public disclosure as an opportunity to explain exactly what happened behind the scenes, demonstrating their competence and professionalism in responding. This would not only aid broad learning and prevention of similar problems in other products, but help rebuild trust in their products.

## *Improving Software Authenticity, Trust, and Responsibility*

Large modern software systems are built from many components, all of which must be authentic and built by trustworthy entities, from secure subcomponents, using a secure tool stack. This chain continues on and on, literally to the dawn of modern digital computing. The security of our systems depends on the security of all these iterations that have built up our modern software stack, yet the exact chains of descent have by now faded into the mists of computing history, back to a few early self-compiling compilers that began it all. The classic paper "Reflections on Trusting Trust" by Ken Thompson elegantly demonstrates how security depends on all of this history, as well as how hard it can be to find malware once it's deeply embedded. How do we really know that something untoward isn't lurking in there?

The tools necessary to ensure the integrity of how our software is built are by now freely available, and it's reasonable to assume they work as advertised. However, their use tends to be dismayingly ad hoc and manual, making the process susceptible to human error, if not potential sabotage. Sometimes people understandably skip checking just to save time. Consider, for example, validating the legitimacy of a *nix distribution. After downloading an image from a trusted website, you would also download the separate authoritative keys and checksum files, then use a few commands (obtained from a trustworthy source) to verify it all. Only after these checks all pass should installation proceed. But in practice, how thoroughly are administrators actually performing these extra steps, especially when instances of these checks failing for a major distro are unheard of? And even if they always are, we have no record of it as assurance.

Today, software publishers sign released code, but the signature only assures the integrity of the bits against tampering. There is an implication that signed code is trustworthy, yet any subsequent discovery of vulnerabilities in no way invalidates the signature, so that is not a safe interpretation at all.

In the future, better tools, including auditable records of the chain of authenticity, could provide a higher assurance of integrity, informing the trust decisions and dependencies that the security of our systems relies on. New computers, for example, should include a software manifest documenting that the operating system, drivers, applications, and so on are authentic. Documenting and authenticating the software bill of materials of components and the build environment require a major effort, but we shouldn't let the difficulty deter us from starting with a subset of the complete solution and incrementally improving over time. If we start getting serious about software provenance and authenticity, we can do a much better job of providing assurance that important software releases are built from secure components, and the future will thank us.

## Delivering the Last Mile

*The longest mile is the last mile home.*

—Anonymous

If you diligently follow every best practice, apply the techniques described in this book, code with attention to avoid footguns, perform reviews, thoroughly test, and fully document the complete system, I wish that I could say your work will be perfectly secure. But of course, it's more complicated than that. Not only is security work never finished, but even well-designed and well-engineered systems can still fall short of delivering the intended levels of security in the real world.

The "last mile," a term taken from the telecommunications and transportation industries, refers to the challenge of connecting individual customers to the network. This is often the most expensive and hardest part of delivering services. For example, an internet service provider might already have high-speed fiber infrastructure in your neighborhood, but acquiring each new customer requires a service call, possibly running cables, and installing a modem. None of this scales well, and the time and expense become significant additional upfront investments. In much the same way, deploying a well-designed, secure system is often only the beginning of actually delivering real security.

To understand these "last mile" challenges for security, let's take an in-depth look at the current state of the art of mobile device data security through the lens of a simple question: "If I lose my phone, can someone else read its contents?" After years of intensive engineering effort resulting in a powerful suite of well-built modern crypto technology, the answer, even for today's high-end phones, seems to be, "Yes, they probably can get most of your data." As this is perhaps the largest single software security effort in recent times, it's important to understand where it falls short and why.

The following discussion is based on the 2021 paper "Data Security on Mobile Devices: Current State of the Art, Open Problems, and Proposed Solutions," written by three security researchers at Johns Hopkins University. The report describes several important ways that delivering robust software security often remains elusive. I will simplify the discussion greatly in the interests of highlighting the larger lessons for security that this example teaches.

First, let's talk about levels of data protection. Mobile apps do all kinds of useful things—too much for a single encryption regime to work for everything—so mobile operating systems provide a range of choices. The iOS platform offers three levels of data protection that differ mainly in how aggressively they minimize the time window that encryption keys are present in memory to facilitate access to protected data. You can think of this as analogous to how often a bank vault door is left open. Opening the big, heavy door in the morning and shutting it only at closing time provides the staff convenient access throughout the day, but it also means the vault is more exposed to intrusion when not in use. By contrast, if the staff has to find the bank manager to open the vault every time they need to enter, they trade that convenience for increased security: the vault is securely locked most of the time. For a mobile device, asking the user to unlock the encryption keys (by password, fingerprint, or facial recognition) in order to access protected data roughly corresponds to asking the bank manager to open the vault.

Under the highest level of protection, the encryption keys are only available while the phone is unlocked and in use. While very secure, this is a hindrance for most apps, because they lose access to data when the device is locked. For example, consider a calendar app that reminds you when it's time for a meeting. A locked phone renders the app unable to access calendar data. Background operations, including syncing, will also be blocked during the locked state. This means that if an event were added to your calendar while the phone was locked, then you would fail to get the notification unless you happened to unlock the phone beforehand so it could sync. Even the least restrictive protection class, known as *After First Unlock (AFU)*, which requires user credentials to reconstitute encryption keys after booting, presents serious limitations. As the name suggests, a freshly rebooted device would not have encryption keys available, so a calendar notification would be blocked then, too.

We can imagine designing apps to work around these restrictions by partitioning data into separate stores under different protection classes, depending on when it is needed. Perhaps for a calendar, the time would be unprotected so as to be available, so the notification would vaguely say, "You have a meeting at 4 PM," requiring the user to unlock the device to get the details. Notifications lacking titles would be annoying, but users also expect their calendars to be encrypted for privacy, so a trade-off is necessary. The sensitivity of this information may vary between users and depend on the specifics of the meeting, but making the user explicitly decide in each case isn't workable either, because people expect their apps to work on their own. In the end, most apps opt for increased access to the data they manage, and end up using lower levels of data protection—or, often, none at all.

When most apps operate under the "no protection" option for convenience, all that data is a sitting duck for exfiltration if the attacker can inspect the device. It isn't easy, but as the Johns Hopkins report details, sophisticated techniques often find a way into memory. With AFU protection, all the attacker needs to do is find the encryption key, which, since devices spend most of their time in this state, is often sitting in memory.

Confidential messaging apps are the main exception to the rule; they use the "complete protection" class. Given their special purpose, users are predisposed to put up with the missing functionality when the device is locked and the extra effort required to use them. These are a minority of apps, comprising a tiny proportion of locally stored user data, yet most phone users (those who even think about security at all) probably believe all of their data is secure.

As if the picture wasn't already bleak enough, let's consider how important cloud integration is for many apps, and how it is antithetical to strong data protection. The cloud computing model has revolutionized modern computing, and we are now accustomed to having ubiquitously connected datacenters at our fingertips, with web search, real-time translation, image and audio storage, and any number of other services instantly available. Functionality such as searching our photo collections for people using facial recognition vastly exceeds even the considerable compute power of modern devices, so it very much depends on the cloud. The cloud data model also makes multi-device access easy (no more syncing), and if we lose a device, the data is safely stored in the cloud so all we need to do is buy new hardware. But in order to leverage the power of the cloud, we must entrust it with our data instead of locking it down with encryption on our devices.

Of course, all of this seamless data access is antithetical to strong data protection, particularly in the case of a lost cloud-connected phone. Most mobile devices have persistent cloud data access, so whoever recovers the device potentially has access to the stored data too. That data most likely isn't encrypted; even if we tried to envision, say, a photo app that stored end-to-end encrypted data in the cloud, that would mean only opaque blobs of bits could be stored, so we'd lose the power of the cloud to search or provide photo sharing. And since the decryption key would have to be strictly held on the device, multi-device access scenarios would be difficult. Also, if something happened to the key on the device, all the data in the cloud would potentially be useless. For all these reasons, apps that rely on the cloud almost completely opt out of encrypted data protection.

We've only scratched the surface of the full technical details of the effectiveness of data protection in mobile devices here, but for our purposes, the outlines of the more general problem should be clear. Mobile devices exist in a rich and complicated ecosystem, and unless data protection works for all components and scenarios, it quickly becomes infeasible to use. The best advice remains to not use your phone for anything that you wouldn't greatly mind possibly leaking if you lose it.

The lessons of this story that I want to emphasize go beyond the design of mobile device encryption, and in broad outlines apply to any large systems seeking to deliver security. The point is that despite diligent design, with a rich set of features for data protection, it's all too easy to fall short of fully delivering security in the last mile. Having a powerful security model is only effective if developers use it, and when users understand its benefits. Achieving effective security requires providing a useful balance of features that work with, instead of against, apps. All the data that needs protection must get it, and interactions with or dependencies on infrastructure (such as the cloud in this example) shouldn't undermine its effectiveness. Finally, all of this must integrate with typical work flows so that end users are contributing to, rather than fighting, security mechanisms.

Years ago I witnessed a case of falling short on the last mile with the release of the .NET Framework. The security team worked hard getting Code Access Security (CAS)—described in Chapter 3—into this new programming platform, but failed to evangelize its use enough. Recall that CAS requires that managed code be granted permissions to perform privileged operations and then assert them when needed—an ideal tool for the Least Privilege pattern. Unfortunately, outside of the runtime team, developers perceived this as a burden and failed to see the feature's security benefit. As a result, instead of using the fine-grained permissions that the system provided only where needed, applications would typically assert full privilege once, at the start of the program, and then operate entirely without restrictions. This worked functionally, but meant that applications ran under excess permissions—with the bank vault door always open, if you will—resulting in any vulnerabilities being far more exposed to risk than they would have been if CAS had been used as intended.

These considerations are representative of the challenges that all systems face, and are a big reason why security work is never really done.

Having built a great solution, we need to ensure that it is understood by developers as well as users, that it is actually used, and that it is used properly. Software has a way of getting used in novel ways its makers never anticipated, and as we learn about these cases, it's important to consider the security ramifications and, if necessary, adapt. All of these factors and more are essential to building secure systems that really work.

## Conclusion

Software has the unique and auspicious property of consisting entirely of bits—it's just a bunch of 0s and 1s—so we can literally conjure it out of thin air. The materials are free and available in unlimited quantities, so our imagination and creativity are the only limiting factors. This is equally true for the forces of good as it is for those who seek to harm, so both the promise and the daunting challenge are unbounded.

This chapter provided a call to action and some forward-looking ideas. When developing software, consider security implications early in the process, and get more people thinking about security to provide more diverse perspectives on the topic. An increased awareness of security leads to healthy skepticism and vigilance throughout the software lifecycle. Lessen your dependence on manual checking, and provide more automated verification. Keep auditable records of all key decisions and actions along the way to realizing a system, so the security properties of the system are well defined. Choose components wisely, but also test assumptions and important properties of the system. Reduce fragility; manage complexity and change. When vulnerabilities arise, investigate their root causes, learn from them, and proactively reduce the risk going forward. Critically examine realistic scenarios and work toward delivering security to the last mile. Publish the details as fully as is responsible so others can learn from the issues you encounter and how you respond. Iterate relentlessly in small steps to improve security and honor privacy.

Thank you for joining me on this trek through the hills and valleys of software security. We certainly did not cover every inch, but you should now have a grasp of the lay of the land. I hope you have found useful ideas herein and, with a better understanding of the topic, that you will begin to put them into practice. This book isn't *the* answer, but it offers *some* answers to raising the bar on software security. Most importantly, please don your "security hat" from time to time and apply these concepts and techniques in your own work, starting today.

# A

## SAMPLE DESIGN DOCUMENT

The following document is a hypothetical design provided to illustrate the process of performing a security design review (SDR) on an actual design. Intended as a learning tool, it omits many details that would be present in a real design, focusing instead on security aspects. As such, it is not a complete example of a real software design document.

**NOTE** *Bold text highlights security-related content: examples of good security practice in a design, what features a good designer adds, or points that security reviewers should be raising. Italic text is intended as meta-descriptions about this design document. I use it to remark on the document's pedagogical purpose and explain shortcuts I've taken.*

# Title – Private Data Logging Component Design Document

**Table of Contents**

## Section 1 – Product Description

This document describes a logging component (herein called Logger) that provides standard software event logging facilities to support auditing, system monitoring, and debugging, designed to mitigate risks of inadvertent information disclosure. **Logger will explicitly handle private data within logs so that non-private data can be freely accessed for routine uses. In rare cases when this access level is insufficient, limited access to protected, private log data can be provided, subject to explicit approval and with restrictions to minimize potential exposure.**

*The notion of explicitly handling private data separately within the context of a logging system is an example of security-centric design thinking. Adding this feature to an existing system would be less efficient and require considerable code churn, compared to designing it in from the start.*

## Section 2 – Overview

For baseline project design assumptions, see the documents listed in Section 10.

### 2.1 Purpose

All applications in the datacenter need to log details of important software events, and since these logs potentially contain private data, careful access control needs to be enforced. Logger provides standard components to generate logs, store logs, and enforce appropriate access to authorized staff while maintaining a reliable and **non-repudiable** record of what access does occur. Since the logging, access, and retention requirements of systems vary, Logger operates based on a simple policy configuration that specifies an access policy.

### 2.2 Scope

This document explains the design of the software components of Logger without mandating the choice of implementation language, deployment, or operational considerations.

### 2.3 Concepts

The notion of a filtered view of logs is core to the design. The idea is to allow relatively free inspection of the logs with any private details filtered out, an access level which should suffice for most uses. Additionally, when needed, sensitive data that is logged can be inspected, subject to additional authorization. The access event is logged too, making the fact of inspection auditable. This graduated access lets applications log important private details while still minimizing how that data is exposed for legitimate uses by internal staff. Data so sensitive that it should never appear in logs simply should not be logged in the first place.

For example, web applications routinely log HTTPS requests as a record of system usage and for many other reasons. Often these logs contain private information (including IP addresses, cookies, and much more) that must be captured but is rarely needed. For example, IP addresses are useful when investigating malicious attacks (to identify the origin of an attack), but for other uses are immaterial. A filtered view of logs hides, or "wraps," private data while showing nonsensitive data. Designated pseudonyms in a filtered view can show that, for instance, the IP addresses of all events labeled "IP7" are identical without disclosing the actual address. Such a filtered view often provides sufficient information for the purposes of monitoring, gathering statistics, or debugging. When that is the case, it's advantageous to have avoided exposing any private data at all. The logs still contain the full data, and in rare cases when the protected information is required, the unfiltered view is available in a controlled manner with proper authorization.

Suppose that a web application receives a user login attempt which triggers a bug that causes the process to crash. Here is a simplified example of what the log might contain:

```
2022/10/19 08:09:10 66.77.88.99 POST login.htm {user: "SAM", password: ">1<}2{]3[\4/"}
```

The items in this log are: timestamp (not sensitive), IP address (sensitive), HTTP verb and URL (not sensitive), username (sensitive), and password (very sensitive). An investigation potentially needs to consider all this information in order to reproduce the bug, but you don't want to display this data in plaintext unless absolutely necessary, and then only to authorized agents.

To address the security needs of a wide range of systems, the sensitivity of various kinds of log data should be configurable, and the logging system should only selectively reveal confidential data. For example, as a best practice URLs should not contain sensitive information, but a legacy system might be known to violate this rule of thumb and require protection not usually necessary—which makes the filtered view less useful for some debugging. In the case of a URL, regular expressions could facilitate configuring certain URLs as more sensitive than others.

A filtered view of the previous example log that omits or wraps the sensitive data might look like this:

```
2022/10/19 08:09:10 US1(v4) POST login.htm {user: USER1(3), password: PW1(12)}
```

The IP address, username, and password are all wrapped as identifiers to hide the data, but the substituted identifiers could be used in context to query other requests with matching values. In this example, US1 designates an IP address in the US; USER1 designates the username associated with the event without divulging it specifically; and PW1 stands for the password submitted. The suffixes in parentheses indicate the format or length of the actual data, adding a hint without revealing specific details: we can see that it's an IPv4 address, the username has 3 characters, and the password has 12. **For example, if an excessively long password caused a problem, this fact would be apparent from its surprising length alone. Knowing the length of the password leaks a little information but should not be compromising in practice.**

When the filtered view is insufficient for the task at hand, an additional request to unwrap an identifier such as US1 can be made. This makes seeing the sensitive data an explicit choice, and allows a graduated revealing of data. For example, if only the IP address is needed, the username and password values remain undisclosed.

## 2.4 Requirements

Logs are reliably stored, immediately accessible with authorization, and destroyed after the required retention period. To support high volumes of use, the log capture interface must be fast, and once it reports success, the generating application is rightly assured that the log is stored.

Logs can be monitored without knowledge of private details, so a filtered log view can be made widely available for most uses, with special authorization needed to see the full data (including private data) only when strictly necessary.

An important goal of this design is to allow the logging of very sensitive private data that can be made available for investigating possible security incidents or, in rare cases, debugging issues that only occur in production. Complete mitigation against an insider attack is an impractical goal, but it's important to take all reasonable precautions and preserve a reliable audit trail as a deterrent.

Storage for logs is encrypted to protect against leaks if the physical media is stolen.

Software generating logs is fully trusted; it must correctly identify private data in order for Logger to handle it correctly.

## 2.5 Non-Goals

As Logger is intended for use by admins, a slick UI is unnecessary.

**Insider attacks such as code tampering or abuse of admin root privilege are out of scope.**

**To be effective, Logger requires careful configuration and oversight. How this is implemented must be defined by system management but should include a review process and auditing with checks and balances.**

## 2.6 Outstanding Issues

Details of log access configuration, user authentication, and grants of unfiltered access authorization remain to be specified.

**Querying encrypted private data is inherently slow. This design envisions that log data volumes are sufficiently small that a brute-force pass (that is, without reliance on an index) decrypting records on demand will be performant. A more ambitious future version might tackle indexing and fast querying over encrypted data.**

Error cases need to be identified and handling specified.

Enhancements for future versions of Logger to consider include:

- Defining levels of filtered views that provide more or less detailed information

- Providing a facility to capture portions of the log for long-term secure storage that would eventually be routinely deleted

## 2.7 Alternative Designs

**The final design chosen is based on fully trusting Logger to store all sensitive information in logs, putting "all eggs in one basket." An alternative was considered that allowed sensitive information to be compartmentalized by source. This was not pursued for a few reasons (briefly explained below) that did not appear compatible with important use scenarios, but it is important to note that this would arguably be a more secure logging solution.**

### Alternative design

Log sources would create an asymmetric cryptographic key pair and use it to encrypt the sensitive data portions of log records before sending to Logger. If this were done carefully, Logger could (probably) still generate pseudonyms for filtered views (for example, US1 for a certain IP address in the US). Authorized access to unfiltered views would then require the private key in order to decrypt the data. The main advantage of this approach is that disclosure of stored log data would not leak sensitive data that was encrypted, and Logger would not even have the necessary key(s).

### Reasons not chosen

This design puts the burden of encryption and key management on both log sources and authorized accessors. The designation of what data is sensitive and how it should be partitioned is determined by the log source and fixed at that time. By centralizing trust in Logger, both of these aspects can be reconfigured as needed, and fine-grained access can be controlled by authenticating the log viewer.

## Section 3 – Use Cases

Applications in the datacenter generate logs of important software events using Logger. Routine monitoring software and appropriate operational staff are allowed filtered access (data views without disclosure of any private data) for their routine duties. Operational statistics including traffic levels, active users, error rates, and so forth are all generated from filtered log views.

Rarely, when support or debugging requires access to the unfiltered logs, authorized staff may get limited access subject to policy. Access requests specify the subset of logs needed, their time window, and the reason for the access. Once approved, a token is issued that permits the access, which is logged for audit. Upon completion, the requester adds a note describing the result of the investigation, which is reviewed by the approver to ensure propriety.

Reports detailing summaries of requests, approvals, audit reviews, log volume trends, and confirmation of expired log data deletion are generated to inform management.

## Section 4 – System Architecture

Within the datacenter, Logger service **instances run on physically separate machines operated independently** from the applications they serve, via a standard publish/subscribe protocol. Logger is constituted from three new services organized as the following functions:

### Logger Recorder

A log storage service. Applications stream log event data **over an encrypted channel** to the Logger Recorder service, where they are written to persistent storage. One instance may be configured to handle logs for more than one application.

## Logger Viewer

A web application that technical staff use to manually inspect filtered logs, with the ability to reveal unfiltered views subject to authorization according to policy.

## Logger Root Recorder

A special instance of Logger Recorder that logs events of Logger Recorder and Viewer. *For simplicity we omit the details of filtered and unfiltered views of this log.*

# Section 5 – Data Design

Log data is collected directly from applications that determine what events, with what details, should be logged. **Logs are append-only records of software events and are never modified other than being deleted upon expiration.**

Applications define a schema of log event types, with zero or more items of preconfigured data, as illustrated by the following example. All log events must have a timestamp and at least one other identifying data item.

```
{LogTypes: [login, logout, ...]}
{LogType: login, timestamp: time, IP: IPaddress, http: string,
 URL: string, user: string, password: string, cookies: string}
{LogType: logout, timestamp: time, IP: IPaddress, http: string,
 URL: string, user: string, cookies: string}
{Filters: {timestamp: minute, IP: country, verb: 0, URL: 0,
 user: private, password: private, cookies: private}}
```

*Many details regarding built-in types, formatting, and so forth are omitted since the basic idea of how these would be defined should be clear from this partial example.*

**Requests and responses must be UTF-8-encoded valid JSON expressions less than 1 million characters in length. Individual field values are limited to at most 10,000 characters.**

The first line (LogTypes) enumerates the types of log events this application will produce. For each type, a JSON record with the corresponding LogType entry (the second line is for LogType: login) lists the allowable data items that may be provided with such a log.

The fourth line (Filters) declares the disposition of each data item: **0** for nonsensitive data, **private** for private data to be "wrapped," and other special types of data handling, including:

minute

Time value is rounded to the nearest minute (obscuring precise times)

country

IP addresses are mapped to country of origin in the filtered view

Filters should be defined by pluggable components and easily extended to support custom data types that various applications will require.

**Note that "nonsensitive" data should be used for limited internal viewing only; this designation does not mean that this data should be publicly disclosed.** The requirement that all data items be declared, including disposition (private or not), is to ensure that explicit decisions are made about each one in the context of the application. **It is critical that these definitions and any updates have careful scrutiny to ensure the integrity of the log processing.**

Here is an example log entry in the unfiltered view for this schema:

```
2022/10/19 08:09:10 66.77.88.99 POST login.html {user: "SAM", password: ">1<}2{]3[\4/"}
```

And this is the corresponding filtered view:

```
2022/10/19 08:09 US1(v4) POST login.html {user: USER1(3), password: PW1(12)}
```

Data is stored persistently and available until the policy-configured expiration date is reached, measured as time elapsed since the event log timestamp.

Logs are transient data only intended for monitoring and debugging or for forensic purposes in the case of a security breach, and as such are only kept for a limited time. **Potential data loss is mitigated by storing the data on a dedicated machine, using a RAID (or similar) disk array for redundant persistent storage. Logs are intended as short-term storage for auditing and diagnostic purposes. Long-term storage of any of this data should be stored separately.**

## Section 6 – API

The Logger Recorder's network interface accepts the following remote procedure calls:

**Hello**

Must be the first API call of the session; identifies the application and version

**Schema**

Defines the log data schema (see Section 5)

**Log**

Sends event data (see Section 5) to be recorded to the specified log

**Goodbye**

Sent when the application terminates, ending the session

Each application connects to its logging service via a dedicated channel. **HTTPS secures API invocations between authenticated endpoints; the preconfigured server name authenticates (by its digital certificate) that clients are connected to valid Logger service instances.** The following are the request types.

## 6.1 Hello Request

Any process that will use the Logger service sends this request to initiate the logging:

```
{"verb": "Hello", "source": "Sample application", "version": "1"}
```

The following response acknowledges the request with an OK or error message and provides a string token for the session:

```
{"status": "OK", "service": "Logger", "version": "1", "token": "XYZ123"}
```

The token is used in subsequent requests to identify the context of the initiating application corresponding to the `Hello`. **Tokens are generated randomly with sufficient complexity and entropy to preclude guessing: the minimum recommended token size is 120 bits, or about 20 characters in base64 encoding. Shorter tokens are used here for brevity.**

## 6.2 Schema Definition Request

This request defines the data schema for subsequent logging, as described in Section 5:

```
{"verb": "Schema", "token": "XYZ123", ...}
```

*Details of this request are omitted for brevity.*

The schema defines the field names, types, and other attributes that will appear in the log contents, as illustrated by the sample event log request shown in the following section (which includes the fields `timestamp`, `ipaddr`, `http`, `url`, and `error`).

## 6.3 Event Log Request

This request actually logs one record with the Logger service:

```
{"verb": "Event", "token": "XYZ123", "log": {
 "timestamp": 1234567890, "ipaddr": "12.34.56.78",
 "http": "POST", "url": "example", "error": "404"}}
```

The `log` JSON presents content to be recorded to the log that must match the schema.

The response acknowledges the request with an OK or error message:

```
{"status": "OK"}
```

*Error details are omitted for brevity.* **Logging errors (for example, insufficient storage space) are serious and require immediate attention, since system operation is not auditable in the absence of logging.**

## 6.4 Goodbye Request

This request completes a session of logging:

```
{"verb": "Goodbye", "token": "XYZ123"}
```

The response acknowledges the request with an OK or error message:

```
{"status": "OK"}
```

The token thereafter is no longer valid. To resume logging, the client must first make a `Hello` request.

## Section 7 – User Interface Design

The user interface to the Logger is a web interface served by Logger Viewer that is used to examine the logs. **The web app is only accessible by authorized operations staff and authenticated by enterprise single sign-on.** Authenticated users see a selection of logs they are allowed to access, with links to browse or search the most recent filtered log entries or, when allowed, to request access to unfiltered logs subject to approval.

*For brevity, only a high-level description of the web interface is provided for this example.*

Approval requests are queued for processing in a web form that provides basic information:

- The reason access is requested, including specifics such as customer issue ticket numbers
- The scope of access requested (typically a specific user account or IP address)

Approval requests trigger automated emails sent to approvers with a link to the web app page to review these requests. When each decision is taken, an email notifies the requester with the following:

- An approval or denial
- Reason for denial, if applicable
- Time window for approved access

Filtered and unfiltered logs are visible on a page corresponding to each log. Queries may be entered specifying which log entries to view. An empty query shows the most recent entries with Next/Previous links for paging through the results.

Queries specify log entry fields and values, combined with Boolean operators to select matching log entries. Most recent first is the default order, unless an explicit ordering is given in the query. *For brevity, the details of query syntax are omitted.*

Filtered logs are displayed with symbolic identifiers (see Section 2.3) instead of the raw log contents. Queries may use symbolic identifiers present in filtered log content; for example, if a filtered log entry shows the IP address US1, a query of [IP = US1] would find other logs from that IP address without disclosing the address itself.

**Queries over filtered logs must disallow searches on filtered fields with exact values. For example, even if IP addresses are not shown, if the user can guess [IP = 1.1.1.1] (and so forth) they may eventually hit a log entry that will show it as something like USA888 and then be able to infer the actual value.**

Even when unfiltered access is approved, users must select an option to begin unfiltered viewing and querying. **Best practice maximizes use of filtered logs, only revealing filtered values on an as-needed basis, and it is important that the user interface encourage this.**

Users can renounce the right to unfiltered log access when the task is completed. The user interface should promote this after a period of inactivity to minimize risk of unnecessary access.

**Web pages displaying log contents should not be locally cached by user agents to avoid inadvertent disclosure and to ensure that, on expiry, the log data is no longer available.**

## Section 8 – Technical Design

The Logger Recorder service consists of a write-only interface for applications to stream log event data that will be written to persistent storage, and a query interface to get views of those logs. Storage is a sequence of write-append files consisting of UTF-8 lines of text, with one line per log event. Log data as described by the relevant schema (see above) maps to/from a canonical representation as text. *Details of formatting are omitted for this example.*

**Log data fields subject to filtering should be stored in the filtered representation in addition to the raw data encrypted with an AES key generated by the service, using a new key every day. Use a hardware key storage or suitable means of securely protecting these keys.**

Since exhausting available storage represents a fatal error for a logging service, the write rate is measured against free space (free_storage_MB / avg_logging_MB _per_hour) and a priority operational alert is raised if space for fewer than 10 hours of data, assuming constant write volumes, remains (this number of hours to alert is configurable).

For performance, consider a SQL database recording filtered log event information (timestamp, log type, filename, and offset), supplementing the actual log files for efficient access.

Filtered logs hide private data with symbolic identifiers (for example, US1 for an IP address in the US). **To avoid storing unfiltered private data, these maps go from a secure digest of the unfiltered data value to the filtered moniker.** This mapping is temporary and maintained by Logger Viewer separately for each user context per log. Users have the ability to clear mappings for a fresh start, or after 24 hours of non-use, they are automatically cleared to prevent useless buildup over time.

## Section 9 – Configuration

Log retention is configured as follows. **Data is automatically, securely, and permanently deleted beyond the retention period (not just moved to trash; use the** shred(1) **command or similar).**

```
Retention: {
  "Log1": {"days": 10},
  "Log2": {"hours": 24},
}
```

Log access is granted by configuring lists of authorized users:

```
Access: {
  "Log1": {"filtered": ["u1", "u2", "u3", . . .],
          "unfiltered": ["x1", "x2", "x3", . . .]},
          "approval": ["a1", "a2", "a3", . . .]},
}
```

Users allowed filtered access to the log denoted Log1 are listed within brackets, as shown above (for example, u1, u2, u3). Users permitted unfiltered access are then similarly listed. These users will be granted access only following an approved request. Finally, users with the power to grant approval for limited unfiltered access are listed in the same manner.

## Section 10 – References

The following documents are useful for understanding this design document.

*These are fictional.*

- Enterprise baseline design assumptions document (referenced in Section 2)
- Enterprise general data protection policy and guidelines
- Publish/subscribe protocol design document (referenced in Section 4)

## END OF DOCUMENT

# B

## GLOSSARY

Terminology that is specific to software security may seem straightforward, but nuances are important to get right. I have evolved the following security-specific meanings of terms based on my experience across multiple companies and many diverse projects, and while these definitions are generally accepted, don't be surprised if you find diversity in the terminology used in the wild. If you pay close attention, you'll notice that security specialists define and use the same terms in slightly different ways, bringing their own unique perspectives to the foundational precepts of the field. Expect to hear many variations, because there is no accepted standard vocabulary; usually, however, these variations are easy to deduce in context.

### Affected users

An assessment of the proportion of users potentially impacted by the exploitation of a specific vulnerability. (Component of *DREAD*)

### Allowlist

An enumeration of safe values that should be allowed. (Cf. *Blocklist*)

### Assessment report

The written results of a security design review (SDR), consisting of a ranked summary of findings and recommendations, including specific design changes and strategies to improve security.

### Asset

Valuable data or resources, especially likely targets of attack, to be protected.

### Asymmetric encryption

Data encryption with separate keys for encryption (public key) and decryption (private key). (Cf. *Symmetric encryption*)

### Attack

Action taken in an attempt to violate security.

### Attacker

A malicious agent working to violate the security of a system. (Also known as *Threat actor*)

### Attack surface

The aggregate of all potential points of entry to a system for attack.

### Attack vector

A sequence of steps forming a complete attack, starting from the attack surface and culminating in access to an asset.

### Auditing

Maintaining a reliable record of actions by principals, for regular inspection, to detect suspicious behavior indicative of improper activity. (Component of the *Gold Standard*)

### Authentication (authN)

High-assurance determination of the identity of a principal. (Component of the *Gold Standard*)

### Authenticity

Assurance that data is genuine, a stronger claim than data integrity.

## Authorization (authZ)

Security policy controls ensuring that privileged access is restricted to certain authenticated principals. (Component of the *Gold Standard*)

## Availability

Assurance that data access is always available to authorized principals; in other words, that the system avoids significant delays or outages hindering legitimate access. (Component of *C-I-A*)

## Backtracking

Behavior of algorithms, such as regular expression matching, where progress may advance and regress, exponentially repeating. Potential security issues result when backtracking incurs excessive computation that degrades availability.

## Block cipher

A symmetric encryption algorithm that processes fixed-length blocks of data, as opposed to a bitstream.

## Blocklist

An enumeration of unsafe values that should be disallowed. Not generally recommended because, unless exhaustive, there is risk of vulnerability. (Cf. *Allowlist*)

## Bottleneck

A single point in the code execution path that guards all access to a specific asset. Bottlenecks are important for security because they ensure that uniform authorization checks happen for all accesses.

## Buffer overflow

A class of vulnerabilities involving invalid access outside the bounds of allocated memory.

## Certificate authority (CA)

An issuer of digital certificates.

## Chokepoint

See *Bottleneck*.

## Chosen plaintext attack

Analysis of encryption where the attacker is able to learn the ciphertext for a plaintext of their choice, and thereby weaken the encryption.

## C-I-A

The fundamental information security model. (See *Confidentiality*, *Integrity*, and *Availability*)

### Ciphertext

The encrypted form of a message that is meaningless without the key. (Cf. *Plaintext*)

### Code Access Security (CAS)

A security model that dynamically adjusts authorization according to the privileges of all callers to mitigate Confused Deputy vulnerabilities.

### Collision

When two different inputs produce the same message digest value.

### Collision attack

An attack that uses a known collision to subvert authenticity relying on the uniqueness of cryptographic message digest values.

### Command injection

A vulnerability allowing malicious inputs to result in running arbitrary commands controlled by an attacker.

### Confidentiality

The fundamental information security property of enforcing only authorized access to data. (Component of *C-I-A*)

### Confused Deputy

A vulnerable pattern where an unauthorized agent can trick an authorized agent or code to perform a harmful action on the former's behalf.

### Credentials

Evidence of identity, attributes, or authority, as a basis for authentication.

### Cross-site request forgery (CSRF or XSRF)

An attack that modifies web server state, typically using a POST request with the victim client's cookies context.

### Cross-site scripting (XSS)

A web-specific injection attack where malicious input alters the behavior of a website, typically resulting in running unauthorized script.

### Cryptography

The mathematical art of reversibly transforming data so as to conceal it.

### Cryptographically secure pseudo-random number generator (CSPRNG)

A source of random numbers considered unpredictable enough that guessing is infeasible, which is thus suitable for cryptography. (Cf. *Pseudo-random number generator*)

**Damage potential**

An assessment of how much harm can be done by exploiting a specific vulnerability. (Component of *DREAD*)

**Deanonymization**

Analysis of supposedly anonymous data that infers identifying traits to compromise the degree of anonymity.

**Decryption**

The process of transforming a ciphertext back into the original plaintext message.

**Denial of service (DoS)**

An attack that consumes computing resources in order to degrade availability. (Also a component of *STRIDE*)

**Dependency**

A software library or other component of a system that software requires in order to operate.

**Dialog fatigue**

The human response to repetitive or uninformative software dialogs, often leading to reflexive responses to get past the dialog in order to accomplish a goal. The security impact occurs when users fail to understand or consider the security consequences of their actions.

**Digest**

A unique numerical value of fixed size computed from an arbitrarily large data input. Different digest values guarantee the inputs are different, but collisions are possible. (Also known as *Hash*)

**Digital certificate**

A digitally signed statement asserting a specific claim by the signer. Common digital certificate standards include TLS/SSL secure communications (both for the server and the client side), code signing, email signing, and certificate authorities (root, intermediate, leaf).

**Digital signature**

A computation demonstrating knowledge of a private key, proving the authenticity of the signer.

**Discoverability**

An assessment of how easily the existence of a specific vulnerability could be learned by a would-be attacker. (Component of *DREAD*)

**Distributed denial-of-service attacks (DDoS)**

Coordinated denial-of-service attacks, typically orchestrated using a large herd of bots.

## DREAD

An acronym for a five-component system used to assess a vulnerability to gauge its severity. (See *Damage potential*, *Reproducibility*, *Exploitability*, *Affected users*, and *Discoverability*)

## Electronic code book (ECB) mode

A block cipher encryption mode where each block is encrypted independently. Since identical blocks result in identical outputs, ECB is weak and usually not recommended.

## Elevation of privilege

Any means by which an agent acquires increased privileges, especially when an attacker exploits a vulnerability. (Component of *STRIDE*)

## Encryption

An algorithm transforming plaintext into ciphertext to secretly convey a message.

## Entropy source

A source of random input that generates an unpredictable bitstream.

## Exploit

The recipe for a working attack that violates security, causing harm.

## Exploitability

An assessment of how easy it is to exploit a specific vulnerability. Often this is a subjective guess due to many unknowns. (Component of *DREAD*)

## Fact of communication

Knowledge of whether or not two communicants exchanged information, such as by an eavesdropper observing encrypted messages they cannot decipher.

## Flaw

A bug that might or might not be a vulnerability, either in design or implementation.

## Footgun

A software feature that makes it easy to introduce a bug, especially a vulnerability.

## Fuzz testing

Automated brute-force testing with arbitrary inputs to discover software flaws.

## Gold Standard

A nickname for the three basic security enforcement mechanisms. (See *Auditing*, *Authentication*, and *Authorization*)

**Guard**

An authorization enforcement mechanism in software that controls access to a resource.

**Hardware random number generator (HRNG)**

A hardware device designed to produce highly random data efficiently. (See *Cryptographically secure pseudo-random number generator*)

**Hash**

See *Digest*.

**Hash message authentication code (HMAC)**

A class of message digest functions where each key value determines a unique message digest function.

**Incident**

A specific instance of a security attack.

**Information disclosure**

An unauthorized information leak. (Component of *STRIDE*)

**Injection attack**

A security attack that uses malicious input to exploit a vulnerability where part of the input is interpreted in an unexpected manner. Common forms include SQL injection, cross-site scripting, command injection, and path traversal.

**Input validation**

Defensive checking of input data to ensure that it is of a valid format that will be correctly processed downstream.

**Integration testing**

Software testing of multiple components operating together. (Cf. *Unit testing*)

**Integrity**

The fundamental information security property of maintaining data accurately, or only allowing authorized modification and deletion. (Component of *C-I-A*)

**Key**

A parameter to a cryptographic algorithm that determines how the data is transformed. (See *Private key*, *Public key*)

**Keyed hash function**

See *Hash message authentication code (HMAC)*.

### Key exchange
A protocol for two communicants to establish a secret key that is secure even if the content of all messages exchanged is revealed to an attacker.

### Message authentication code (MAC)
Data accompanying a message as evidence that it is authentic and has not been tampered with. (Cf. *Hash message authentication code*)

### Message digest
See *Digest*.

### Mitigation
A preemptive countermeasure to prevent a potential attack or reduce its harm, such as by minimizing damage, making the attack recoverable, or making it easily detectable.

### Nonce
An arbitrary number used once, such as in a communications protocol to prevent replay attacks.

### One-time pad
A shared secret key for message encryption that can only be used once because reuse weakens its security.

### Overflow
The incorrect result of an arithmetic instruction when the value exceeds the capacity of the variable. When overflow happens undetected, it often results in a vulnerability by introducing unexpected results.

### Path traversal
A common vulnerability where malicious input injects unexpected content into a filesystem path that allows it to designate files outside the bounds of intended access.

### Plaintext
The original message before encryption, or after decryption by the intended recipient.

### Preimage attack
An attack on a message digest function attempting to find an input value that produces a specific message digest value.

### Principal
An authenticated agent: a person, business, organization, application, service, or device.

### Private key
A parameter needed for decryption, kept secret by the authorized recipient.

### Provenance

A reliable history of the origin and chain of custody, providing confidence in the validity of data.

### Pseudo-random number generator (PRNG)

A "pretty good" random number generator that is vulnerable to prediction by sophisticated analysis. These random numbers are useful for many purposes, such as simulations, but are unsuitable for cryptography because they are not sufficiently random. (Cf. *Cryptographically secure pseudo-random number generator*)

### Public key

A widely known parameter needed to encrypt a message for a particular recipient.

### Random number

An arbitrarily chosen number that cannot be reliably predicted.

### Rate limiting

A method of slowing down a process, commonly used to mitigate attacks that rely on brute-force repetition to succeed.

### Replay attack

Attacking an secure communication protocol by resending previous authentic messages. A replay attack succeeds if an attacker resends a copy of a previous authentic communication that is mistaken as a subsequent identical message sent by the original sender.

### Reproducibility

An assessment of how reliably the exploitation of a specific vulnerability will work over a number of repeated attempts. (Component of *DREAD*)

### Repudiation

Plausible deniability for actions, specifically allowing an attacker to evade responsibility. (Component of *STRIDE*)

### Root certificate

The self-signed digital certificate authorizing trust in a certificate authority.

### Same Origin Policy (SOP)

A set of restrictions enforced by web clients to limit access between different windows of different websites.

### Sandbox

A restricted execution environment designed to limit the maximum privilege available to code executing within it.

### Security design review (SDR)

A structured review of the security of a software design.

## Security hat

An expression for intentionally focusing with a security mindset to think about how things might go wrong.

## Security regression

The recurrence of a known security bug that was previously fixed.

## Security test case

A software test case that checks that a security control is properly enforced.

## Security testing

Software testing to ensure that security controls work properly.

## Side channel attack

An attack that deduces confidential information indirectly, as opposed to by directly defeating protection mechanisms. For example, reliably deducing knowledge of the results of a computation from the time delay to produce the result.

## Speculative execution

The optimization method used in modern processors whereby future instructions are executed early to potentially save time, with backtracking logic to discard results later if unneeded. The impact of speculative execution on the cache state potentially leaks information not otherwise accessible, making it a security threat.

## Spoofing

The subversion of authentication where an attacker pretends to be an authorized principal. (Component of *STRIDE*)

## SQL injection

A vulnerability allowing an attacker to craft malicious inputs to run arbitrary SQL commands.

## STRIDE

An acronym for the six basic kinds of software security threats, useful to guide threat modeling. (See *Spoofing, Tampering, Repudiation, Information disclosure, Denial of service, Elevation of privilege*)

## Symmetric encryption

An encryption method where the same key is used to encrypt or decrypt. The symmetry is that anyone who can encrypt can also decrypt.
(Cf. *Asymmetric encryption*)

## Tainting

A process of tracing the origin of data through software used to mitigate untrusted inputs, or data influenced by those inputs, from being used in privileged operations such as for an injection attack.

### Tampering

The unauthorized modification of data. (Component of *STRIDE*)

### Threat

A potential or hypothetical security problem.

### Threat actor

See *Attacker*.

### Threat modeling

Analysis of the model of a system used to identify threats needing mitigation.

### Timing attack

A side channel attack where information can be inferred from measuring the timing of an operation.

### Trust

The choice to rely on a principal or component without recourse in the event of a failure to protect.

### Underflow

Lost precision in the result of a floating-point computation.

### Unit testing

Software testing of individual modules in isolation from other components.

### Untrusted input

Input data originating from untrusted sources, in particular from a potential attack surface.

### Vulnerability

A software flaw that makes a security attack possible.

### Vulnerability chain

A collection of vulnerabilities that, when combined, constitute a security attack.

### Weakness

A bug that causes fragility and hence may be a vulnerability.

# C

## EXERCISES

*Exploration is the engine that drives innovation.*
—Edith Widder

 This appendix contains some ideas for further exploration, open questions, and challenges for readers who want to go beyond the material covered in this book.

**Chapter 1: Foundations**

- The book focuses on information security in conventional computer systems, but appliances and devices also run on software, and these are increasingly connected to the internet. How do we extend principles such as C-I-A to secure software that interacts with the physical world?

**Chapter 2: Threats**

- Threat model an existing software design, or just one component of a large system.

- For fun, threat model a favorite movie or scene from a book where adversaries battle over a prized asset.

### Chapter 3: Mitigations

- Write helper functions to limit the exposure of sensitive data in memory as described in "Minimize Data Exposure" on page 47.
- Intentionally code a Confused Deputy and try to exploit it, or challenge a colleague to do so. Fix the vulnerability and confirm that the code is secure.
- Design a library to enforce an extensible access policy for an existing data access API.

### Chapter 4: Patterns

- Take an existing design, or undertake a new one, and see how many of the chapter's patterns you can use to make it as secure as possible.
- What additional security patterns and anti-patterns can you think of? Keep a running list, adding to the ones presented in the chapter, and share them with colleagues.
- Are allowlists always better than blocklists? Think of an exception, or explain why none exist.

### Chapter 5: Cryptography

- An easy way to play around with real crypto tools is with the OpenSSL command line (*https://wiki.openssl.org/index.php/Main_Page*). You can use it to experiment with symmetric and asymmetric crypto, as well as MACs (called *digests* in openssl(1)), or even create and check your own certificates.
- Find a high-quality crypto library and try using it to implement the basic operations described in the chapter. How was the API in terms of ease of use, and how confident are you that your implementation is secure?
- If the previous exercise proved difficult, how could you redesign the API to be easier to use, as well as more foolproof?
- Code the crypto API improvements you thought of, or wrap the original library to provide a better API.

### Chapter 6: Secure Design

- Explore Google's design document writing guidance (*https://www .industrialempathy.com/posts/design-docs-at-google/*).
- If you haven't written a software design document before, try it out the next time you get an opportunity to do so (making it as informal and high level as you like).
- If you work on a codebase that has no written design document, retroactively create one. For large systems, create designs for one component at a time, focusing on whatever components are most important to security or otherwise of interest.

## Chapter 7: Security Design Reviews

- Find existing designs and review them as a learning exercise. Don't just look for vulnerabilities; create a broad assessment of both strengths and weaknesses, including places where security matters most, ways the design enhances security, mitigation alternatives, and ways in which security could be improved or made more usable.

- Share and discuss your findings from the preceding exercise with colleagues.

## Chapter 8: Secure Programming

- To get a feel for realistic examples of security vulnerabilities, look for security bugs that have already been found and fixed in your codebase or in open source software projects. I suggest focusing on open source projects because vulnerabilities are usually described in detail and you can see the code. The US Department of Homeland Security sponsors a large database of publicly known vulnerabilities (*https://cve.mitre.org/*). The Chromium bug database is another good source of public vulnerabilities (*https://bugs.chromium.org/p/chromium/issues/list/*). A good starting point is to filter these databases for fixed security bugs so you can see the actual code changes.

- *Underhanded coding*, also known as *obfuscated coding*, is the fine art of using footguns and other trickery to write code that works differently from what a casual inspection of the code would indicate. Underhanded coding contests challenge programmers to show off their creativity in pushing programming languages to their limits. But the same techniques used to camouflage malicious code as benign can also, if stumbled upon inadvertently, become footguns. Check out these sites for a start, or try to craft your own: *http://www.underhanded-c.org/* and *https://underhandedcrypto.com/*.

## Chapter 9: Low-Level Coding Flaws

- Why don't languages that provide fixed-width integer types provide any mechanism to detect overflow? Would it help? If so, how would you extend the C language to take advantage of it?

- Explore how analysis tools such as Valgrind detect issues with memory management (*https://valgrind.org/docs/manual/mc-manual.html*).

- Write a little program that includes a few kinds of memory management vulnerabilities, such as both read and write buffer overflows. Use a tool like Valgrind to see if it detects the bugs. Try varying the code to make it harder for the tool to analyze, and see if you can sneak a bug past it.

## Chapter 10: Untrusted Input

- Identify the untrusted inputs on the main attack surface of the system you work on and see how thoroughly input validation is implemented and tested.

- If you find that untrusted inputs may represent vulnerabilities, implement input validation.

- Often, input validation for a system is repetitive. Look for opportunities to use common code or helper functions to handle it reliably. Consider ways of baking input validation into frameworks so it cannot be accidentally forgotten.

### Chapter 11: Web Security

- Write security requirements for a component that creates and authenticates a web session. Design and threat model it, and find a friend to security review it.

- Build an implementation of your web session into a simple web app. Try to impersonate another session, or steal the necessary session state. Better yet, find a friend to "attack" your implementation.

- Add a CSRF protection mechanism to the component and test it in your web app.

- Explore ways of securing web sessions without the use of cookies as an experiment to understand the essence of the security challenge.

- Find the source code (and ideally, a written design document) for a web framework and learn how it implements sessions, prevents XSS and CSRF vulnerabilities, and ensures that HTTPS secures all web interactions. By threat modeling or other means, can you find any vulnerabilities? If you want to try attacking it, put up your own test server to do that.

### Chapter 12: Security Testing

- In the codebase of your choice, locate some area where security is important and look for additional security test cases that should be added. Write and contribute new security test cases.

- Consider this alternative example of a vulnerability in GotoFail that the security tests we wrote wouldn't catch—in place of the extra goto fail;, instead insert the line:

```
if (expected_hash[0] == 0x23) goto fail;
```

This sort of technique might be used to secretly include a vulnerability that requires a specific trigger as a kind of backdoor. Detecting this would require a test case with an expected hash whose first byte was 0x23. Can you write tests to detect this sort of vulnerability without knowing the specifics?

- Check out an old version of an open source software project with a known vulnerability. Run the test suite and ensure that all tests pass. Write a security regression test to confirm the vulnerability. Sync up to the next version that fixes the vulnerability, merging in your regression test. Your security regression test should now pass; if not, fix it. Then, check for additional, related vulnerabilities in the latest version.

## Chapter 13: Secure Development Best Practices

- Explore easy ways to make incremental code quality improvements, such as using lint or code scanning tools, as well as checking the test coverage of error and exception handling.

- See how well the security aspects of your codebase are documented and make needed improvements.

- Whenever you do code reviews, put on your security hat for another pass when appropriate.

- Consider security when you do bug triage, or perhaps browse your bug database with security in mind to see if bugs that have security implications are being punted.

## Afterword

- Look for opportunities to make improvements along the lines mentioned in the conclusion, even if this means taking small steps: broader security participation, earlier integration of a security perspective and strategy, reduction or management of complexity, improvement in transparency about security practice, and so on.

- Identify a unique security challenge and design and develop a reusable component that addresses it.

- Pursue other ideas of your own to raise the security bar and spread the word.

# CHEAT SHEETS

*Your conscious mind should be used as a focusing tool, not a storage place.*
—David Allen

## Chapter 1

### Classic Security Principles

**Information Security (C-I-A)**

| | |
|---|---|
| Confidentiality | Allow only authorized data access—don't leak information |
| Integrity | Maintain data accurately—don't allow unauthorized modification or deletion |
| Availability | Preserve the availability of data—don't allow significant delays or unauthorized shutdowns |

**Gold Standard**

| | |
|---|---|
| Authentication | High-assurance determination of the identity of a principal |
| Authorization | Reliably only allowing an action by an authenticated principal |
| Auditing | Maintaining a reliable record of actions by principals for inspection |

# Chapter 2

## *The Four Questions*

- What are we working on?
- What can go wrong?
- What are we going to do about it?
- Did we do a good job?

## *STRIDE*

**Table 2-1:** Summary of STRIDE Threat Categories

| Objective | STRIDE threats | Examples |
|---|---|---|
| Authenticity | Spoofing | Phishing, stolen password, impersonation, replay attack, BGP hijacking |
| Integrity | Tampering | Unauthorized data modification and deletion, Superfish ad injection |
| Non-repudiability | Repudiation | Plausible deniability, insufficient logging, destruction of logs |
| Confidentiality | Information disclosure | Data leak, side channel attack, weak encryption, residual cached data, Spectre/Meltdown |
| Availability | Denial of service | Simultaneous requests swamp a web server, ransomware, memcrashed |
| Authorization | Elevation of privilege | SQL injection, xkcd's *"Exploits of a Mom"* |

# Chapter 4

## *Secure Design Patterns*

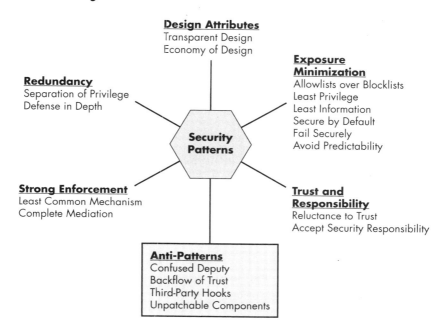

**Design Attributes**
Transparent Design
Economy of Design

**Exposure Minimization**
Allowlists over Blocklists
Least Privilege
Least Information
Secure by Default
Fail Securely
Avoid Predictability

**Redundancy**
Separation of Privilege
Defense in Depth

**Security Patterns**

**Strong Enforcement**
Least Common Mechanism
Complete Mediation

**Trust and Responsibility**
Reluctance to Trust
Accept Security Responsibility

**Anti-Patterns**
Confused Deputy
Backflow of Trust
Third-Party Hooks
Unpatchable Components

# Chapter 7

## *Security Design Review*

The six stages of a security design review:

1. *Study* the design and supporting documents to gain a basic understanding of the project.

   - First, read the documentation to get a high-level understanding of the design.
   - Next, put on your "security hat" and go through it again with a threat-aware mindset.
   - Take notes, capturing your ideas and observations for future reference.
   - Flag potential issues for later, but at this stage it's premature to do much security analysis.

2. *Inquire* about the design and ask clarifying questions about basic threats.

   - Ensure that the design document is clear and complete.
   - If there are omissions or corrections needed, help get them fixed in the document.
   - Understand the design enough to be conversant, but not necessarily at an expert level.
   - Ask members of the team what they worry about most; if they have no security concerns, ask follow-up questions to learn why not.

3. *Identify* the most security-critical parts of the design for closer attention.

   - Examine interfaces, storage, and communications—these will typically be central points of focus.
   - Work inward from the most exposed attack surfaces toward the most valuable assets, just as determined attackers would.
   - Evaluate to what degree the design addresses security explicitly.
   - If needed, point out key protections and get them called out in the design as important features.

4.  *Collaborate* with the designer(s) to identify risks and discuss mitigations.

    - As a reviewer, provide a security perspective on risks and mitigations where needed.

    - Consider sketching a scenario illustrating how a security change could pay off down the line to help convince the designer of the need for mitigations.

    - Offer more than a single solution to a problem when you can, and help the designer see the strengths and weaknesses of these alternatives.

    - Accept that the designer gets the last word, because they are ultimately responsible for the design.

    - Document the exchange of ideas, including what will or will not go into the design.

5.  *Write* a summary report of findings and recommendations.

    - Organize the report around specific design changes that address security risks.

    - Spend most of your effort and ink on the highest-priority issues, and proportionally less on lower priorities.

    - Suggest alternatives and strategies, without attempting to do the designer's job for them.

    - Prioritize findings and recommendations, using priority rankings. (Classify points as Must/Ought/Should.)

    - Focus on security, but feel free to offer separate remarks for the designer's consideration as well.

6.  *Follow up* with subsequent design changes to confirm resolution before signing off.

    - For major security design changes, you might want to collaborate with the designer to ensure that changes are made correctly.

    - Where opinions differ, the reviewer should include a statement of both positions and the specific recommendations that weren't followed to flag it as an open issue.

# Chapter 13

## *DREAD*

**Damage potential**

If exploited, how bad would it be?

**Reproducibility**

Will attacks succeed every time, some of the time, or only rarely?

**Exploitability**

How hard, in terms of technical difficulty, effort, and cost, is the vulnerability to exploit?

How long is the attack path?

**Affected users**

Will all, some, or only a few users be impacted?

Can specific targets be easily attacked, or are the victims arbitrary?

**Discoverability**

How likely is it that attackers will find the vulnerability?

# INDEX

untrusted inputs, 206

web security, 206

writing test cases, 211

Separation of Duty pattern, 67, 232

Separation of Privilege pattern, 67

serialization, 143

SHA-256 hash, 200

Shostack, Adam, 25

side-channel attack, 11, 30, 141

Snowden, Edward, 100

software quality, 237

software security, 5

software supply chain, 225

SOP (Same Origin Policy), 193–196

Spectre, 141

speculative execution, 141

spoofing, 36. *See also* STRIDE

SQL injection, 176–179

stories

auto salesman, 4

driver's ed, 75

"No Game Scheduled", 176

street crossing, 6

strcpy function, 161

STRIDE, 35–38

definition, 35

origins, 35

relation to information security
principles, 37

repudiation, 37

strlcpy function, 161

strtol function, 160

sudo, 57

# T

tainting, 132

tampering, 13, 37, 78, 143. *See
also* STRIDE

prevention with MAC, 79

Taylor, Jason, 229

test-driven development (TDD), 219

The Most Dangerous Code in the
World, 226

Third-Party Hooks anti-pattern, 74. *See
also* Backflow of Trust anti-
pattern

Thompson, Ken, 240

threat modeling, 78, 101–103

asset prioritization, 29

balancing security needs, 102

definition, 26

early efforts, 24

essential threat model, 102

granularity, 28

incorporating into design, 101

iterative process, 27

methodology varieties, 27

overview, 26

personally identifiable
information, 102

real-life applications, 41

real world, 40

real world versus digital, 27

working from a model, 27

threats, 23–41 *See also* attacks

addressing, 44

availability, 13

brute-force guessing, 16

categorizing with STRIDE, 35

fact of communication, 50

identifying, 33

mitigation, 38, 43–52

privacy, 39

threat taxonomy. *See* STRIDE

timing attack

forgot password example, 142

Meltdown, 141

mitigation, 142

Spectre, 141

speculative execution example, 141

toolbox. *See* crypto toolbox

transparency, 238

Transparent Design pattern, 56, 77

Transport Layer Security (TLS),
89, 162

Heartbeat Extension, 162

triage. *See* vulnerability triage

trust, 5

actions, 10

being trustworthy, 10

decisions, 8

decision tree, 8

features, 10

feeling trust, 6

## Y

Y2k38 bug, 218
Y2K bug, 218

## Z

ZIP code, 12

*Designing Secure Software* is set in New Baskerville, Futura, Dogma, and TheSansMono Condensed. The book was printed and bound by Sheridan Books, Inc. in Chelsea, Michigan. The paper is 60# Finch Offset, which is certified by the Forest Stewardship Council (FSC).

Never before has the world relied so heavily on the Internet to stay connected and informed. That makes the Electronic Frontier Foundation's mission—to ensure that technology supports freedom, justice, and innovation for all people—more urgent than ever.

For over 30 years, EFF has fought for tech users through activism, in the courts, and by developing software to overcome obstacles to your privacy, security, and free expression. This dedication empowers all of us through darkness. With your help we can navigate toward a brighter digital future.

# RESOURCES

Visit *https://nostarch.com/designing-secure-software/* for errata and more information.

*More no-nonsense books from*  **NO STARCH PRESS**

**THE MISSING README**
**A Guide for the New Software Engineer**
*BY* CHRIS RICCOMINI *AND*
DMITRY RYABOY
288 PP., $24.99
ISBN 978-1-71850-183-6

**BLACK HAT PYTHON,**
**2ND EDITION**
**Python Programming for Hackers**
**and Pentesters**
*BY* JUSTIN SEITZ *AND* TIM ARNOLD
216 PP., $44.99
ISBN 978-1-71850-112-6

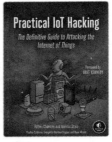

**PRACTICAL IOT HACKING**
**The Definitive Guide to Attacking**
**the Internet of Things**
*BY* FOTIOS CHANTZIS ET AL.
464 PP., $49.99
ISBN 978-1-71850-090-7

**BUG BOUNTY BOOTCAMP**
**The Guide to Finding and Reporting**
**Web Vulnerabilities**
*BY* VICKIE LI
416 PP., $49.99
ISBN 978-1-71850-154-6

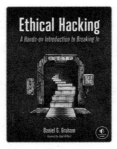

**ETHICAL HACKING**
**A Hands-on Introduction to Breaking In**
*BY* DANIEL G. GRAHAM
376 PP., $44.99
ISBN 978-1-71850-187-4

**HOW TO HACK LIKE A GHOST**
**Breaching the Cloud**
*BY* SPARC FLOW
264 PP., $34.99
ISBN 978-1-71850-126-3

**PHONE:**
800.420.7240 OR
415.863.9900

**EMAIL:**
SALES@NOSTARCH.COM

**WEB:**
WWW.NOSTARCH.COM